John Edward Campbell

Getting It On Online
Cyberspace, Gay Male Sexuality, and Embodied Identity

Pre-publication
REVIEWS,
COMMENTARIES,
EVALUATIONS . . .

"John Edward Campbell's *Getting It On Online* invites us to rethink some of the core methodological and theoretical questions that have concerned cyberculture studies over the past decade, including the status of online ethnography, the nature of 'virtual communities,' and the absence or centrality of the body to our cyber-identities. This book offers startling insight into the construction of gay male sexuality, taking an approach that is theoretically informed but never loses sight of the real-ity of participants' experiences—online and offline. Campbell's own role as an active participant in the online communities being discussed allows him to share an incredible degree of intimacy with the people who choose to hang out at these 'virtual gay bars.' Campbell writes cautiously, carefully, avoiding easy generalizations, capturing the richness and complexity of this online culture. Few other ethnographers have captured gay men speaking with this degree of frankness and openness about their bodies, their desires, their fantasies, and their fears. This book marks the debut of an important new talent in the field of media and cultural studies."

Henry Jenkins, PhD
Director, Comparative Media,
John E. Burchard Chair in the Humanities,
Massachusetts Institute of Technology

More pre-publication
REVIEWS, COMMENTARIES, EVALUATIONS . . .

"Campbell's work puts to rest awkward and untenable assertions about disembodiment in cyberspace. Like other communicative scenes, cyberspace invites the body in and out, responding to the desires and relationships of those who participate, and bringing offline habits to new forms of mediation. *Getting It On Online* also keeps the sex in queer studies, with a playwright's sensitivity to sexual dialogue, a social researcher's sensitivity to sexual community, and a lover's sensitivity to erotic tastes and practices. Gay masculinities are admirably diversified and deconstructed, and the book contributes sharp methodological and ethical insights to the burgeoning but under-explored field of virtual ethnography. This is queer cyberstudies at its best—fond, critical, and illuminating."

Lisa Henderson, PhD
Associate Professor of Communication,
University of Massachusetts at Amherst

HPP

Harrington Park Press®
An Imprint of The Haworth Press, Inc.
New York • London • Oxford

Getting It On Online
*Cyberspace, Gay Male Sexuality,
and Embodied Identity*

HAWORTH Gay & Lesbian Studies
John P. De Cecco, PhD
Editor in Chief

Getting It On Online
Cyberspace, Gay Male Sexuality, and Embodied Identity

John Edward Campbell

HPP

Harrington Park Press®
An Imprint of The Haworth Press, Inc.
New York • London • Oxford

Published by

The Harrington Park Press®, an imprint of The Haworth Press, Inc., 10 Alice Street, Binghamton, NY 13904-1580.

Cover design by Marylouise E. Doyle.

Library of Congress Cataloging-in-Publication Data

Campbell, John Edward.
  Getting it on online : cyberspace, gay male sexuality, and embodied identity / John Edward Campbell.
    p. cm.
  Includes bibliographical references and index.
  ISBN 1-56023-431-8 (hard : alk. paper)—ISBN 1-56023-432-6 (soft : alk. paper)
  1. Gay men—Computer network resources. 2. Computer sex. 3. Dating (Social customs)—Computer network resources. 4. Body image. 5. Internet—Social aspects. 6. Online chat groups. I. Title.

HQ75.14.C36 2004
025.04'086'642—dc21

2003012259

To the memory of my grandmother, Naomi O. Campbell,
for her unyielding love and for asking,
"Johnny, what exactly is a drag queen?"

ABOUT THE AUTHOR

John Edward Campbell, MA, is a doctoral candidate at the Annenberg School for Communication at the University of Pennsylvania. Working under the rubric of cultural studies, he examines how people incorporate new communication technologies into their everyday lives. His research has been published in the *International Journal of Cultural Studies,* the *Journal of Broadcasting and Electronic Media,* and the *Electronic Journal of Communication.*

CONTENTS

Foreword

In the first chapter of *Cities of the Plain* (as Moncrieff translated the French title, *Sodome et Gomorrhe*) Proust's (1927, p. 9) protagonist introduces his observations of "the men-women, descendents of those of the inhabitants of Sodom who were spared by the fire from heaven" with the analogy of an orchid that awaited the arrival of "an extremely rare insect" to "bring it that rare pollen without which it must die a virgin." In the instance Proust recounts, the favorable conjunction is that of Baron de Charlus and the young tailor Jupien, one of those "predestined to exist in order that [Charlus] may have [his] share of sensual pleasure on this earth; the man who cares only for elderly gentlemen." Whereas the fortuitous meeting—and mating—Proust imagines takes place under the dual signs of nature and destiny, in real life those whose erotic inclinations or physical attributes do not match the preferred templates of fashion and moment may not be so lucky.

John Edward Campbell introduces us to another set of protagonists who do not readily find their desires reflected in the mirrors and the dreamscapes of contemporary media but for whom cyberspace offers the same miraculous prospect Proust imagined in the conjunction of orchid and insect. As Campbell notes, his informants and fellow participants in the virtual environments of #gaymusclebears and #gaychub found in these channels "an opportunity to speak of bodies commonly marginalized or rendered completely invisible in the media—to speak of the obese body, to speak of the hairy body, to speak of the older body—in a context that affirmed their own desires and self-image."

Campbell's exploration of these communities was conducted as a participant as well as an observer, and the method used was more "observant participant" than "participant observer"—a small difference, perhaps, but an important one. Beginning in the 1960s as part of a radical rethinking of anthropology (see Hymes, 1969), and continuing with the ongoing critique of ethnography that has become a cottage industry of theorizing about knowledge, power, and narrative (see Clifford and Marcus, 1986), field researchers have increasingly recognized that the details of their own participation and relationships cannot responsibly be left out of their accounts. By the time the opportunities to study computer-mediated communities began to proliferate, social researchers were aware of the possibilities available to those wishing to combine acknowledged personal engagement with analysis. Computer-mediated discussion groups actually make it easy to passively observe—"lurking" is an accepted role in these virtual environments, even if the label carries a somewhat sinister connotation—but active participation is necessary if the researcher is to get beyond the surface and engage members in directed conversation (i.e., informal or even formal interviewing). Thus, it is not unusual for scholars to research online communities in which they have been active, even longtime members, even at the risk of exposing themselves as, say, soap opera fans (see Baym, 1999). Still, because erotic and sexual interests are among the more private and personal facts about an individual, conducting and reporting research that is predicated on one's membership in communities organized around such interests requires no little amount of courage. It also offers the researcher—and the readers—rich rewards in that it puts us in touch with matters of the utmost importance to most people: the stuff of art and literature more often than social science.

Campbell's research makes an important contribution to sexuality studies as well as the growing literature on computer-mediated communities. His account of communities formed around images of the muscular male body highlights one of the most controversial aspects of the new electronic frontier—its ability to transmit sexually explicit images and words. Every new communications technology has been put to work in the service of humanity's boundless interest in sex. "Sometimes the erotic has been a force driving technological innovation; virtually always, from Stone Age sculpture to computer bulletin boards, it has been one of the first uses for a new medium" (Tierney, 1995, p. 1E). But the Internet has particular importance to sexual minority communities. Some researchers have described gay men and lesbians as the largest and most loyal population segments using the Internet today. As quoted in Lewis (1995, p. D3), Tom Rielly, the founder of PlanetOut, explained, "Traditional mass media is very cost-intensive. Gays and lesbians don't have a high level of ownership of mainstream media properties. The Internet is the first medium where we can have equal footing with the big players." For those who are, with or without good reason, afraid to visit gay establishments or subscribe to gay publications, Web sites, chat rooms, and other online services oriented toward the gay community create a safe venue for private, at-home exploration and entertainment, away from prying eyes.

The social history of lesbian and gay people in the United States in the twentieth century has documented the importance of the bar as the cradle of identity and solidarity in a hostile world. As a lesbian musician quoted by Joan Nestle (1987, p. 113) put it, speaking about a working-class lesbian bar in Lowell, Massachusetts, in the 1950s, "If there hadn't been little Moody Gardens all over the world, we wouldn't even be allowed to get together as we do today and feel, in a small way, we are being accepted and we are not alone." Today, for many who do not find themselves welcomed in or validated by the increasingly commercialized and mainstreamed institutions of the newly respectable GLBT communities, the Internet may serve as their virtual Moody Garden. Computer-mediated communication offers possibilities for the exploration and expression of identity, for affiliation and solidarity among otherwise isolated and even stigmatized individuals. At the same time, cyberspace's public real estate is being developed and exploited by corporate entities, and there are grounds for concern that as single companies begin to control both Internet content and systems for gaining access to that content, the Web could resemble an enclosed shopping mall.

Lesbian author and Internet innovator Patricia Nell Warren (2000) warned, "If the Net continues to nurture the 'gay community,' and keep it inclusive, it's important not to forget the original reasons why the Net attracted us: low cost, grassroots access, ease in finding each other, inclusiveness, the dignity of the individual." Campbell's account of three Internet Relay Chat communities comprising "men who utilize Internet technologies to find others who share their erotic predilections" offers a valuable and important glimpse into virtual spaces that fulfill Warren's prescription for the promise of online community.

Larry Gross
Annenberg School for Communication
University of Southern California

REFERENCES

Baym, N. (1999). *Tune in, log on: Soaps, fandom, and online community.* Thousand Oaks, CA: Sage Publications.

Clifford, J. and G. Marcus (Eds.) (1986). *Writing culture: The poetics and the politics of ethnography.* Berkeley: University of California Press.

Hymes, D. (Ed.) (1969). *Reinventing anthropology.* New York: Random House.

Lewis, P. (1995). "Planet Out's Gay Services on Virtual Horizon." *The New York Times,* August 21, p. D3.

Nestle, J. (1967). *A restricted country.* Ithaca, NY: Firebrand.

Proust, M. (1927). *Cities of the plain.* Trans. C. K. Scott Moncrieff. New York: The Modern Library.

Tierney, J. (1995). "From the Stone Age to the Information Age SEX SELLS." *The Baltimore Sun,* July 23, p. 1E.

Warren, P. N. (2000). "Chasing Rainbows: GLBT Identity and the Internet." March 2000, available at <http://www.cybersocket.com>.

Acknowledgments

This work would not have come to be without the assistance, advice, and guidance of many remarkable individuals. The original study from which this book emerged was conducted as my master's thesis under the guidance of Lisa Henderson, whose patience, energy, and untiring encouragement will forever remain a wonder to me. It was my advisor at the Annenberg School for Communication at the University of Pennsylvania, Larry Gross, who recommended developing this initial study into the book you now hold. His insights have proven invaluable to this project, and I'm extraordinarily fortunate to have him as a mentor. I'm also grateful to John De Cecco for his support of this project and his keen observations on how it could be brought to fruition. Valuable contributions to this book were also made by Jarice Hanson and Justin Lewis as members of my thesis committee at the University of Massachusetts.

I owe a debt of thanks to Richard F. Hentz, whose feedback significantly improved this text and whose friendship profoundly enriches my life, and Frank Schaap, whose words so often served to inspire. Likewise, I would like to express my appreciation to Julia Chang and Lee Humphreys for their introspective contributions and steadfast friendships. I also extend my gratitude to Ian Reyes, for so eagerly serving as a theoretical sounding board; Ignacio Lopez-Vicuña, for debates, musings, and hot-fudge sundaes; James Allan, for thoughtful discussions on Foucault, Butler, and cute guys at the gym; and Les Wright for being such a generous repository of bear history. For always providing a sympathetic ear, I offer a nod and a smile to Carol Bonura, who herself has a promising future as an ethnographic scholar. A special note of appreciation is owed to Jillian Mason, for so promptly answering my many questions regarding the publishing process, and Amy Rentner, for her boundless patience and unflagging assistance with this manuscript.

I want to acknowledge all those members of the IRC channels #gaymuscle, #gaychub, and #gaymusclebears for their cooperation, friendliness, and interest in this study. Though I am unable to list their names here, I am deeply indebted to those individuals who spoke to me so openly and honestly about their experiences in cyberspace. Their words and stories constitute the soul of this work.

Finally, I wish to thank Henry Jenkins, whose guidance and friendship made graduate school a possibility for me. The debt I owe him is too great to be adequately expressed in words. Without him, I am sure none of this would have come to be.

Thank you all.

Chapter 1

Bodiless Exultation?

For Case, who'd lived for the bodiless exultation of cyberspace
. . . the elite stance involved a certain relaxed contempt for the
flesh. The body was meat.

William Gibson
Neuromancer, 1984

Revelations can be found in the most mundane of moments. At
least this was the experience in my thinking about cyberspace. My
rather modest revelation occurred during a bright and otherwise un-
eventful afternoon in the fall of 1997, just after the air had taken on
that invigorating crispness so characteristic of New England au-
tumns. Returning home from the gym, still sweaty and sore from my
workout, I mixed a protein shake, sat down at my computer, and
connected to the Internet, intending only to check my e-mail before
showering. But when my modem made those familiar beeps and
hisses as it reached out over the phone lines, something was aroused
in me—curiosity perhaps—that would divert me from my innocent
aims. I was drawn to a place that had become a fixture in my daily
life, a place that was at times comfortable and reassuring, like a well-
worn easy chair, and at other times exhilarating and intimidating, like
a less-than-savory bar that holds the promise of carnal discovery.
That place was a chat room—a virtual environment in cyberspace—
known to its patrons simply as #gaymuscle.

The first thing I noticed upon entering was the topic of the day—
"We're going to pump *clap* you up!"—which, not surprisingly, reflected **Brutus**'s fondness for the *Saturday Night Live* characters
Hans and Franz. The next thing I noticed was one of the regulars, a
weight lifter of considerable strength and girth named **NCLifter,**
conspicuously scratching his groin and spitting. **Plutarch,** another

1

recognized patron of this place, took the opportunity to comment on **NCLifter**'s macho performance. The two have a long-standing rivalry and are well matched not only in personality and wit but also in build. Although such a display may have put off newcomers, I had grown accustomed to such antics and engaged in my customary greetings. To my surprise, #gaymuscle was quite active for a weekday afternoon, with the competing conversations of a dozen or so people lending the place a boisterous atmosphere. A small smile worked its way across my face when two of my closest friends returned my greetings, their presence providing me with a certain sense of satisfaction.

Someone new to the scene was inquiring about the place to see if anyone else was in Phoenix. Publicly calling out, he asked if there were any "desert rats" in attendance, to which **NCLifter** quickly countered that only "gym rats" were present. A moment later, **Plutarch** revealed that he was in Sierra Vista, only a few hours away from Phoenix, adding that he visits Tucson most weekends. Characteristic of his sense of humor, **Smilee** contributed a crass remark about **Plutarch**'s sex life, to which **NCLifter** added an inarticulate expression of his dismay. No doubt the new guy quickly learned that there is little sense of propriety in this place.

Although they were not participating in any of the conversations, two others in the place drew my attention. **Umgawa,** who usually involves himself in any discussion, maintained a silent vigil from the sidelines. I considered privately messaging him but decided against it. Not only had our relationship become overshadowed by an emotional awkwardness, but also I suspected that he was at that moment too engrossed in his work to pay attention to any online activities. Several patrons do this—hang out here while at work, alternating their attention between #gaymuscle and their professional responsibilities. Often such people are present during weekdays in name only.

The other individual attracting my attention was **Msclfreak**. He, like **Umgawa,** was not participating in any of the energetic exchanges, but this was not unexpected. **Msclfreak** seldom engaged in public conversations anymore, preferring private chats with those who already knew him. Unable to resist, I sent him a private message, attempting to initiate a brief tête-à-tête of our own. My pulse quickened the instant he responded to my invitation. It is well known among my friends that I harbor an intense attraction for **Msclfreak,** and our conversations generally carry sexual undertones. I told **Msclfreak** about my workout in hopes that he, as an experienced bodybuilder, could offer a few training tips and perhaps a few words of encouragement. Of course, discussions of training often serve as preludes to more erotic discussions of bodily performances.

In the next moment, a competitive bodybuilder named **PECS** entered and was immediately greeted by many of the regulars, including myself. Possessing one of the most muscularly developed bodies on #gaymuscle, **PECS** has garnered a certain celebrity among the patrons, a celebrity he most assuredly encourages. In keeping with his flamboyant image, **PECS** began giving out roses to his friends and fans. He offered roses to **Younghung, Britannic,** and me before stopping to comment that **NCLifter** is too "butch" to appreciate such a gesture. When **NCLifter** confirmed this, **Plutarch** had an outburst of laughter. I couldn't help laughing as well and, with a prodigious grin on my face, made a brief comment on how amusing I found all of this. With a fading chuckle, I reclined back into my chair and savored the sensation of being someplace familiar, the sensation of being among friends, just as another old chum entered the room.

Well, at least that's how it all *felt* at the time. In actuality, it looked like this:

```
*** Now talking in #gaymuscle
*** Topic is 'We're going to pump *clap* you up!'
*** Set by Brutus on Wed Sept 29 15:19:04
<BUffbutt> Minnesota here
*NCLifter spits and scratches his balls
<Plutarch> So butch, NJ.
<NCLifter> yea well you know how it is
<John> Hey guys!
*** BigNY has joined #gaymuscle
<Younghung> hey john!
<Brittanic> john! how ya doing?
<sk8rboy21> <—Phoenix
<sk8rboy21> any desert rats here?
<NCLifter> nah just gym rats
<John> Hey younghung, hey brittanic—doing well thanx!
<sk8rboy21> hmmm
<Plutarch> A few hours southeast of ya, sk8rboy
<sk8rboy21> where you at Plutarch? Tucson?
<Plutarch> Sierra Vista, actually. Although I get into Tucson most ev-
    ery weekend.
*** topme-20 has quit IRC (Ping timeout: 180 seconds)
```

<Smilee> still cruisin for cock out in AZ huh plu
<Smilee> can't you take a hint? :)
<NCLifter> uuuuuuuuuuuuuuuuuuuuuuuuuuuuuuuuuuuuuuh
*** PECS has joined #gaymuscle
<Younghung> PECS!
<John> PECS!
<Brittanic> hey pecs!
<NCLifter> hey jimmy
<PECS> kiddies!
* PECS gives Younghung a rose
* PECS gives John a rose
* PECS gives Brittanic a rose
<PECS> lifter youre to butch for a rose
<NCLifter> damn right!
<Plutarch> LOL
<John> too funny! :)
*** Mastertop has joined #gaymuscle

I recall that as I continued to chat into the late afternoon, I felt the sweat drying on my skin and the growing pressure on my bladder from the protein shake. I also remember how those bodily demands were countered by the elation I experienced as **Msclfreak** described what he could do to me with his body—perhaps a different form of physical imperative. Indeed, it seemed that bodies were involved in every aspect of this online experience. Those sensations originating from my own body—the sweat drying on my skin, the pressure building in my bladder, the blood rushing to my groin—only heightened my awareness of the distant bodies of those I was interacting with but could not physically see. I was reading text on the screen, but I was thinking and feeling in terms of flesh. While **Msclfreak** may have been some 3,000 miles away from me at the time, my thoughts were focused on the qualities of his body: its thickness, its hardness, its capacity for growth. Although I had never met either **NCLifter** or **Plutarch** in person, I held a substantial impression of their considerable bulk and strength. **PECS** may have been giving me a virtual rose in a virtual space, but my mind never questioned the tangibility of his sculpted physique sitting before the keyboard. It was in this moment that revelation was found: bodies remain very much a part of the experience of the virtual.

BODIES IN CYBERSPACE . . .

As this brief recollection illustrates, my experience of cyberspace exists in sharp contrast to those fantastical images of technological disembodiment found in so much science fiction. For those I have encountered online, cyberspace is about anything but the "bodiless exultation" William Gibson envisioned in his dystopic novel, *Neuromancer.* Yet this seductive image of bodily transcendence in cyberspace has proliferated not only in the pages of cyberpunk fiction and such Hollywood fare as *The Lawnmower Man* (1992), *Johnny Mnemonic* (1995), and *The Matrix* (1999)—ironic that the notion of disembodied existence should prove so sexy in the popular consciousness—but also in the pages of many academic works. In the final decade of the twentieth century, a number of Western intellectuals began postulating that a new subjectivity was evolving from online interaction. Perhaps prematurely, some argued that this emerging online subject would be like the Greek god Proteus, possessing the ability to transform the self at will. For these social scientists and philosophers, the capacity to transcend the corporeal constitutes the liberating potential of cyberspace and the technological panacea for oppressive social hierarchies. Freed from our burdensome material selves, they proclaim, we become fluid entities, overcoming those societal stigmas inscribed on the body—race, gender, age, size, beauty, what have you.

Whether it is proclaimed to offer our salvation or our ruin, the more extreme arguments surrounding cyberspace are based on a fundamentally similar supposition conflating online interaction with bodily transcendence. This conflation, in turn, rests on an essentialized understanding of "the body" as solely a physical object—a corporeal shell containing and confining some ethereal and cognitive self. Thus to interact where, in theory, the body is absent is to be liberated from those social prohibitions imposed on the body. In essence, these arguments, condemnatory and celebratory alike, are predicated on the conviction that there is a radical disjuncture between experiences in the physical world and those found in cyberspace. I identify this position as the *online disembodiment thesis.*

The story I relate in this book counters this enticing vision of bodiless exultation with a more sensual portrait of cyberspace. Here I will tell the story of a group of men who utilize Internet technologies to find others that share their erotic predilections. This is a story of carnal exploration and community formation, as well as a story of bodybuilders and musclebears and chubby chasers. Specifically, this is a story of three distinct social scenes on Internet Relay Chat (IRC): #gaymuscle, a community formulated around images of the muscular male body; #gaychub, a community celebrating male obesity, where—in diametric opposition to #gaymuscle—fatness holds considerable value; and finally, #gaymusclebears, a space representing the erotic convergence of the obese and muscular male body emerging out of the gay male "bear" subculture. The channels that serve as the nexuses for these social scenes represent virtual spaces constructed by gay men for the discussion, exploration, and eroticism of the male body. This is the story of how it is that the body remains present in these virtual spaces replete with their own vernaculars and conventions, cultural practices and social taboos. And as with all good stories, this story endeavors to make a point.

Examining the vital role the body plays in defining these online spaces offers insight into how individuals negotiate their relationship to their physical-world self through computer-mediated communication technologies. Indeed, the social practices emerging in these virtual environments expose the critical role of culture and language in constituting what we understand as "the body." Investigating how the body is (re)incorporated into social relations in these online communities also allows me to complicate the online disembodiment thesis. As I will demonstrate, for interactants on these channels, the body is both a shared reference for online communication and a primary component of online identity. The body remains present in cyberspace because what we refer to as "the body" is at once a physical form and a discursive configuration apprehending the physical, and it is this discursive configuration that accompanies individuals into these virtual environments and shapes online interaction.

Of interest here is not only the formulation of online communities around particular conceptions of the desirable body but also the very intensity of the discussions surrounding the body in spaces generally purported to be lacking all physicality. Because each channel—#gaymuscle, #gaychub, and #gaymusclebears—is oriented toward the exploration and eroticism of various images of the male body, these online interactants have had to devise textual means of reconstructing the body in cyberspace. I endeavor to complicate simplistic understandings of the body as a "natural" basis of identity by examining how the body is experienced on these channels. I also attempt to challenge some of the generalizations surrounding social relations in cyberspace, especially in regard to gender and sexuality, by assuming a grounded approach to these very particular online communities. My observations suggest that gay men have been quick to employ computer-mediated communication technologies to expand their social networks, and I want to understand how this adoption of Internet technologies is fueled by physical-world needs. That is, I am keenly interested in how offline social relations shape online behavior. In pursuing this goal, I find ethnography a particularly useful mode of inquiry.

Historically, ethnography has been understood as a method of anthropological investigation based on immersion in a particular cultural community. The investigation of ethnographic research is not only to observe and record a community's ostensible social structures and practices but also to gain an appreciation for the more elusive tacit cultural assumptions of a particular population. Conventionally, this immersion involved living in proximity to the community of study (in the so-called field) and participating with community members in key social institutions. More recently, however, understandings of proximity have been complicated as anthropologists use ethnography as a means of studying communities with which they already identify (see, for instance, the insightful work of Kath Weston [1991, 1998]). Although initially associated with cultural anthropology, ethnography has become a critical mode of inquiry for those working under the rubric of cultural studies, exemplified in the work of Paul Willis (1977), Dick Hebdige (1979), Janice Radway (1984), Henry Jenkins (1992), and Angela McRobbie (1991). In my use of ethnography, I endeavor to extend this line of scholarship into the realm of the virtual.

Cultural studies scholars are not so much interested in examining specific cultural phenomena in isolation, but rather seek to understand how particular (sub)cultural communities and practices relate to and reflect the larger social and political context. Central to scholarly work following in the intellectual trajectory of the Birmingham Centre for Contemporary Cultural Studies is the theory of "articulation" (Sterne, 1999). This theory holds that all social institutions are complexly interconnected and that seemingly independent economic and political spheres do in fact influence each other (such as the mili-

tary and the commercial media). Therefore, by studying specific cultural artifacts, insights can be gained into the institutions producing
such artifacts and, indirectly, into the broader power dynamics shaping those producing institutions. The cultural studies commitment to
theory—that is, the commitment to relating the concrete and particular to a more holistic and abstract reality—arises from the imperative
to understand how social hierarchies are deployed and maintained
and how they can be resisted and subverted. An important dimension
of this larger intellectual project is comprehending how individuals
incorporate cultural artifacts (such as mass-media products) into their
negotiation of daily life and how those artifacts influence the ways
people make sense out of the world they live in. As Paul Willis (1978)
poignantly points out,

> it is one of the fundamental paradoxes of our social life that
> when we are at our most natural, our most *everyday*, we are also
> at our most cultural; that when we are in the roles that look the
> most obvious and given, we are actually in roles that are con-
> structed, learned and far from inevitable. (p. 184, emphasis orig-
> inal)

A notable influence in this study of everyday life is the French philosopher Michel de Certeau, who explores how individuals employ
cultural products in ways unforeseen by their producers. For de Certeau,
although individual consumers exercise little control over what is
produced and distributed, they can adopt subversive strategies that allow them to appropriate those aspects of cultural products they find
meaningful into their own narratives of life. Referring to this practice
as "poaching," de Certeau offers a useful departure from the deterministic models of the Frankfurt School which positioned media consumers as cultural dupes easily manipulated by the ruling classes.

Media scholars drawing on de Certeau abandon deterministic assumptions about the activities of media consumers in favor of more
complex and nuanced understandings of the cultural roles of mass
media.[1] For instance, Roger Silverstone (1989) draws on the thought of
de Certeau in arguing for a more comprehensive approach to the
study of television reception: "[I]f we are to gain a more mature understanding of television's place in contemporary culture then we
need to study in detail the mechanisms of its penetration into the warp
and weft of everyday life: into the ways in which it enters, and is

transformed by, the heterogeneity—the polysemy and the polymorph-ology—of daily experience" (p. 78). Despite studying a medium very different in technological design, I hold a position intellectually aligned with Silverstone's—to gain a significant appreciation of the phenomenon of computer-mediated communication, we must exam-ine how individuals incorporate these technologies into their everyday experiences. Although a growing body of research into the develop-ment of cyberspace exists, meaningful understandings of how the diverse social positions of individuals inform their use of communi-cation technologies has, like the integration of television into daily life, "somehow slipped through the net of academic scrutiny" (Silver-stone, 1989, p. 77). Thus I am interested in how gay men incorporate Internet technologies into their negotiation of everyday life and how their uses of these technologies are shaped by their physical-world circumstances. By assuming an exploratory approach to my subject, I hope to avoid the intellectual pitfalls found in more deterministic positions, particularly the analytical dangers of technological deter-minism so common in discussions of new media.

Unfortunately, technological determinism has been a central fea-ture of early research on cyberspace. In her study of a Usenet newsgroup devoted to television soap operas, Nancy Baym (1995) in-terrogates this initial research that denies recognition to the social, playful, and expressive potential of online interaction, commenting that too much of the work on computer-mediated communication "assumes that the computer itself is the sole influence on communi-cative outcomes" (p. 139). Carolyn Marvin (1988) identifies this view as the "instrument-centered perspective" (p. 4). Marvin compli-cates this artifactual approach in which the technology itself is viewed as the sole determinant of the social uses surrounding it, not-ing that new social "practices do not so much flow directly from tech-nologies that inspire them as they are improvised out of old practices that no longer work in new settings" (p. 5).

Marvin's claim constitutes an important corollary of this study: the uses to which individuals put emerging technologies are often very different from those envisioned by either the developers of such tech-nologies or those policymakers directing their deployment in society. It is doubtful that the computer engineers designing ARPANET (the precursor to the Internet) for the U.S. military ever envisioned gay men utilizing such technologies to explore their erotic desires. Arguably, these particular social activities emerge less out of the technologies of computer-mediated communication and more out of such established queer practices as tearoom trade, cruising, and public sex (Califia, 1994; Chauncey, 1994). I would also contend that there is a certain technological determinism inherent in those arguments perpetuating the image of disembodiment in cyberspace. This point will perhaps be more obvious if I provide some explanation of what I have in mind when referring to the "online disembodiment thesis."

INTERROGATING THE ONLINE DISEMBODIMENT THESIS

According to the editor of *Mondo 2000,* R. U. Sirius, we are increasingly "creatures of mind-zapping bits and bytes moving around at the speed of light" (quoted in Terranova, 2000, p. 271). Certainly many of those writing about cyberspace in the 1990s perpetuated this image of the online self as a digital entity of pure thought unadulterated by the experiences of the physical world, and this image all too often leads to celebratory discussions of cyberspace as some virtual utopia. For instance, in her cyberfeminist treatise, Sadie Plant (1996) contends that online interaction is undermining "the material reality of two thousand years of patriarchal control" (p. 171). Not surprisingly, Plant avoids outlining exactly how this undermining is happening or what precisely constitutes this feminist "cyberrevolution." What is clear, however, is that Plant sees a radical rupture between the mundane physical world we presently inhabit and those realities emerging in cyberspace. Nowhere is the rhetoric of bodily transcendence more apparent than in her claim that as "man" enters cyberspace, "the phallic dream of eternal life and its fantasy of female death are interrupted by the abstract matters of a cybernetic space which has woven him into its own emergence" (p. 182). The problem with Plant's claims is that they have little grounding in what people actually do with computer-mediated communication technologies. Rather, her speculations are reminiscent of the seductive images of cyberspace found in the pages of cyberpunk fiction. By leveling such criticism, I am not suggesting that speculation cannot be fruitful. However, I become concerned when grand claims based on fanciful imagery are uncritically incorporated into scholarly discourse. Although Plant contends that "cyberspace is out of man's control" (p. 181), it is just as possible that Internet technologies and virtual realms can serve to reinforce patriarchal schema, as some feminist writers have suggested (Balsamo, 1995; Kendall, 2002; O'Brien, 1999).

Not all discussions of bodily transcendence are as celebratory as Plant's treatise. Dan Thu Nguyen and Jon Alexander (1996), for instance, contend that achieving the "human dream of transcending materiality" comes at an "unforeseen cost," abstracting "us from our existence as physical beings in the world" and undermining the possibility of a democratic public sphere (p. 99). For writers such as Nguyen and Alexander, the very transcendence of the physical that they claim Internet technologies make possible undermines our humanity; when our own bodies cease to matter, so do our social relations. Although politically critical of cyberspace, their discussion is not itself critically grounded. Like Plant, Nguyen and Alexander's arguments are based more on speculation than empirical evidence. Essentially, their critique rests on the hypothesis that an online interactant "initially experiences a bodiless exultation that may shortly settle into the armature of addiction" (p. 102). Though this is very much the case in Gibson's fictitious world, it is not clear that this is what individuals are actually experiencing in cyberspace.

Whether describing cyberspace in utopian or dystopian terms, arguments such as Plant's or Nguyen and Alexander's are predicated upon what I identify as the online disembodiment thesis. This thesis rests on the notion that there is an absolute demarcation between the real and the virtual, and therefore a radical disjuncture between experiences in cyberspace and those in the physical world. Scholars subscribing to this proposition characterize cyberspace as a sovereign realm, distinct from and unaffected by the cultural, political, and economic forces shaping the mundane world we inhabit. Thus some social scientists may see online experiences transforming offline perceptions, but seldom do these same researchers examine the ways in which offline circumstances inform online interactions.

The demarcation between cyberspace and the physical world underlying the online disembodiment thesis is based on a certain binary logic. In other words, either/or thinking is at hand: if the physical world is real, then cyberspace must be virtual and therefore something other than real; if the body is present in the physical world, then the body must be absent in the virtual world; if oppressive social constructs such as race, gender, and sexuality are based on the body, then when the body is absent these constructs must also be absent. This logic is often implicit in those arguments promoting the disembodiment thesis. For instance, it is by employing such binary logic that Plant sees cyberspace as feminist space precisely because the physical world is male-dominated space. Such binary thinking fails to recognize the complex ways in which online and offline experience, or the real and the virtual, bleed into each other.

As I will demonstrate, for at least some people, new and complex but no less critical relationships to the physical body are developing through online interaction. These relationships may unsettle certain societal notions surrounding the body, but they do not appear to challenge our existence as embodied entities. More than a mere physical shell containing and confining some ethereal essence, the body is a principal component of our identity—it is one of the predominate means of how we identify ourselves and how we are identified by others—and I would contend that this holds true in cyberspace. This is not to suggest that social experiences in cyberspace cannot help us to envision how we can apprehend this material existence differently. Indeed, I will argue that social formations emerging in the virtual can expose dominant discourses surrounding the body as artificial, socially constructed, and therefore alterable. Cyberspace as a social phenomenon can prove invaluable, for it can help us imagine how social relations could be different and perhaps more egalitarian. Even the most fanciful writings of cyberpunk fiction prove to be useful cultural products, for they broaden our notions of what is possible, or at least reveal what is possible to imagine at a particular historical moment. However, scholarship becomes problematic when it confuses such conceptual possibilities with what is actually occurring online.

In this study, I make every effort to avoid this online disembodiment thesis and the binary logic it encompasses. I do not see an either/or relationship between online interaction and offline experiences. Rather, I see individuals integrating their online and offline experiences into a broader understanding of the reality of everyday life. One means of circumventing the online disembodiment thesis is to avoid essentialized understandings of the body itself. Informed by both poststructuralist and feminist thought, my understanding of the body is both of a physical presence (bodies occupy physical space and have materiality) and a discursive figuration or performance (bodies also occupy discursive space and have expressive significance). We communicate with our bodies through speech, hand gestures, and facial expressions, but our bodies also act as objects of communication in terms of skin color, facial features, and somatotype, which may signify racial, ethnic, gender, or even sexual identities beyond our intent. As feminist thinkers have well established, society generally frames what is spoken based on the body that does the speaking (Butler, 1990a,b, 1993; Grosz, 1994).

It would be a mistake to understand this distinction between the physical body and the discursive or performative body in terms of some problematic mind/body dichotomy. Rather, we make meaningful our corporeal existence—our experience of embodiment—through discourse, as discourse takes on physical consequence through bodily performance. Perhaps it would be more useful to understand this in terms of what Don Ihde (2002) identifies as the "body one/body two distinction" (p. 16). Drawing on phenomenological thought, Ihde's "body one" is our motile, perceptual, and emotive experience of embodiment, while his "body two" is how such direct "being-a-body" experience is understood in a social and cultural sense. It is through this "body two"—"the body of the condemned in Foucault, body upon which is written or signified the various possible meanings of politics, culture, the socius" (p. 70)—that the experiences of "body one" are incorporated into social relations. However, in our negotiation of life, these two modes of bodily experience are rendered indistinguishable, "keep[ing] any clear line of demarcation between body one and body two from being drawn" (p. 17).

The indistinguishability of "body one" and "body two" in daily life is evident in the experience of being the target of an abusive epithet. On those occasions when I, as a gay man, have been subjected to hurtful epithets regarding my sexuality, the experience has been by no means a purely discursive one. I have in mind a particularly offensive word that I have heard hurled at me from a passing car on more than one occasion while walking out of a gay bar. Upon hearing that unmistakable word, and noting the tone with which it was uttered, I have the sensation of physical harm—my pulse races, my stomach tightens, my gait stumbles, and my body shivers. In essence, I have the visceral experience of fear. Although the act in question is a discursive one, my experience of that event is as much physical as it is cerebral. In terms of cyberspace, the text appearing on the computer screen can, like the violent epithet, invoke visceral responses. Thus, rather than seeing ourselves as disembodied when online, I find it much more useful to conceptualize ourselves as experiencing the possibility of relating to our bodies in new ways—finding new ways to speak about and think about embodiment.

A particularly useful concept I will explore in this book is that of the cyborg. This is not the fantastical image of the cyborg emerging from popular science fiction and such films as *The Terminator* (1984) or *Blade Runner* (1982). Rather, I refer to the feminist articulation of the cyborg offered by Donna Haraway as a way of understanding what it is that we are becoming in our increasingly technological society. This understanding of the cyborg complicates such binary figurations as natural/synthetic and self/other. Indeed, we may already be in the state of becoming this cyborg subject, and as a result we may need to rethink our views of the body, the self, and the other. Throughout this book, I will revisit the question of (dis)embodiment in cyberspace, endeavoring to demonstrate that in addition to containing flesh and bone and genetic material, bodies also bear social and political significance. First, however, the question of why I focused my study on the online experiences of gay men merits comment.

WHY GAY MEN?

In composing this study, I am sensitive to the disproportionate representation of gay men in queer scholarship. To date, queer theory has been based primarily on the experiences of gay men who are both white and middle class, fostering a theorizing of sexuality that often lacks direct relevance to the experiences of lesbians, bisexuals, and transsexual and transgendered individuals, as well as those whose "nonnormative" sexual identity intersects with nondominant racial, ethnic, or class identities. I do not intend this study to perpetuate this problematic trend by suggesting that the experiences of these specific individuals are immediately generalizable to broader queer populations. Rather, my aim is to provide a more complex, albeit incomplete, understanding of how members of a sexual minority manage their identities through communication technologies.

A key reason for focusing on communities constructed by gay men is that the online experiences of sexual minorities have been largely absent in the existing literature on cyberspace. This is particularly striking when one considers the substantial (and perhaps disproportionate) representation of gay-oriented Web sites as well as queer-identified chat rooms on both Internet Relay Chat (IRC) and America Online (AOL). To date, there has been a general collapse of online sexuality with straight sexuality and, arguably, online communities with online white, straight communities. Some of the only studies to look at the experiences of gays and lesbians in cyberspace include David F. Shaw's (1997) uses and gratifications examination of emotional expressions in the online discourse of gay men on IRC; Shelley Correll's (1995) investigation into the formation of an online lesbian community around a particular electronic bulletin board service; Nina Wakeford's (1996) discussion of postings on "Sappho," a lesbian-oriented electronic mailing list; and Randal Woodland's (2000) overview of the defining features of queer space on four distinct computer systems. Beyond these few studies, however, remains a general absence of investigation into expressions of queer sexuality online or the formation of gay and lesbian communities in cyberspace.

Examining those distinct practices central to these online queer communities also allows me to complicate hasty generalizations made by earlier cyberspace researchers based on the activities of more mainstream (read "straight") online collectives. However, one generalized claim I will make is that cyberspace has proved to be a hospitable sphere for the discussion and exploration of sexuality, particularly sexualities deemed nonnormative by the dominant society. In his study of gay male discourses online, Shaw (1997) notes that "IRC's 'gaysex' and 'jack-off' (also gay) channels are usually among the most populated IRC channels—sometimes surpassing the population of 'sex,' the complementary heterosexual chat room" (p. 136). Data gathered for this project indicate that on a typical night on the IRC network where the channels studied here reside,[2] more than 38,000 users are on more than 15,000 channels, and more than 1,000 of these channels are devoted to some form of nonnormative sexuality.[3] Of course, these figures do not encompass the many more chatting on the private service America Online, the single largest Internet provider with an estimated membership of more than 35 million, according to their corporate Web site <www.corp.aol.com/whoweare.html>. If we know that large numbers of people are entering cyberspace to discuss their sexual desires, then a need arises for theoretical explanations addressing the possible physical-world conditions motivating people to engage in virtual-world erotic interactions.

One possible explanation for the proliferation of online spaces dedicated to erotic discussions may be a general dissatisfaction with how sex is apprehended in the discourses of daily life. Pat Califia (1994) contends that there "is something unsatisfying and dishonest about the way sex is talked about (or hidden) in daily life" (p. 11). Although I would hold that sex is far from hidden in daily life (rather, it would seem that sex is omnipresent, invested in every social relation), I agree there is something unsatisfying and profoundly dishonest, or perhaps artificial, underlying mundane discussions of sex. Some sense of why these day-to-day discussions about sex prove so unsatisfying may be found in the writings of French historian and philosopher Michel Foucault. Contesting the conventional view of Western history in which sexuality has been progressively liberated from the repression and denial of Victorian times—a view he identifies as the "repressive hypothesis"—Foucault (1978) examines the proliferation of institutional discourses surrounding sexuality since the eighteenth century. Foucault notes how those discourses produced by key Western institutions—schools, prisons, clinics, asylums, and universities—superficially appear only to confine sex, restricting it to an object of scientific study and regulation. However, this view remains incomplete, for sex has not been so much repressed through such institutional discourse as it has been incorporated into the modern mechanisms of power.

By interrogating these institutional discourses, Foucault's (1978) objective is not simply to "liberate desire" but rather to "show how deployments of power are directly connected to the body" (p. 152). For Foucault, the Western institutional incitement to speak about the sexual did more than render sex an object of study; more profoundly, it extended institutional power over our "bodies and their materiality, their forces, energies, sensations, and pleasures" (p. 155) by apprehending bodily sensations through the social construct of sexuality. Thus, these proliferating discourses of the sexual do not so much unshackle desire as they regulate our relationships to our bodies, effecting the "displacement, intensification, reorientation, and modification of desire itself" (p. 23). In short, this social construction of sexuality succeeded in "penetrating bodies in an increasingly detailed way" and in "controlling populations" by subordinating bodily sensations to cultural imperatives (p. 107).

This discursive colonization of the body and bodily pleasures remains in the terms available to speak of sex, rendering "sexual liberation" an impossibility. As Foucault (1978) points out, "saying yes to sex" should not be equated with saying "no to power" (p. 157). On the contrary, resisting such power relations resides not in the sexual per se but in "bodies and pleasures" (p. 157). Perhaps this provides an explanation as to why some people—including those represented in this study—turn to cyberspace as a forum to explore the erotic, not necessarily as it relates to institutional examination or social proscription, nor to talk about sex for its own sake, but rather to speak more directly of their own personal desires, fantasies, fetishes, and pleasurable practices. Perhaps some turn to cyberspace as an arena in which to explore their bodies and bodily pleasures outside the conventions of daily life. This may prove especially true for those who find themselves members of a sexual minority, and particularly for those marginalized within their respective sexual minority due to race, age, body type, or desire.

To be clear, the mere abundance of sexual discussions through this new medium should not be read as immediately representing a radical departure in the ways sex(uality) is apprehended in Western societies. In examining *how* sex is discussed in these virtual spaces, it is vital to confront such questions as what new discourses regarding the erotic are possible within these novel contexts and what new conceptualizations may emerge out of social relations conducted through this new medium. Ultimately, some determination will need to be made as to whether those discourses emerging online reinforce the oppressive deployment of sexuality in Western societies or undermine naturalized understandings of sex and sexuality.

In conducting this study, I began with the premise that a general dissatisfaction for the way sex is apprehended in mundane offline discussions constitutes a strong motive for these interactants to construct their own virtual spaces. In addition to a general dissatisfaction with prosaic discussions of sex, I would also suggest that some might be turning to cyberspace out of a discontentment with how the body is represented in the mainstream media. Each of the three IRC channels examined in this study provides not only an affirming space for erotic exploration but also an alternative means for speaking of the body. It is this diverse range of discourses surrounding embodiment that, I argue, subverts essentialized conceptions of physical beauty and normative sexual practices. Although the multifarious understandings of what constitutes the sexual in these virtual spaces complicate comfortable truisms in Western society, I acknowledge that the majority of those interacting on these channels are not necessarily aware of the political implications of their online activities. While unsettling naturalized conceptions surrounding the erotic body, these same interactants can produce discourses reinforcing oppressive understandings of the racial or gendered body. It is vital then to avoid collapsing online engagement in nonnormative erotic practices with a conscious attempt to subvert the cultural and political status quo.

My intent in examining these IRC channels is neither to celebrate nor condemn these gay men as political subjects, but rather to ascertain what discourses converge in these distinct cyberspaces that are absent (or rendered invisible) in the norm of physical-world interaction. From this it is possible to conceptualize society's investment in maintaining certain lines of discourse surrounding sex, sexual identities, and the body, while concealing and suppressing others. In addition, the discourses emerging from these particular virtual environments allow me to explore online embodied experiences that subvert those conceptions of beauty, health, and the erotic depicted in more mainstream media. Finally, the online practices of these individuals complicate the problematic thesis equating social interaction in cyberspace with bodiless interaction. As I will demonstrate, the flesh continues to hold broad currency in the virtual.

COMING ATTRACTIONS

In Chapter 2, I discuss how it is that I came to participate in and ultimately study the online communities central to this book. In doing so, I provide an overview of IRC, including a brief outline of its historical development, as well as some explanation of why I elected to study social relations on IRC rather than on that form of synchronous computer-mediated communication represented in so many online studies: MUDs (multiuser dungeons). I conclude the chapter by touching on many of the methodological and theoretical issues confronting the ethnographic researcher in cyberspace. In Chapter 3, "Virtual Gay Bars," I turn to the IRC channels central to this study, exploring the characteristics of their populations as well as their norms and conventions (particularly those surrounding gender and sexuality). I also argue for the particularity of online experience by demonstrating how the offline social positions of individuals (in terms of race, gender, class, sexuality, and age) shape social dynamics in cyberspace. In examining the complex reasons individuals cite for first venturing online, and particularly for chatting on these specific channels, I hope to counter notions that cyberspace exists as a sovereign realm independent of social relations in the physical world.

Chapter 4 focuses on the role of the body in online interaction. Here I theorize about the discursive apprehension of embodiment as I show how some individuals in cyberspace are reincorporating the corporeal into their online interactions and, in so doing, complicating certain dominant understandings of the erotic and the sexual. Building on this analysis, I deconstruct the problematic online disembodiment thesis by demonstrating the vital role the body plays in defining social relations on these channels. Chapter 5 examines what I identify as the "gay male beauty myth." Although many of those I interviewed indicated a general frustration with how the attractive male body is represented in mainstream straight media as well as many of the prevailing modes of gay media, I hold that members of these communities have not necessarily escaped oppressive beauty hierarchies online. Rather, patrons have simply constructed new beauty hierarchies in these virtual spaces, resulting in a broader but not boundless constellation of idealized images of the male body. In the final chapter, I attempt to synthesize my online observations and experiences into some concluding, but not necessarily exhaustive, inferences. In my attempts to complicate particular truisms in contemporary Western culture by extrapolating from online social relations, I hope to make evident how rich and fertile a terrain cyberspace is for the social scientist. I also offer some speculation about the future of those communities represented in this study, IRC as a medium, and the trajectory of computer-mediated communication scholarship.

Before proceeding, however, I need to comment on how I distinguish between online experiences and those had offline in this text. Conventionally, those employing computer-mediated communication technologies will describe their social interactions occurring through Internet technologies as happening "online" or "in cyberspace." Conversely, those experiences had offline are often identified as happening in "the real world," "real life," or even "RL" for short. This means of demarcating between online and offline experience will be apparent in the online interviews presented throughout this book. However, I have elected to make an effort to refer to offline events as occurring in the "physical world" as opposed to using the expressions "real world" or "real life." The reason for my preference of the designation "physical world" is to avoid suggesting that online experiences are any less real or meaningful than experiences offline. Though in my observations, online interactants are not necessarily privileging their offline experiences by using the expression "real life," I avoid this term because of how the reader may perceive its use on my part. However, by referring to offline experiences as occurring in the physical world, I should not be read as implying that online experiences are without physicality. As I endeavor to demonstrate in the following chapters, our physical selves profoundly shape how we understand our encounters in cyberspace.

Chapter 2

Getting Online

When we read ethnographic studies, there is always a point at which we need to ask who is speaking, and for whom.

Graeme Turner
British Cultural Studies: An Introduction, 1990

It is a gray Sunday morning in Boston. Though my calendar proclaims late spring, the weather outside my window suggests late autumn. It is the sort of day that dissuades one from pursuing any productive endeavor, a day better spent huddled in one's home, reading a favorite book while still cocooned in the warmth of the bedcovers. On this particular morning, however, it is my curiosity that beckons me out of bed and to the desk in the corner of my living room. On the desktop is a modest computer, which recently has been equipped with a state-of-the-art 14,400-baud modem. Although I have had access to the Internet through my place of employment for years, the ability to enter cyberspace at home still carries a certain novel thrill.

Within the past few months, several of my friends have begun chatting online, and dialing up my Internet connection, I am eager to ascertain the allure of this activity. Once online, I seek out the Web site for mIRC that my close friend Mike has told me about. Over dinner last evening Mike explained to me that before one can actually start chatting online, one must first obtain a suitable IRC client. A client, I was told, is an interface program designed to make synchronous (i.e., "real-time") chatting functional by providing a graphic representation of the data streaming between different servers on a network. Locating the mIRC site, I read the introductory information explaining how to download, install, and use the program. This is the first time I've downloaded software from the Internet, and I suddenly feel a bit tech savvy. Of course, the instructions are so explicit I doubt any twelve-year-old would have problems following them.

I find the download complete when I return from making breakfast in the kitchen. It starts raining hard outside my window as I anxiously run the installation program. What new experiences await me in cyberspace, I wonder? What new people will I encounter there? What new places will I explore? Fortunately, the program is designed to detect and select the correct settings for my modem and Internet connection. This is one of the primary reasons Mike—a software programmer who often refers to me as "computer challenged"—recommended this particular IRC client. The installation proves quicker than anticipated, and, rather suddenly, I find myself preparing to log on to IRC for the first time.

Before the client will connect me with an IRC network, the program prompts me to select a nickname—an online handle that will be used to identify me to others on the network. I've been warned by my friends not to use my real name, and, to be honest, I'm intrigued by the notion of online anonymity. My first choice, the name of a mythological figure, is apparently not a terribly original one, as the interface indicates that the handle is already in use. I ponder for a moment the significance that will be assigned to this name before deciding on something simple, playful, and far less pretentious: **Big-boy**. As I will come to discover, this seemingly innocent name carries unexpected connotations on certain channels. This time the interface successfully connects to the network and suddenly I find a brave new world of textual interaction opening to me.

In the center of my interface is a large window with the word "status" in the title bar, and within this window is an initial welcome message indicating how many servers there are on the network and how many users are currently logged on. There are also some technical announcements that I neither understand nor pay much attention to. After this initial greeting, nothing more happens. Wondering what to do now, I sit for a moment and listen to the rain pattering against the window like an impatient driver's fingers on a steering wheel. Staring at the motionless screen feels rather like floating in a void—empty, alone, lost. I'm finally here, although I'm not quite sure where here is, or what one does when one arrives. Is this Gibson's "consensual hallucination"? Where is the infinite cityscape of data? It is all a bit disappointing and not much of a distraction from the rainy day outside.

Above the main window, on the top row of the interface, is a series of drop-down menus and, under those, a series of icons. Because I don't understand the functions of any of the icon buttons, I scan across the selection of drop-down menus. I simply stare at the interface for awhile. Although my friend (the computer professional) described this client as intuitive, for me the technology is incomprehensible. Even though I notice there is a "help" menu, I resolve to approach this software application like I have all others before—just play around with it until I figure out what I'm doing. I start reading the options on the different drop-down menus until I find under the "commands" menu the "join channel" function. This seems to be the next logical step once on IRC—joining a channel. But what channel? My friend, the computer programmer, commented about spending most of his time chatting on the channel #gayboston. From the mIRC homepage, I learned that the term "channel" was derived from citizen's band (CB) radio and that all channel names are preceded by a hash mark (#). Recalling this, I type #gayboston into the "join channel" dialogue box.

A new window appears in my interface with the name #gayboston in the title bar. Next to the channel's designation is a topic line indicating that today's subject of conversation is supposed to be "How to make the world's most fabulous martini!" Different colored text is scrolling swiftly by as I try to orient myself. Enlarging the window, I notice that the channel window is divided vertically in two—a larger column to the left and a considerably smaller one to the right. In the larger section, messages appearing at the bottom are quickly pushed up and through the top of the window as new messages proliferate beneath them. Someone is raving about the Italian restaurant that opened last week on Boylston Street; someone else is wondering if anyone is going to tea dance tonight at Chaps. It rather resembles a colorful and chaotic teleprompter.

The narrower section to the right appears to list all the names of people chatting on the channel. Scanning down the perhaps thirty or forty names listed, I recognize one as the nickname my friend told me he goes by online: **JohnnyQuest**. Assuming it is in fact him, I'm not sure how to let him know I'm here. I don't want to type a message on the main window of the channel. I'm afraid any message I type will be lost in the flood of conversation rushing by. I'm also a bit hesitant to draw attention to myself just yet. This is all so new to me that I'm not prepared to be engulfed by this social scene. I move the cursor over to his name and click, highlighting the handle. I try double clicking and, to my surprise, a new dialogue box appears with his online handle in the title of the window. In this new window, I type a terse question:

> **Big-boy:** Is that you Mike?[1]

A moment passes, and then a response appears.

> **JohnnyQuest:** yeah who's this?

A sudden sense of relief mingled with excitement surges through me. I am having my first online conversation.

> **Big-boy:** It's me John. How are you?
> **JohnnyQuest:** hey john! cool, you made it on everything go smoothly? the install and all
> **Big-boy:** Yes, very straightforward. Just one question though . . .
> **JohnnyQuest:** what's that
> **Big-boy:** What do I do now?

Although I am reconstructing this account several years later, that day in the spring of 1996 remains remarkably vivid in my mind. Perhaps it is true that you never forget your first time online. At that moment, however, it would have been impossible to anticipate that this inauspicious event would come to symbolically mark my advent into the "field." Like the traditional cultural anthropologist who has a distinct moment of arrival in the field—such as first entering the village of the "native" culture under study—I could identify my logging on to IRC that day as my entry into the social world I would later come to write about.

OF VIRTUAL TENTS ON CYBERBEACHES . . .

The romantic image of the ethnographer in the field is perhaps best exemplified by the Polish anthropologist Bronislaw Malinowski. Credited with initiating the technique of "participant observation," Malinowski arrived on the beach of the Trobriand Island people he wanted to study in 1915 and, for the next three years, endeavored to live among the "natives." For much of the twentieth century, the image of Malinowski setting up his tent near the Polynesian village under study served as the paradigm for the ethnographic fieldworker, a model remarkably removed from my experiences as researcher. Two significant differences distinguish me from the traditional image of the ethnographer epitomized by Malinowski. First, I entered IRC not as a researcher but as a gay man looking to expand my social networks. In fact, at the time I initially ventured into cyberspace I was working the conventional nine-to-five job in a corporate setting, having yet to return to school to pursue graduate study. Unlike Malinowski, I never intended to leave my home in the quest to discover some distant and exotic "Other." Quite the contrary, I was hoping to discover others like myself where I already lived.

The second important distinction between the traditional image of the cultural anthropologist and myself is that I never actually left the field. In contrast to Malinowski, there is no point at which I returned home to "civilization" with my collection of notes, photographs, physical artifacts, and other forms of documentation to be used in composing a scholarly account of some exotic people. Rather, I continue to chat on the very channels I write about, maintaining those friendships I have already established and fostering new relationships with people I am now meeting. For me, these channels are as much communities in which I share membership as they are subjects of study. In light of these critical distinctions, I am less an academic gone native than a native gone academic.

Despite the many significant differences between Malinowski's position and mine, important insights can be garnered from examining his experiences in the field. For instance, Malinowski took pains to record the minutia of everyday life while they were still new and foreign. Discussing what he terms the "inponderabilia of actual life," Malinowski (1922) warned that the researcher must document impressions "early in the course of working out a district" since "certain subtle peculiarities, which make an impression as long as they are novel, cease to be noticed as soon as they become familiar" (pp. 20-21). Indeed, more quickly than I would have anticipated, I became accustomed to the particularities of online interaction. When I first logged on to IRC, even a simple one-on-one conversation was a strange and technologically wondrous event. However, at some point I cannot now place, the technology of online chatting became transparent to me, and I transitioned from seeing IRC as a vast computer network relaying textual messages in the form of electronic data bits to seeing it as a window onto a newfound social scene. Becoming adept at participating in group conversations on the channel while concurrently carrying on multiple private conversations, I learned to relate my thoughts in terse statements and acronyms to maintain the appearance of real-time interaction. I found that my online use of grammar was changing as capitalization and punctuation became less of a concern than speed in composing messages. Almost instinctively I began emulating other channel members in their use of unique combinations of keyboard characters (known as "emoticons") to textually represent facial expressions such as smiles, frowns, or winks. The more time I spent chatting online, the more this form of communication came to feel remarkably "natural."

My acculturation to online interaction included more than adapting to the distinctive structure of online communication, however; it also included a growing comfort with the disposition of the channels I interacted on. When I first started chatting online, I spent most of my time on the channel #gayboston, which seemed logical because I was living in Boston at the time. I expected this to be a space populated by men self-identifying as "gay," much like any gay bar in the physical world. During my first month on the channel, I became familiar with those notable #gayboston personalities who regularly initiated conversations on the channel, greeting them when they arrived much like those greeting George Wendt's character, Norm Peterson, on the television series *Cheers*. In many respects, the channel reminded me of a gay online version of the Boston bar in that long-running situation comedy, except patrons were doing something other than playing pool in the back room. I also became aware of those who logged on to the channel only to observe, a practice derogatively referred to as "lurking." In time, I realized that the majority of people logging on to the channel seldom participated in group conversations. For many the channel functioned primarily as a space to meet other individuals for private online conversations and, potentially, offline rendezvous. None of this was particularly unexpected.

What was unexpected, however, was the explicitness surrounding sexual discussions. I was amazed at how easily people inquired into my particular erotic predilections, desires, and fantasies. Questions such as "What turns you on?" or "What are you into?" were common in private conversations and not unheard of even in the public discourse of the channel. At first I found this a bit disconcerting. I never would imagine having such an unabashed conversation with a person I had just met face to face in a gay bar. Yet, in time, I grew fully accustomed to the candor of online interaction, gaining confidence in expressing my sexual interests. In fact, I began to appreciate the straightforwardness of these conversations, seeing how such candor could offer a liberating alternative to the more reserved quality of offline discussions. Oddly, I found I had become more wont to have a sexually intimate tête-à-tête with an individual I had just met online than I was to have such a conversation with friends I had known for years offline. All of this—the technology of online communication, the economy of online conversations, and the openness of online sexual discussions—began to feel quite ordinary to me.

Thus when I assumed the role of researcher, I was placed in the difficult position of having to make the familiar novel again in order to critically address the more fundamental aspects of online interaction. One of the strategies I employed in doing this was to account for how it was that I came to interact on the channels I would later study. In retrospect, it proved to be some time after first logging on to IRC before I discovered #gaymuscle, #gaychub, or #gaymusclebears. What drove me to seek out these particular channels which I did not know existed when I first ventured onto IRC? Part of the explanation rests with a growing dissatisfaction I had in chatting only on #gayboston. I recall harboring the feeling that I was treading in only the shallowest waters of a vast cybernetic ocean awaiting exploration. I was sure there had to be more out there, wherever there actually was.

My suspicions regarding IRC's unexplored depths were confirmed when I discovered the "list" feature on my mIRC client. By entering a simple command (/list), my interface would present an inventory of all publicly accessible channels on the network. Through experimentation, I learned that this "list" function could be refined to display only those channels with a particular word in their designation, such as "gay" or "lesbian." One night, for the sake of curiosity, I listed all of the channels with "gay" in their title. To say the least, I was surprised by the immensity of gay-identified channels. The following is only a partial listing of some of the more interesting gay-identified channels I've happened across on IRC (in addition to channel names, captions appearing in the title bar are provided where available):

Gay_skinheads (We're skinheads and we're gay—so FUCK U!)
Gay3wayChicago (blk&wht male couple need a black third)
Gayarmpits (The sweatier the better!)
Gayboysex
Gaycigars (Feed me Your Smoke, Sir!!)
Gay-cowboys (Welcome to Gay Cowboys—Now bend over please)
GayDad/son/sex (it's not about incest, it's about one more day to Hump Day)
Gaydirtyjockstraps
Gaydogsex (Where dogs get attached to their men)
Gayfeet (Big shoes, big feet, big. . . .)
Gayfisting
Gaygainers
Gayleathersex (Where the only color leather is black)
Gaymuscle-n-gut (Big, Beefy boys into Pumping Up and Pigging Out!)
GayNippleTorture
Gaypainpigs (Erotic and Exotic Torture)
Gayphonesex
Gay-pumpingbears
Gayrape
Gayraunch (Ripe pits, dirty feet, sweaty Jocks)
Gayraw_fuck (no rubbers, just raw raunchy sex!!!)
Gaysci-fi
GaySir/Boy
GaySlaveMarket (The place to meet Adult slaves & Masters, not boys!)
Gaysons4dads
GayToiletSex
Gayuncut
GayWaterSports

Though such listings would give me a sense of the diversity of gay spaces on IRC, I would be introduced to the first channel I studied by one of the most outspoken regulars on #gayboston. **PECS,** a self-identified bodybuilder and a well-known personality on the channel informed me of another channel he regularly chatted on and, in many respects, preferred over #gayboston. From our conversations, **PECS** surmised my interests in both weightlifting and muscular men and suggested that I may find others sharing such interests on a channel called #gaymuscle. Intrigued by the name of the channel, I began chatting on #gaymuscle and was immediately amazed at how different two online spaces could *feel.* Unlike #gayboston, most of the patrons of #gaymuscle were geographically dispersed throughout North America, Europe, and Australia. This was my first experience with a channel that was organized around particular spheres of interest as opposed to geographical location. By virtue of being on the channel, interactants ostensibly shared not only a sexual identity but also more particular interests in bodybuilding, weight training, and the muscular male body. In referring me to the channel, **PECS** was guiding me to an on-line community better matched to my interests and demonstrating the tutelage veteran individuals on IRC sometimes offer novices.

As with #gaymuscle, I was introduced to both #gaymusclebears and #gaychub by friends sharing their online experiences. There is a certain quality whereby individuals on IRC share their online travel narratives, telling others of new spaces to be explored and experienced in cyberspace. To date, I have been chatting on the #gaymuscle channel for over six years and the #gaymusclebears channel since it was formed in the summer of 1998. Finally, I have been participating on #gaychub for approximately four years but would not characterize myself as a regular on the channel. Although I have visited a wide range of gay-identified channels since my introduction to IRC, I find I tend to spend most of my online time on either #gaymuscle or #gaymusclebears.

Before discussing the distinct characteristics of these particular channels, it may be useful to provide more contextual information regarding online chatting in general and IRC in particular. In the remainder of this chapter, I will construct a brief overview of the historical development of IRC and discuss how this mode of computer-mediated communication differs from another popular form of online communication, MUDs. In doing so, I will explain my reasons for examining social activities on IRC rather than on MUDs. Finally, I will examine some of the methodological and theoretical considerations I confronted in conducting this study.

A BRIEF HISTORY OF IRC

At its most basic, IRC is one of the earliest modes of multiuser synchronous computer-mediated communication. In less technical language, IRC was one of the first means by which more than two individuals could communicate in real time through computer networks in the form of textual messages. The historical development of IRC is complex and a bit chaotic. It is generally agreed, however, that Internet Relay Chat came into being in August 1988 when Jarkko

Oikarinen, a member of the Department of Information Processing Science at the University of Oulu, developed a new mode of online communication based on the existing bulletin board system (BBS). Oikarinen recounted some of the circumstances surrounding the development of IRC in his own account:

> I was working in the Department of Information Processing Science in University of Oulu during summer '88. I guess they didn't have much for me to do. I was administering the department's sun server, but it didn't take all time [sic]. So I started doing a communications program, which was meant to make OuluBox (a Public Access BBS running on host tolsun.oulu.fit, administered by me) a little more usable. The purpose was to allow USENET News-kind of discussion and groups there in addition to real time discussions and other BBS related stuff. (Oikarinen, 2000)

This early version of the IRC program was run on a single server with no more than ten users. Although Oikarinen had originally planned to incorporate nonsynchronous messages features into the program so it could also function as a bulletin board service, the ability to have real-time chatting proved so demanding that the bulletin board extension was discarded (Oikarinen, 2000). After this modest beginning, Oikarinen arranged for IRC servers to be established at the University of Helsinki and the University of Tampere, significantly expanding the infrastructure of the IRC network and the number of users. Within a few months, IRC was being used across the entire Finnish university network (Funet). The successful deployment of IRC in Finland led to its incorporation into the Scandinavian branch of the Internet (NORDUnet) in the following months. By the end of 1988, IRC was being distributed across the global Internet, run primarily on servers located at major universities (Stenberg, 2002).

As the number of global IRC users grew, separate networks emerged to accommodate their online activities. The most well-established networks include EFnet (Eris Free network), Undernet (the underground network), and DALnet (established in 1994, when Undernet split, and named after its founder, Dalvenjah). Similar to vast highway systems, these networks are subnets composed of dozens of servers located primarily in industrially developed nations such as the United States, Japan, Canada, Great Britain, France, Germany, and Israel. Modeled after citizens' band radio, the servers hosting these networks were originally operated from the computer facilities of major research universities with the intent of offering a means of "public" online communication. Indeed, the decentralized, nonhierarchical architecture of IRC reflects the initial open and anarchistic philosophy of the Internet before its operation was primarily assumed by commercial entities. However, as the cost of maintaining such networks increased, many universities began disconnecting their servers from IRC, leaving private corporations to host these networks. Today, many system administrators donate their time and Internet service providers donate space on their commercial servers to maintain this mode of "public" communication.

When logging onto any IRC network, one is greeted by an automated announcement known as the "message of the day" ("motd" for short). The system administrator of the particular server employed to connect to the network sets this message, using it to post important announcements. The following example is from a server on the EFnet network on July 17, 2002:

Welcome to the Internet Relay Network John
Your host is irc.mindspring.com [207.69.200.132/6667], running version
2.8/hybrid-6.3.1.
This server was created Mon Apr 29 2002 at 02:50:38 EDT
Irc.mindspring.com 2.8/hybrid-6.3.1 o0iwszcrkfydnxb biklmnopstve
WALLCHOPS PREFIX=(ov)@+ CHANTYPES=#and MAXCHANNELS=20
MAXBANS=25 NICKLEN=9 TOPICLEN=120 KICKLEN=90
NETWORK=Efnet CHANMODES=be,k,l,imnpst EXCEPTS KNOCK
MODES=4 are supported by this server

There are 7405 users and 73545 invisible on 44 servers
273 Vanity Haxorz (IRC Operators) online
7 unknown connection(s)
33737 channels formed
I have 542 clients and 1 servers

Current local users: 542   Max 869
Current global users: 80950   Max 93172
Highest connection count: 870 (869 clients) (241406 since server was
(re)started)

Message of the Day, irc.mindspring.com

*** This is the short motd ***
End of /MOTD command

Although the message of the day often carries technical information not of interest to the majority of IRC users, it does display the number of people interacting on a network at any one time. For instance, this motd indicates that this particular network is composed of 44 servers administered by 273 operators, and that there are currently over 33,000 channels on the network and more than 80,000 people logged on to the network globally. The message also indicates that since this server was connected to this particular IRC network, more than 240,000 individuals have used it to connect to IRC. Such information provides a sense of the population size of these networks. In addition, the message of the day will occasionally relate information concerning technical problems with the network, such as "net-splits" or network servers that are temporarily unavailable.

Contributing to the popularity of IRC, the development of sophisticated clients or interface programs made this mode of online communication more convenient for a less technologically savvy population. The most prevelant clients, notably mIRC and pIRCh (Polargeek's Internet Relay Chat Hack), provide graphical representations of online activity. Although there are hundreds of commands on IRC, all of which are distinguished by a forward slash mark ("/"), these interfaces attempt to make online interaction more intuitive by providing icons for key functions. IRC clients are often forms of "shareware," which means individuals can use them for free for up to thirty days and then are expected to voluntarily pay a small fee to register the copy downloaded onto their computer. In all IRC clients, channels have tabs either across their top, side, or bottom. On my mIRC client, for instance, this tab appears as the title bar to the window of the channel (see Figure 2.1). The tab allows the user to determine which channel he or she is on at a given moment, listing the channel's designation (such as #gayboston) and the topic that was last set for that channel (such as "How to make the world's most fabulous martinis!"). It is not uncommon, however, for the topic appearing in the tab to lack relevance to the current conversation on that channel. Despite the development of these graphic interfaces, the true technological key to IRC's success was the implementation of the channel itself. Elizabeth Reid (1991) discusses how the novel concept of the "channel" was central to the proliferation of IRC, noting that in earlier modes of synchronous computer-mediated communication, such as "talk," in which only two interactants could communicate with

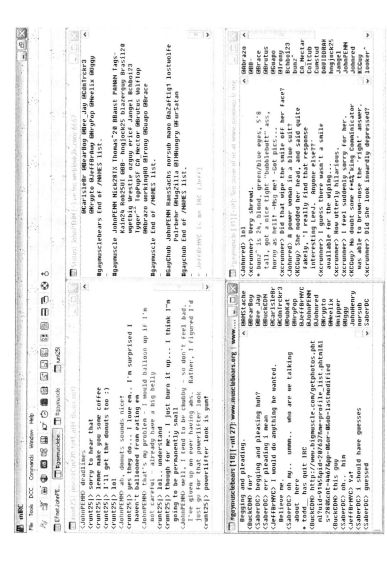

FIGURE 2.1. The mIRC interface showing two different channels (#gaymusclebears and #gaymuscle), a private one-on-one conversation with **runt25**, and the status window

33

each other at a time, there was little problem with their messages simply appearing on each other's computer screens. However, this existing model for synchronous computer-mediated communication would not work with a large population of online users:

> It was therefore necessary to devise some way of allowing users to decide whose activity they wanted to see and who they wanted to make aware of their own activity. "Channels" were the answer. On entering the IRC program, the user is not at first able to see the activity of other connected users. To do so he must join a channel. (p. 7)

The advent of the "channel" allowed IRC to be segregated into a conceivably infinite topography of topics. Originally, channels were simply assigned numerical values (e.g., channel #12 or channel #34), and thus one had to know the designated number to a particular topic. **Umgawa,** who has been chatting online longer than anyone else interviewed in this study, commented on the original form of channel names:

> **John:** How long have you been chatting on IRC?
> **Umgawa:** I started IRC back in 1989 or so . . .
> **Umgawa:** this was before #named channels existed
> **Umgawa:** channels were numbered
> **Umgawa:** 25 is what is now #hottub—general chat
> **Umgawa:** 33 is what later became #gblf, which became #gaysex, which split into ten thousand channels
> **Umgawa:** 43 was all finnish
> **John:** ah, interesting
> **Umgawa:** channels 100+ were invite only
> **Umgawa:** negative channels were private

Today, channels are given actual names, although the hash mark (#) remains in all channel designations as a memento of IRC's less user-friendly past. Any individual logged onto IRC can create a channel and thereby construct a discreet online space. The system is designed to grant the individual creating a channel special privileges over that channel—often referred to as operator privileges (or ops). Such operator privileges can be used to restrict the space to "invited" guests, remove guests from the channel, and set the topic of discussion in the tab of the channel window. The channel operator can also extend these privileges to other members of the channel. In addition to speaking on more "public" channels, individuals on IRC can open private channels for one-to-one conversations. It is not uncommon for interactants to meet in the "public" space of a channel and then create separate private spaces for more intimate interaction.

Although the focus of this study is the social interaction occurring through IRC, it is important not to naturalize or dismiss the technological structure of this medium. Communication technologies, like all technologies, emerge within particular social contexts and therefore reflect particular cultural orientations. As Langdon Winner (1986) argues, technologies are not innocent but, rather, resonate with the cultural biases of their designers. For instance, Winner observes how the unusually low overpasses on the parkways of Long Island, New York, were deliberately designed to exclude particular populations from specific regions of the greater metropolitan area. He notes how Robert Moses, the master builder of New York City's transportation system during the mid-twentieth century, wanted to ensure that "[a]utomobile-owning whites of 'upper' and 'comfortable middle' classes, as he called them, would be free to use the parkways for recreation and commuting," while "[p]oor people and blacks, who normally used public transit, were kept off the roads because the twelve-foot tall buses could not handle the overpasses" (Winner, 1986, p. 23). The result was a city infrastructure—a technological schema— that maintained class and race segregation. Drawing parallels between concrete highways and the information superhighway seems more apt when one considers the military genesis of the Internet in the United States. Indeed, both modes of technologies were originally designed to facilitate certain flows of communication.

Clearly IRC's channel protocol is indicative of how the medium's technological development was shaped by a set of cultural assumptions regarding the uses people would make of this new mode of mediated communication. Although IRC has proved to be a particularly flexible medium, this has not been the case with all forms of computer-mediated communication technology. With AOL, for instance, the technological protocol of their online chat service restricts the number of interactants within a chat room at any one time to less than twenty-five, which ultimately shapes the social dynamics occurring in those chat rooms. Certainly the technological structure of IRC fosters different social relations than the technological structure of those virtual environments known as MUDs—a term originally standing for multiuser dungeons as given by Richard Bartle and Roy Trubshaw in 1979 to the textual computer game of their design. Frank Schaap (2002) notes how the social interaction possible within a particular MUD environment is constricted by the software code of that MUD, which is ultimately determined by the designer (i.e., programmer) of that MUD. As Schaap (2002) indicates, the outcome of the designer's efforts is "a program based on the programmer's common sense understanding of how 'the world' works and how the text-only abstraction of the code can still meaningfully represent the players and offer them meaningful avenues for interaction" (p. 102). In other words, the MUD will ultimately reflect the cultural values of the designer with regard to what forms of online interaction are meaningful and what variety of (virtual) environments should frame social relations.

The central feature of IRC is, quite simply, chatting—socializing through the exchange of textual messages between geographically diverse individuals in real time. In contrast to IRC, MUDs are designed to be comprehensive theme environments, providing an elaborate sense of movement as users progress from one virtual space to another, encountering new settings and characters along the way. On MUDs, individuals primarily interact through "characters," which function as constructed representatives of the offline individual within the virtual world of the MUD, providing an added layer of identity in contrast to IRC chat rooms in which individuals are, ostensibly, themselves online. This more elaborate construction of space and identity on MUDs, however, can prove disorienting to newcomers, as Kendall (2002) notes in her study:

> Newbies [newcomers] are likely to spend some time wandering around before they find things to do or figure out where people congregate. My own first experiences with muds included several days of fumbling around before I could consistently locate groups of people to talk to. It was months before I had any real facility with mud commands. (p. 33)

The significant differences between MUDs and IRC as modes of computer-mediated interaction are demonstrated in the differences between Kendall's online experiences and my own. Unlike Kendall, I garnered a basic understanding of how to function on a channel after my first day on IRC. Once I located a particular channel, I was present with all others on that channel, not needing to seek out "where" everyone was. For me, social relations on IRC *felt* more immediate than those found in the more technologically complex environments of MUDs, where role-playing is often the central objective (Schaap, 2002).

Problematically, some computer-mediated communication research fails to acknowledge the complexities of mastering social interaction on MUDs. For instance, Sherry Turkle (1995) contends that making the connection to these virtual environments "is not difficult; it requires no particular technical sophistication" (p. 11). My observations suggest very much the opposite; for many of those I interviewed on IRC, MUDs proved too technical and required too great a time investment to be attractive forms of online socializing. Because MUDs are comprehensive textual environments requiring proficiency with specific commands in order to successfully interact with others, it is not surprising Turkle observes that "MUD players are often people who work all day with computers at their regular jobs" (1995, p. 12). This is not necessarily the case with those individuals interacting in online chat rooms, as observed in this study.

The most significant difference between IRC and MUDs, however, may be found in the expectations of their users. Owing to their origins, on MUDs individuals (referred to as "players") are often expected to be performing constructed characters; in essence, those interacting on MUDs are expected to be engaging in a form of role-play. Regardless of how close an online character is to an individual's perception of his or her offline identity, the tacit understanding remains on the part of those on the MUD that the individual is interacting as a constructed persona. With IRC, however, the implicit understanding is that individuals are simply speaking as themselves. Although this may prove not to be the case if the person is acting out a constructed persona in cyberspace, the expectation remains that the individual is using IRC as a medium of communication rather than as a site of performance. Obviously, any mode of group interaction involves managing the presentation of self, for, as Erving Goffman (1959) demonstrates, we present different images of ourselves in different settings. However, as with offline interaction, all those facets of the self we present to others on IRC are generally expected to be a genuine part of our identity. On MUDs, individuals can assume unqualified fantasy personae—elves, wizards, aliens, animals—while on most IRC channels, the assumption of such fantastical forms would likely be considered, frankly, ludicrous.

Another important contrast between MUDs and IRC concerns population size. Markham (1998) notes that "LambdaMOO, the most popular Multi-User Dimension to date, has over three thousand members" (p. 35). As noted previously, the average number of users on just *one* IRC network on a typical night numbers more than 38,000, some ten times the population of LambdaMOO, and yet much of the social science inquiry into online interaction continues to focus on social relations on MUDs. Although MUDs can indeed be fruitful grounds for scholarly inquiry, demonstrated recently by the work of Lori Kendall (2002) and Frank Schaap (2002), my decision to focus on social interactions on IRC partially derives from the belief that inadequate attention has been paid to this mode of online communication.

NEGOTIATING THE INSIDER/OUTSIDER DUALITY IN CYBERSPACE

Concerned with anthropology's origins in the European colonial enterprise, Malinowski (1922) advised ethnographers to assume an objective position in relation to those studied, arguing that sound fieldwork must be conducted under the auspice of "real scientific aims" (p. 6). While Malinowski warned future fieldworkers about approaching their subjects with "preconceived ideas," his own writings (especially his posthumously published diaries) reveal how cultural biases can shape understandings of the subject in ways that often go unnoticed by the researcher. During the latter half of the twentieth century, the work of feminist and poststructuralist thinkers led some cultural anthropologists to reject this notion that a researcher can truly assume an "objective" position in relation to the subject. As Weston (1991) points out, "Recent work in cultural anthropology has stressed the importance of recognizing the researcher as a positioned subject" (p. 13). Indeed, Malinowski's own writings are evidence of the inescapability of our own cultural subjectivity.

In light of this, I acknowledge that my research is informed by not only my own personal experiences on these channels—experiences I believe provide me with a deep appreciation of what these virtual spaces mean to their patrons—but also by the social positionality I share with many of these interactants as a gay, white man living in the United States. Those invested in more traditional approaches to research may contend that my close identification with these individuals results in the loss of academic distance central to critical scholarship. Inversely, I would suggest researchers need to unpack this collapse of distance and judiciousness. Maintaining academic distance does not necessarily ensure a more critical research approach, and, as Henry Jenkins (1992) indicates in his work concerning media fandom, such distance allows scholars "either to judge or to instruct but not to converse with" the communities they study (p. 6). By relinquishing pretenses to such distance I am able to converse with those I study, to gain a more complex understanding of their online practices, and, hopefully, to provide a more comprehensive and nuanced representation of their experiences.

I fully acknowledge, however, that there are analytical dangers to studying any subject to which one has such a close identification. In her work on gay kinship, Weston (1991) discusses this challenge of conducting research within a community with which one has "a common frame of reference and shared identity," noting that the greatest difficulty confronting such a researcher is in the "process of making the familiar strange" (p. 14). In this regard, my strategy in online interviewing has been to keep conversations open ended, asking participants to explain to me the significance of online social practices to which I was already accustomed. In this process of making the implicit explicit, I hoped to be surprised by the connotations of things I thought I already understood. In the written account, I allow as much as possible the "voices" of those participating in this study to "speak" directly to the reader, endeavoring to have members of these online communities explain their practices in their own words. This is not to deny the constructedness of ethnographic representations, for, as Bette Kauffman (1992) effectively argues, my social position in regard to race, class, gender, and sexuality is already implicated in the very decision to study these particular channels. As Kauffman (1992) contends, "the particularities of the ethnographer shape the very selection of what constitutes a 'problem' worthy of study, whose reality or social knowledge will be construed as 'answer,' and what techniques will be privileged for the selection of 'facts' from the flow of things" (p. 192).

More pragmatically, there are obvious methodological challenges to conducting interviews with individuals with whom the researcher is already acquainted, particularly in regard to negotiating the researcher-researched relationship. Specifically, when asking for very basic demographic information, some of those interviewed questioned the necessity of such inquiries, since presumably I already knew the answers. Further, in many instances I had had very open, casual discussions with individuals (as friends) about topics that would prove important to my study, only to find that when I asked them to discuss these topics under the auspice of a formal interview, their answers were terse and unrevealing. Other times, any distinction between my role as researcher and my role as friend or even sexual interest blurred, and participants would turn interviews into opportunities to flirt or play. An example of this blurring of roles is demonstrated during a "formal" interview with **TechnoBear:**

> **John:** well, the question is, how would you describe muscle worship?
> **TechnoBear:** You will have to find the answer to that one out IN PERSON.
> **TechnoBear:** ;-)
> **John:** ok..

On this particular occasion, **TechnoBear** was in a playful mood and it took some time before he would provide a serious answer to my query. This instance is indicative of the sexual tensions underlying the negotiation of power between myself as both researcher and community member and those participating in this study. It became evident at points that there were unexpressed contentions over who dictates whether an online interaction will be a serious interview or flirtatious encounter. At other times, there were significantly deeper emotional (and erotic) tensions underlying interviews—tensions originating from the history I shared with a particular subject. This was certainly the case with **Umgawa** as suggested in the initiation of my first formal interview with him:

> **John:** This is an open-ended interview and I want you to feel free to share any experiences you've had online that are important to you
> **Umgawa:** sehr gut.
> **Umgawa:** do I need to be naked during the interview?
> **Umgawa:** sorry :)
> **John:** that's OK

Unlike **TechnoBear**'s playful comments, **Umgawa**'s sexually charged question carries emotional gravity because of the brief but intense relationship we shared prior to the advent of the study. His apology after a moment of online silence serves to acknowledge the emotional strain underlying both our friendship and our researcher-subject dynamic. On several occasions the sexual tensions permeating our online interactions led me to question whether it was appropriate to include him in the study. However, the tremendous insights offered by someone who is not only one of the most experienced IRC users I've encountered but also one of the founders of the channel #gaymuscle ultimately overrode my reservations. Indeed, **Umgawa** would prove an invaluable addition to the core group of participants in this study.

David Bell and Gill Valentine (1995) discuss the power dynamics inherent in the researcher-researched relationship in regard to queer research. Specifically, they warn of collapsing a shared marginalized sexual identity with a shared power position in conducting research:

> The relationships we have with respondents ooze power, and must therefore be handled sensitively. The privilege of "insider status" is open to abuse if groups are misunderstood or misrepresented, while the potential for appropriating marginal voices is ever present. . . . And at a different level, our research relationships and the way we report them cannot (indeed must not) be kept impersonal and clinical. We must also be reflexive about how we feel about our respondents—owning up if we feel sexually attracted to them rather than struggling to maintain a false front of objectivity. (p. 26)

Bell and Valentine's discussion attempts to open a space for more critical and positioned ethnographic work in which the researcher reflexively interrogates his or her own role as researcher *and* as positioned subject, acknowledging that although reflexivity makes the potential audience more aware of power inequities, it *does not* erase them. As Weston (1998) insightfully comments, "Reflexivity reminds the reader to view the circumstances of the anthropologist in relation to the circumstances of the people studied," but "is not, in itself, an equalizing act" (p. 201). Thus, I acknowledge that some of those participating in this study (such as **TechnoBear**) exhibited a sexual interest toward me. Equally, there was a sexual interest on my part toward some of my subjects, though I made an effort to *bracket* such interest while in the mode of researcher.

By "bracketing," I refer to my methodological efforts to monitor my own online discourse, communicating clearly to participants whether I was speaking to them as a researcher or as a friend and community member. Within the context of formal interviews, I avoided initiating any discussions I suspected would be construed as libidinous or even as deeply personal. If I wanted to engage in a personal (sexual) discussion with an individual, it would have to wait until another occasion when we were not interacting under the auspice of research. This is not to suggest that my personal experiences as a member of these online communities do not shade my observations or interpretations. Indeed, it would be dishonest to suggest that one can "bracket out" all of one's expectations and sentiments regarding a group with which one has significant personal investment. Furthermore, as the dialogue with **TechnoBear** demonstrates, those participating in an interview did not always observe such bracketing themselves. Thus, my methodological strategy in approaching these sexually charged relations between myself as researcher and my subjects is simply to be honest with the reader—to include these very social dynamics as objects of analysis and critique. Of course, I cannot deny that the sexually charged atmosphere surrounding many of the interviews central to this study made conducting fieldwork a stimulating experience, to say the least.

Yet another danger confronts the online researcher: constructing an ethnographic account that constitutes participants as subjects existing only in cyberspace. Although there is an inherent liability in any mode of social science inquiry of creating two-dimensional representations of subjects, this intellectual hazard is compounded in computer-mediated communication research by presenting participants as noncorporeal subjects with no material consequence. This appears to be precisely the shortcoming Annette Markham (1998) falls into in her discussion of the frustration experienced arranging online interviews. For instance, in her first conversation with **andrewm,** an interactant on NetMeeting (a form of synchronistic online communication much like IRC), Markham immediately attempts to orchestrate an interview. Later, when **andrewm** fails to appear online at the agreed-upon time, she indicates her surprise, commenting,

I showed up at the agreed-upon time for my interview with **andrewm** and was surprised that he didn't show up. I had spent ninety minutes with him online, just trying to get him to agree to an interview. I finally got him to commit, and he didn't show up! I waited for a couple of hours and came to another realization: Because people are anonymous [online], they can be as flaky as they want. (p. 34)

Although Markham attributes **andrewm**'s failure to appear to being "flaky," it is more likely indicative of the degree of meaningful access Markham has to this online community. Perhaps because Markham had no apparent social or emotional investment in those communities existing or individuals interacting on NetMeeting, **andrewm** felt no social or emotional investment in being interviewed. The possibility also exists that some event in **andrewm**'s offline life prevented him from being interviewed, as, presumably, he also has offline responsibilities and commitments.

In my own experience, I seldom made formal arrangements concerning when and where to interview. Knowing that those interactants I wanted to interview were regulars on their respective channels, I was able to generally find them online most weeknights. Usually, I would simply mention to participants that I was interested in talking to them about a particular topic when they were up to it, and they, in turn, would suggest meeting online the following afternoon or evening to discuss the matter. We would not set precise times to meet because we expected to see each other on a regular (almost nightly) basis online. In one of the few instances in which I had made formal arrangements to meet two interactants who are roommates for a group interview—**Quixote** and **TechnoBear**—I, too, experienced missed online appointments, not once but twice. Unlike Markham, I did not attribute the failure of **Quixote** and **TechnoBear** to appear online at the agreed-upon time and channel as indicative of some eccentricities on their parts. Rather, as I later learned, the first missed interview was due to their being caught in traffic and not arriving home in time; the second was due to the unexpected visit of friends which left them, as respectful hosts, unable to get online.

That they did not make these interviews was a critical reminder that for **Quixote** and **TechnoBear**—as well as for all the subjects represented here—online interaction constitutes only a single facet of their lives. At risk of stating what should be obvious, this study presents but a solitary dimension of the day-to-day experiences of these individuals. While I would argue that the uses these individuals make of online communication are informed by their offline experiences, it would be problematic to suggest their online activities provide a comprehensive view into their negotiation of everyday life.

CONDUCTING FIELDWORK THROUGH THE ETHER

As previously mentioned, the methods of inquiry employed in this study can be characterized as ethnographic, utilizing the long-established anthropological techniques of interviewing and participant observation. However, unlike anthropological endeavors, physical copresence in the conventional understanding has not been a requirement for this study. In this respect, this study follows in the course of those pioneering social science inquiries into cyberspace, such as the work of Sherry Turkle. When Turkle conducted the empirical research that would come to serve as the basis of *Life on the Screen* (1995), a key question confronting researchers interested in online social phenomenon was "what to make of on-line interviews and, indeed, whether and how to use them" (p. 324). Since that time, theoretical and methodological questions have moved beyond whether to use online interviews to new considerations surrounding the nature of community, embodied presence, and cross-media inquiry. However, a key epistemological assumption found in Turkle's work continues to underlie much online inquiry, and it is one I seek to problematize in this study.

Turkle's decision to exclusively interview individuals she has met physically presents two interesting ramifications. First, it imposes geographic restrictions on a space in which the lack of a physical topography is such a unique and important characteristic. Second, and perhaps more important, it implies that the online persona is distinct from and less valid (less "real") than the offline person. However, this distinction between the offline person (the body in the physical world) and the online persona (the self interacting in cyberspace) is fundamentally flawed. Where does the offline person end and the online persona begin? Is the keyboard a true demarcation between two selves? I would suggest that the very impetus to distinguish between the two originates from a fundamental dualism between the mind (site of the true self) and the body (the site of base physical experience) intrinsic to Cartesian thought. This mind/body dualism is not only problematic but also oppressive, allowing the individual to be conceptualized in fragmented terms and the body to be viewed essentialistically as some presocial given. Judith Butler (1990b) discusses the phallocentrism supported by this dubious distinction: "In the philosophical tradition that begins with Plato and continues through Descartes, Husserl, and Sartre, the ontological distinction between soul (consciousness, mind) and body invariably supports relations of political and psychic subordination and hierarchy" (p. 12). Deconstructing this dualism of mind and body, thought and matter, technology and biology is central to Elizabeth Grosz's (1994) project of reconceptualizing a feminist subjectivity that articulates corpore-ality and sexuality and differences between the sexes in terms other than binary. As Grosz (1994) points out, only "when the relation between mind and body is adequately retheorized can we understand the contributions of the body to the production of knowledge systems, regimes of representation, cultural production, and socioeconomic exchange" (p. 19). It is my hope that this book constitutes a modest contribution to such retheorizing.

Informed by Butler, Grosz, and Foucault, I approached this study from a materialist-constructionist perspective, viewing our selves as culturally constituted amalgamations of the physical and discursive. That is, I view our cultural understandings of the body not as inherent and natural but as originating within human interaction and our attempts to socially apprehend the infinitely complex universe into which we are born. Rather than viewing emerging communication technologies as diminishing the importance of the physical body, I see them as complicating particular truisms in Western thought, particularly uncritical distinctions between the mind and body and the organic and synthetic. In fact, my online experiences prompt me to share Katie Argyle and Rob Shields' conviction that our bodies "cannot be escaped, for we express this part of ourselves as we experience together" (1996, p. 58). The problematic nature of distinguishing between the offline body and the online self is illustrated in this brief excerpt of online interaction between two patrons of the channel #gaymuscle—a brief exchange I would characterize as friendly flirtation:

Younghung: I'M BAAAAAAAAAAAAAAAAACK!!!!!!!!! :-) <HUG>
Britannic: Welcome back, baby!
Younghung: Thanx, Sugar! :-)
Britannic: _lick_
Younghung: hehehehehehe, stop, that tickles oh, wait, DON'T STOP!!!!!
Britannic: _lick_
Britannic: _lick_
Britannic: _lick_
Younghung: hehehehehehehehehehehehehehehehehehehe, ok ok, uncle!!!
Britannic: _lick_
Younghung: no fair, stud! :-) I said uncle!! :-) <BIG BEAR HUG>[2]

The use of emoticons and textual representations of bodily actions (i.e., _lick_ and <BIG BEAR HUG>) demonstrates the complex incorporation of the body into online discourse. **Younghung** and **Britannic** are a considerable geographic distance apart, yet **Younghung** hugs **Britannic** when they are reunited. **Britannic** cannot touch **Younghung**'s physical body, yet he licks him repeatedly until **Younghung** can't take the "sensation" anymore and calls "uncle!" **Younghung** continuously indicates his physical enjoyment of the interaction by smiling, perhaps despite himself: "no fair, stud! :-) I said uncle!! :-) . . . "

It is by drawing on the experience of the biological body that **Younghung** is "tickled" by **Britannic**'s repeated licking. It is by his own offline cultural understanding of a smile that **Britannic** knows **Younghung**'s emoticons indicate his enjoyment. As Argyle and Shields (1996) suggest, emoticons and generic actions in the form of bracketed words "are clues that lead us back to ourselves, back to our bodies to try to understand what it is that a person is trying to say" (p. 67). These online interactants have devised means of textually re-incorporating the physical body into online discourse because it is by drawing upon the physical body that their online experiences are made meaningful.

For these reasons, the interviews for this study were conducted exclusively online, primarily with participants I have never physically met. In addition to my theoretical commitments, the decision to conduct research online reflects a pragmatic consideration articulated by Martyn Hammersley and Paul Atkinson (1995): "With many people, interviewing them on their own territory . . . allows them to relax much more than they would in less familiar surroundings" (p. 150). Indeed, due to the sensitive nature of the topics of discussion, some of those participants within geographical proximity indicated they would be hesitant to be interviewed in person.

VIRTUAL ETHNOGRAPHY, REAL SUBJECTS

I began formal interviewing in the fall of 1997 and continued to interview until the fall of 2000, with supplemental interviews and ongoing conversations extending into the summer of 2002. Despite being a recognized member on all three channels before commencing the research for this study, I elected to post introductions of myself as a researcher in the main window of each channel.[3] In my postings, I indicated the intent of my research project and my request for interested individuals to contact me about being interviewed, assuring them of their anonymity. Although a number of online acquaintances had already agreed to be interviewed, I wanted to obtain the broadest sample possible of online interactants from these channels. My posted messages were kept brief to avoid eclipsing other discussions in the main window (a practice considered rude and referred to as "flooding a channel"). These postings allowed anyone interested in being interviewed to inquire privately about my research project. Furthermore, those I interviewed would occasionally direct me to others they believed could offer important insights about a particular channel. For instance, when conducting interviews on the channel #gaychub, I was referred by two participants (**BIGrGUY** and **Top_ Bear**) to **Big_Wolf,** who they identified as the most senior member of that channel. Similarly, in a conversation with **TechnoBear,** I was referred to **Quixote** as the actual founder of the #gaymusclebears channel.

Although I ultimately conducted formal online interviews in various depths with a total of forty-two interactants, I draw primarily (but not exclusively) from ongoing interviews with twenty-one individuals who frequent at least one of the channels discussed here. Each of these participants was a regular on his respective channel throughout the duration of the primary study (fall of 1997 to fall of 2000) and each was recognized by other channel patrons as an integral member of the respective online community. (For more demographic details concerning these twenty-one individuals, refer to the appendix.) With many of these core individuals, my relationship extended beyond mere interviews. For a period of more than three years, I interacted with them regularly online, often forming intimate friendships. Becoming part of their online lives, I spoke to them not only as a researcher but just as often as a comrade and, in some instances, a trusted confidant.

To ensure the anonymity of participants, I use only online handles in this study and, where requested, substitute a screen pseudonym for the participant's actual nickname. In the case of "public" conversations on the main window, I have substituted pseudonyms for all interactants involved. The use of online nicknames, however, does itself present ethical considerations for the researcher in cyberspace. Brenda Danet, Lucia Ruedenberg-Wright, and Yehudit Rosenbaum-Tamari (1997), in their study of play and performance on IRC, argue that open channels (i.e., those channels that are accessible to anyone connected to the IRC network) are essentially "public" spaces and therefore readily admissible to social science inquiry. In regard to online handles, they conclude that "there is no apparent need for researchers to disguise the identity of participants any more than participants have done so themselves" (p. 8).

The online nickname, however, can prove to be a profoundly personal aspect of an interactant's identity on a given channel and needs to be treated with due care by the researcher. Unlike offline names, which are generally assigned at birth and used in public interaction, online nicknames function as modes of self-expression in textual spaces. In the case of those interacting on queer-identified channels, their nicknames may not be intended to function as public identifiers but rather as identifiers in a very specific social situation (e.g., gay online communities). Although the channels I examine are open to anyone interacting on IRC, their existence as "public" spaces is complicated by their function as queer spaces. Thus, it is possible these interactants do not intend the identities they assume on these queer-identified channels—symbolized by their online nicknames—to be presented *outside* the context of a gay space. For these reasons I have taken pains in giving participants every opportunity to assume a pseudonym for this study and use actual online handles only for those who have explicitly expressed comfort with such use. When devising a pseudonym, an effort was made to capture the characteristics of the original name, and in most cases the participants themselves devised the pseudonym for me. As a general practice, when original handles contained the words *bear, cub,* or *chub,* I incorporated these terms into the pseudonym.

Some online researchers may question my decision to employ *any* actual online handles in this study. However, in raising such objections it is vital to keep in mind that the online handle itself constitutes an important source of data concerning the communities under study. Often it was impossible to devise a screen pseudonym that would accurately reflect the expressive intent of the original name without revealing that individual's actual handle. In instances in which interactants themselves devised the pseudonym used in this study, the substituted handles usefully reflect those attributes individuals felt were central to their online personae.

Despite the prominence of IRC handles, it is not uncommon for the offline or given names of participants to arise during online conversations. This happens most frequently during private interactions between two individuals in which the use of an offline given name functions as an indication of personal knowledge of a third person not participating in that conversation. Building upon the work of Erving Goffman, David Jacobson (1996) examines the use of real names in online interactions as a form of social "cue." Jacobson (1996) observes that in group conversations, the invocation of "real" (i.e., offline) names signals a transition into more sincere and genuine discourse, contending that "if pseudonyms convey the message 'This is not real,' the use of real names conveys the message 'This is real'" (p. 469). I would qualify Jacobson's argument in regard to IRC, for even the use of online nicknames (which he identifies as pseudonyms) still may signal that interaction is "real," though perhaps a different understanding of reality than that found in offline interaction. In other words, individuals can become quite emotionally invested in their online nicknames, and those conversations using these nicknames can feel emotionally authentic to those involved in them. To ensure the anonymity of participants, I have substituted pseudonyms for interactants' offline given names where they appear during group conversations or individual interviews. I have elected, however, to use pseudonym offline names rather than simply substituting the online handle to indicate the conditions under which people shift from using an online handle to using someone's actual offline name.

In addition to substituting pseudonyms for participants' offline given names, I have made minor modifications in how online handles appear in this study. On IRC, a participant's handle appears within angle brackets, such as <BIGrGUY> or <PECS>. To make the resulting transcripts easier to read, I have removed the angle brackets enclosing the nickname, while maintaining the original capitalization, adding a colon, and bolding the print of the name. Thus an original transcript of

> <John> About how often do you chat on IRC?
> <TexMuscle> every day
> <John> ok

becomes

> **John:** About how often do you chat on IRC?
> **TexMuscle:** every day
> **John:** ok

What remains unaltered is the actual "voice" or typography of the online interactants. Endeavoring to provide an accurate representation of online communication, I incorporate the actual responses of interactants directly from the IRC transcripts into my written account.[4] Thus, I present conversations of participants complete with all their typographical errors, misspellings, emoticons, and creative uses of grammar. My intent is to allow the reader to both "hear" the voices of those participating in this study as I did and to gain a finer appreciation for the experience of online communication. There is a particular economy of language in online chatting—a vernacular to the virtual, if you will—and I believe it is important to provide the reader with a sense of this mode of communication. At points, these online conversations may prove difficult to follow, especially when, owing to the unique quality of online communication, conversations appear out of sequence. Notably, as many interactants on IRC use ellipses or trailing periods to indicate pauses or the continuation of a thought onto another line of text, these should not be read as the omission of a segment of conversation. It is also worth noting that by rendering online conversations as text on the page, the text, drained of its urgency, becomes a representation of dialogue but is no longer dialogue itself. This is to remind the reader that not only is this account a (re)construction of a particular social world as opposed to an actual window into that world but also that a certain ephemeral quality to online interaction escapes the printed transcript.

In general, I found those interacting on these channels open, some even enthusiastic, about participating in this project. Arguably, this openness partially stems from the convenience of online interviewing, allowing interactants to engage in their usual social activities while speaking to me. This was apparent in my initial interview with **Bennoe:**

> **John:** How do you identify your gender on IRC?
> **Bennoe:** gay
> **John:** Is that how you identify your gender online? What about your sexuality?
> **Bennoe:** sorry. . . . gay and male
> **John:** Oh, ok
> **Bennoe:** I should READ properly
> **Bennoe:** I have 2 conversations going here if that is ok with you
> **John:** that's OK. I completely understand

An important dimension of this study is understanding that many interactants engaged with me as a researcher much as they would with any other individual on the channel, which often meant they were involved in multiple conversations concurrently.

Christine Hine (2000) has recently applied the term *virtual ethnography* to sociological and anthropological research conducted in cyberspace. In her study of the online activities surrounding the media event of the Louise Woodward trial, Hine attempts to lay "the ground for a particular approach to ethnography which is almost but not quite like the real thing: a virtual ethnography" (p. 10). For Hine, social researchers investing considerable time in examining a particular site or cultural phenomenon on the Internet are engaging in a form of ethnographic enterprise. However, future online research may need to more critically consider precisely what constitutes an ethnographic study in cyberspace and which forms of online research are better positioned under the rubrics of discourse or textual analysis. In this study, I believe myself to be justified in my claim to the term *ethnography,* based on the fact that I was an active part of the social phenomenon I studied. These were not static social formations (such as online bulletin boards or Web pages) but dynamic communities demanding my direct participation.

Although agreeing with Hine's (2000) assessment that ethnography constitutes a particularly useful tool for looking "in detail at the ways in which the technology is experienced in use" (p. 4), I am more

exacting in my understanding of what forms of online inquiry constitute an ethnographic endeavor. I hold that for a work to be ethnographic, the researcher must be directly involved in those social
scenes studied, even when conventions of physical copresence are
complicated. Identifying a work as ethnographic functions equally as
an indicator that the researcher has in some way impacted the very social dynamics under study; that is, the community is in some way altered by the presence of the researcher.

I am also critical of Hine's distinction between offline ethnography and online or "virtual ethnography." As I will demonstrate in the
following chapters, those persons interacting on these channels constitute very real subjects. They are not two-dimensional characters
existing solely in cyberspace but flesh-and-blood individuals with
their own strengths and vulnerabilities, insights and prejudices, desires and needs. To qualify the term *ethnography* with the term *virtual*
is to suggest that online research remains less real (and ultimately
less valuable) than research conducted offline. This, in turn, carries
the impolitic and problematic assertion that subjects studied online
are somehow less consequential than subjects studied offline. As I
endeavor to reveal in this study, online research can provide valuable
insights into how individuals living in mass-mediated societies incorporate emerging communication technologies into their experience
of everyday life.

Chapter 3

Virtual Gay Bars

Communities are to be distinguished, not by their falsity/genuineness, but by the style in which they are imagined.

Benedict Anderson
Imagined Communities, 1983

When asked how he views such IRC channels as #gaymuscle and #gaychub, **PHLguy** invoked the metaphor of a virtual gay bar, "without the smoke, the drinking, the loud music," and where the people are "a little bit less inhibited." **PHLguy** is far from the only patron interviewed to compare these channels to physical-world gay bars, and, in many respects, such a comparison is apt. Like physical-world gay bars, these particular IRC channels function as safe spaces for queer-identified individuals to congregate, fashion friendships, affirm their sexual identities, locate (cyber)sexual partners, and build supportive communities. Also like physical-world gay bars, the communities originating on these channels, though initially formulated around a particular cyberspace, often extend beyond the confines of their respective channels and into the private (virtual) spaces of community members. Considering that bars dedicated to gay and/or lesbian clientele have historically played vital roles in the formation of queer identity and queer-affirming communities in the physical universe, a comparison to these offline establishments may provide a more comprehensive understanding of the role virtual spaces play in the formation of individual queer communities in cyberspace.

The importance of the gay and/or lesbian bar both as a site for community formation and as an entry point into some form of "gay community" for queer-identified individuals has been recognized in historical studies of the experiences of gay men and women (Kennedy and Davis, 1997; Chauncey, 1994; Thorpe, 1997; Retzloff,

1997). This is not to suggest, however, that commercial bars have served as the sole sites for the formation of gay and lesbian communities, nor even as the sole sites for same-sex sexual activity. George Chauncey (1994), for instance, extensively documents the central role New York City's boardinghouses, bathhouses, cafeterias, public parks, and even street corners played as sites for gay men to congregate and formulate some sense of a gay identity in the first half of the twentieth century, commenting that gay men "took full advantage of the city's resources to create zones of gay camaraderie and security" (p. 152). Still, Chauncey (1994) indicates that the rise of "exclusively" gay bars marked a fundamental change in the pattern of gay male socializing: "As more gay men identified themselves as homosexuals interested in *other* men who were homosexuals, bars where they could meet one another became more attractive than bars where they could meet trade [straight men]" (p. 359, emphasis original). Similarly, Brett Beemyn (1997), in his introduction to a collection of historical studies of distinct and regionally diverse lesbian and gay communities, argues that bars "served as important sites for people interested in same-sex sexual relationships to meet and to develop a sense of shared experience" (p. 3).

Thus, during the early half of the twentieth century, the gay bar emerged as an important site where gay men and lesbians could meet others who shared their sexual identity (rather than those interested only in having sex with them), which, in turn, fostered a more communal and political perception of queer identity. Increasingly, to be gay or lesbian represented more than being someone who engaged in particular sexual practices, it also meant membership in some form of larger community, however abstract that sense of community may prove. Notably, it is this sense of community that becomes central to the notion of a shared political position. As Elizabeth Lapovsky Kennedy and Madeline D. Davis (1997) contend in their study of the role of gay bars in the lives of lesbians in Buffalo during the 1930s and 1940s, "bar communities were not only the center of sociability and relaxation in the gay world, they were also a crucible for politics" (p. 27). Returning to my comparison, these IRC channels, like physical-world gay bars, represent safe and affirming spaces where queer-identified individuals formulate communities around common interests, practices, politics, and desires, including shared understandings of the desirable body, spaces in which individuals need not necessarily engage in sexual activities to share a sexual identity. In addition, these virtual gay bars, like their physical-world counterparts, function as sites where isolated or "closeted" individuals exploring their sexual identity can find entry into some form of queer community.

The function of this chapter is to familiarize the reader with these virtual gay bars—#gaymuscle, #gaychub, and #gaymusclebears—and their patrons. Beyond the more facile level of observation, this chapter will explore the key cultural dimensions (such as safety, anonymity, and accountability) defining these virtual spaces in an effort to provide a deeper appreciation of how these online spaces function as the locus for queer community formation. A central argument of this chapter is that the perception of safety constitutes an essential component of both community formation and erotic exploration in cyberspace. Though anonymity has been identified by many computer-mediated communication researchers as the central feature making interactants feel safe in engaging in sexual experimentation online (Reid, 1996a; Bruckman, 1996; Danet, Ruedenberg-Wright, and Rosenbaum-Tamari, 1997; Hamman, 1996; Danet, 1998), I contend that such anonymity alone is not sufficient to foster feelings of safety in the case of queer erotic exploration. Rather, I would suggest it is the more complex convergence of online anonymity, shared presumptions of both a particular gender and sexual identity, the policing of these presumptions, as well as communal efforts to exclude hostile discourses, that has, for queer interactants, made these channels hospitable spaces for erotic exploration.

Where this chapter departs from more conventional studies of online communities is in the specificity of its attributions. To date, many of those studying computer-mediated communication have examined the activities and practices of particular online groups—including Usenet newsgroups (McLaughlin, Osborne, and Smith, 1995; Baym, 1995), MUDs (Turkle, 1995; Bruckman, 1996; Reid, 1996b; Markham, 1998), IRC channels (Reid, 1996a; Danet, Ruedenberg-Wright, and Rosenbaum-Tamari, 1997), and AOL chat rooms (Hamman, 1996)—in an effort to reach universal conclusions concerning online social relations. For instance, Danet, Ruedenberg-Wright, and Rosenbaum-Tamari (1997) build on their analysis of a "virtual party" held on IRC to make various generalizations regarding the nature of interaction in synchronistic textual environments, including the position that online interaction can be characterized as inherently playful. Although some

of their postulations may be substantiated, others, such as their assertion that there "is a tendency to play with gender identity in synchronous chat modes" (p. 9), may well prove unsustainable. This represents the most significant danger of making generalized claims
regarding the experiences of individuals in cyberspace based on the
observations of a particular segment of the online population: such
claims may simply not describe other scenes or, worse, may conceal
conflicting activities.

Although acknowledging the importance of being able to engage
in broader theoretical discussions of the social implications of online
interaction, I share Beemyn's (1997) conviction that the close study
of individual communities is positioned to better understand particular social formations. Despite distinguishing between two differing
bodies of queer scholarship—one focusing on distinct experiences of
individual gay and lesbian communities within a particular historical
context (Chauncey, 1994; Kennedy and Davis, 1997; Johnson, 1997;
Thorpe, 1997; Retzloff, 1997), the other attempting to make broad as-
sessments of *the* "gay experience" in Western society (Browning,
1993; Boswell, 1989)—Beemyn's discussion remains applicable to
studies of online social formations. Concerning queer scholarship,
Beemyn (1997) argues that the "increased focus on individual communities has drawn greater attention to the specificity of gay experience and the importance of place in shaping the lives of lesbians, gay
men, and bisexuals" (p. 2). Similarly, I would suggest that focusing
on the particular characteristics of distinct online communities can
provide a more tangible understanding of how the social positionality
of individuals within the larger cultural context informs their use of
Internet technologies.

Thus, I have elected to ground claims in my examination of these
particular online communities—claims that may be later extrapo-
lated upon to provide some broader understanding of online interaction but should not be taken as indicative of some universal experience of cyberspace. In addition to providing a more complex and
comprehensive representation of social formations in cyberspace, I
endeavor to demonstrate that distinct communities arise in cyberspace which do not necessarily share those characteristics generally
attributed to online interaction.

ENTERING THE VIRTUAL GAY BAR

Unlike chat rooms on AOL, the channels examined here are neither maintained nor moderated by private companies. Rather, each channel represents what I argue is a communal effort to construct a safe and affirming space for the exploration of erotic practices and desirable bodies. Each channel constitutes a stable virtual space[1] and is moderated by a group of interactants who volunteer their time to do so. It would be problematic to identify the interactants on these channels as fixed and discrete communities. Instead, the communities formulated around these channels often permeate one another; those chatting regularly on #gaymuscle may also chat on #gaymusclebears, even #gaychub, either simultaneously or cyclically. In fact, many of the current regulars on #gaymusclebears originally chatted on either #gaymuscle or #gaychub before the creation of this new channel by **Quixote** in the summer of 1998 established an intersecting "common ground." In general, IRC presents a particularly dynamic space, and the parameters defining these channels are in constant flux. Though some of those interviewed indicated a strong commitment to just one channel, the majority demonstrated a fluid sensibility concerning movement between the channels.

On an average night, both #gaymuscle and #gaychub host between forty and fifty interactants at any one time, many of whom frequent their respective channel several times a week. The #gaymusclebears channel, being more recently formed, hosts generally between twenty and thirty interactants at any one time and seems to have a more consistent group of regulars than the other more established channels. The open discussions[2] scrolling by on any of the channels' main windows can be characterized to include greetings, good-natured gossip, joking, flaming, advice on such matters as weight training or dating, and debates ranging from the "true" sexuality of media and sport celebrities to the authenticity of a patron's publicly announced bodily attributes. On all channels, interactants pay no fee, nor do they need permission to enter and participate. In general, the volunteer moderators only "kick" (remove by using privileged commands) those interactants from the channel who enter the space solely to attack others for being gay (a phenomenon I refer to as "online bashing"). By removing hostile individuals the moderators ensure each channel remains a safe and comfortable space for expressions of queer sexuality. In providing this service, channel moderators[3] can be thought of as these virtual gay bars' virtual bouncers.

Often individuals, after joining a channel and seeing who is present, create separate channels for private, one-on-one discussions with other interactants. It is not uncommon for a channel patron to be involved in public conversations on the main window while carrying on multiple intimate conversations in separate private channels. When two individuals establish a private channel, the activities within that channel, as well as its very existence, are concealed from anyone else on IRC, including the moderators on channels such as #gaymuscle or #gaymusclebears. Despite the danger of belaboring the analogy to physical-world gay bars, these private channels can be thought of as the virtual gay bars' virtual back rooms.

GENERAL PROFILE OF THE CHANNELS

From those interviewed, a representative profile of interactants on these channels can be constructed: the vast majority of participants identify either the United States or Canada as their residence, although I have interviewed individuals from Australia, Great Britain, France, and Mexico. The clear majority of those interviewed identify themselves as "white," although some identify themselves as African American or Latino. The lack of Asian-identified individuals in this study represents a deficiency in my sample and not the utter absence of Asian interactants on these channels, but in my experience the number of Asian-identified individuals frequenting these particular virtual spaces is considerably less than the number of individuals identifying themselves as either black or Latino.

Of those interviewed, a slight majority indicated holding professional positions, although there was a surprising range of responses to the question of occupation, including police officer, factory machinist, night security guard, temporary secretary, and "disabled." This range of responses, coupled with the fact that an online researcher has only the demographic information interactants elect to identify, makes any generalization concerning the socioeconomic position of IRC interactants difficult to substantiate. Clearly, the very cost of the equipment and services (i.e., Internet service providers) necessary to connect to the Internet precludes segments of the general population from being represented on IRC. In addition to economic capital, individuals connecting to IRC must also possess a particular type of technological knowledge and skill set—in essence, a specific mode of cultural capital—in order to use a computer to gain access to the Internet and the World Wide Web. Thus, it is reasonable to expect individuals interacting on IRC to reflect those segments of the general population with significant access to material and cultural resources.

However, there were certainly exceptions to this expectation within the core group of participants. **Younghung,** for instance, had graduated from high school two years before I first met him on #gaymuscle and was still living at home with his mother and his older sister in a small town in Florida. In contrast to the predominant image of a heavy computer user, **Younghung** was not attending college but rather was working full-time as a night security guard at a local apart-ment complex. Though he occasionally discussed with me both online and over the phone his aspirations to attend college, he was not foreseeing such a possibility in the immediate future. According to **Younghung,** no one else in his family had ever obtained any formal education beyond high school, and therefore no one in his family could offer guidance on how to pursue a college education. I often felt that one of the reasons **Younghung** and I forged such a strong online friendship was that his experiences reminded me so much of my own, both being raised by a single parent and coming from remarkably similar class backgrounds (though as someone working toward his doctorate, I now occupy an ambiguous position in regard to class). In our conversations, **Younghung** indicated that he was first introduced to computers through his high school and apparently was the most technologically savvy member of his extended family. This latter claim was supported by the fact that although the computer was located in the living room of his home where all members of the household had access to it, he was the only one who actually used it.

Arguably, the declining cost of computers (particularly used computers available through some small, independent computer stores) as well as online service providers (which now generally charge a single fixed monthly fee in the United States) has brought Internet access into the reaches of individuals such as **Younghung.** This is also illustrated in the experiences of **Big_Wolf,** a disabled African-American man living in Maryland, and **BluCollar,** a white male working as a factory machinist in Michigan, who both are now able to

afford access to the Internet and thus to IRC. Like **Younghung,** neither **Big_Wolf** nor **BluCollar** have obtained any formal education
beyond high school, nor have any members of their families. Although I agree with Kendall's (2002) assertion that class background
"may be the single most important factor influencing online participation" (p. 183), future online research needs to consider how the personal priorities of those individuals with modest financial resources
influence whether they will invest in access to the Internet.

Approximately half of those interviewed indicated they log on to
IRC from their place of employment, and the majority, but by no
means all, indicated they own a personal computer. Notably, some
interactants indicated that they are able to gain access to IRC only
from work or school. **Mage78,** for instance, finds his school to be his
primary means of connecting to IRC; although he owns a computer
he does not have access to the Internet beyond his college. The average amount of time these interactants have been chatting on IRC at
the time of the first interview was approximately three years, with responses ranging from as few as six months to as many as eight years.
Most indicated they spend at least five hours per week online (**Bennoe,
IrishCrop, WorkOut**), and some spend as many as twenty-five to
thirty hours per week (**Mage78, Big_Wolf**), though for a few chatting
was now an increasingly sporadic activity (e.g., **Younghung, Britannic, Msclfreak**). The mean age of study participants at the time of the
first interview was thirty-three, although ages ranged from twenty
(**Younghung**) to forty-seven (**BluCollar**).

Unlike the group of MUD users Kendall (2002) studies, individuals interacting on these channels do not formally meet offline for
group activities, though interactants do occasionally meet offline individually as friends or sexual partners. As those interviewed indicated, offline meetings can prove disconcerting experiences, especially if there are expectations of physical attraction. Patrons such as
Umgawa discussed how the mental image they constructed through
online interaction was often incongruous with what they encountered
in person:

> **John:** what is it like when you meet someone offline that you've been
> chatting with online?
> **Umgawa:** Hrmmm . . .
> **Umgawa:** usually only 10% of what you think is correct
> **Umgawa:** there is just so little of a person that comes across in con-
> versational print

When **Umgawa** refers to only "10% of what you think is correct," he is not necessarily suggesting that individuals on these channels intentionally mislead other interactants in describing themselves (though this certainly has been known to happen). Rather, the very imprecision of the written language underlying computer-mediated interplay can lead one to formulate an impression of another person significantly differing from the impression that would be constructed through face-to-face contact. Obviously, this can create an awkward situation if two individuals are meeting for a potential sexual liaison only to discover that, in person, there is no physical attraction. Kendall (2002) discusses the social anxiety that can be experienced when an intense (amorous) online relationship transitions into an offline encounter:

> In the early stages of romantic attraction, people often idealize the object of their affection. This is especially easy to do when you can't see the other person. Thus, looking for the first time at someone to whom you consider yourself attracted can be threatening, both to the relationship itself and to participants' views of how realistic they've been about each other. (p. 161)

Even when individuals meet offline under the pretext of a platonic friendship, expectations remain regarding demeanor and the compatibility of personalities. Although some online affinities develop into offline relationships, many other mediated friendships fail the transition into the physical world.

Of the core group of participants in this study, I have met only two in person—**PECS** and **Umgawa.** In both instances our online friendships were reinforced by our offline contact, but we did not develop enduring physical-world relationships. Even though I found the online physical descriptions of both **PECS** and **Umgawa** congruent with the persons I met offline, I discovered that our interpersonal dynamics were substantially different when we interacted face to face. For instance, with **PECS,** I was surprised by the fact that he, as a dedicated bodybuilder, smoked. In addition, what read as a playful and jocular personality online came across as more of an aggressive and determined personality offline. In person it was much more apparent how central bodybuilding was to his understanding of himself, reflected in the clothes he wore (e.g., tight tank tops intended to conspicuously display his muscularity), in his deportment (regularly flexing his muscles to impress those around him), in the social circles in which he moved (primarily other dedicated bodybuilders), and in his favored topics of conversation. Though I enjoyed our face-to-face interactions, I found that our relationship remained primarily a mediated friendship. In regard to **Umgawa,** although we both initially experienced an intense physical attraction, we discovered that offline our personalities were not well suited for a lasting amorous relationship, despite the fact that we had engaged in intimate discussions online which suggested we were well matched romantically. As these two instances demonstrate, online interaction fosters expectations regarding not only the physical appearance of another interactant but also the social dynamics that will occur in face-to-face contact— expectations that may prove far from the reality encountered offline.

Beyond meeting in person, another, though less definitive, means IRC interactants have of confirming physical characteristics described online is through the online trading of pictures (often referred to as "pics") in the form of electronic files. To date, I have exchanged pictures with approximately half of those interviewed in this study, and these digital images provide a stronger sense of how that person appears offline. However, many individuals still do not have access to the resources (such as a scanner or digital camera) necessary to create digital images of themselves that can be exchanged online. Thus, for those that I have neither met in person nor received a picture of, I must accept those defining characteristics they identify online. Overall, online relationships still remain dependent on what individual interactants select to identify, which substantially shapes the images other interactants will formulate.

As interesting as what *is* identified on these channels are those factors commonly *not* identified: gender and sexuality. This reveals two key presumptions of the communities formulated around these channels: a shared gender and a shared sexuality. The former presumption, as will be demonstrated, is so naturalized as to be unquestioned in social relations on these channels. The latter, however, represents a site of occasional contention and policing. Yet both represent essential aspects of the holistic character of these channels and the communities formulated around them.

WALK LIKE A MAN, CHAT LIKE A MAN . . .

Virtual gender bending, or portraying a different gender in virtual environments, has been an exceptionally celebrated topic of those writing on social interaction in cyberspace. For instance, Amy Bruckman (1996), in her discussion of gender roles on MUDs, identifies online gender swapping as "one example of how the Internet has the potential to change not just work practice but also culture and values" (p. 318). In forms of computer-mediated textual interaction such as MUDs, it is generally held that the offline physical body is concealed and thereby rendered less meaningful in online social relations. As a result, those attributes central to the physical body, such as gender, become sites for experimentation, exploration, and performance, or so some contend. In examining the performance of gendered identities in both MUDs and IRC, Brenda Danet (1998) maintains that cross-dressing is one of the more common forms of "playful expressivity" undertaken in online interaction. From this Danet concludes that such masquerading "promotes consciousness-raising about gender issues and might contribute to the long-term destabilization of the way we currently construct gender" (p. 130). The ease with which an individual can assume a different gender in cyberspace—as Reid (1996b) comments, on "MUDs sex and gender are subverted by the whims of imagination" (p. 337)—has been repeatedly identified, perhaps naively, as indicative of the liberating possibilities of social interactions without the burdensome presence of the physical body.

Jodi O'Brien (1999) is not so convinced of the "consciousness-raising" impact of virtual gender bending. In her investigation of the reincorporation of gender into online interaction, O'Brien contends that regardless of whether an individual is physically present, "we conjure up and make sense of ourselves and others in terms of embodiment" (p. 79). Since, as she indicates, gender as a "social institution" represents "the primary means by which we sort and define self and others" (p. 77), when online interactants are confronted by "instances of gender stretching they tend to snap . . . back into the conventional physical sex dichotomy" (p. 78). O'Brien's contentions were supported by the confused, even irritated responses I sometimes received to the question of gender identification. Though gender may be open to exploration, experimentation, and even subversion in the spaces Bruckman and Danet studied, it is more rigidly ascribed on the channels discussed here.

Indeed, even the spaces of these channels are inscribed with gender norms. The hypermasculine, sexually charged character of public discourse on all three channels mark them as distinctly male cyberspaces. This is illustrated in the following segment of general discussion from the main window of the channel #gaymuscle:

> *** Topic is 'Welcome to gaymuscle! Did you lift today?'
> *** Set by NJLifter on Fri Jul 19 22:18:53
> <john> Hey guys!
> <BigRob> who's gonna top me?
> <Powerhaus> I will
> <Umgawa> hey john
> <growing> hey john
> <john> hey Umgawa, growing! How are ya?
> <puppydog> That's what I always said. We're going to have a baby and I don't care if you have to fuck me until babies fall from the sky. If it doesn't work the first time, I'll try again . . . and again . . . and again.
> <Umgawa> that could be a lot of cum, PH . . . remember that I am now 33, and can't do it any more than nine times a night or so, anymore
> <puppydog> :P
> <puppydog> I always thought your 30s were the peak of your sexuality?
> <growing> john: I'm well, thanx
> *** wrkmynips has joined #gaymuscle
> <Umgawa> for me it was 17
> <Powerhaus> Umgawa, that's ok, I'll work with you, even in your weizened state
> <Umgawa> *shrug* :)
> <puppydog> 17 times a days? :oP
> <Powerhaus> For hormones and cum volume, it's supposed to be 17
> <Powerhaus> 17 years old
> <Powerhaus> as in, FELONY
> * NJbulge NNJ 4 same
> <puppydog> Hrm.
> <Umgawa> yes, but I looked 21 at the time
> <Umgawa> so it never was a problem
> <Powerhaus> Don't think the judge will buy it
> <puppydog> Well, I lost my virginity when I was 15. :oP
> <BigRob> I've had more sex in the past 6 years than I did the 10 years prior
> <Umgawa> well, that's too late :)
> *** MAX30 has joined #gaymuscle
> <Powerhaus> I lost mine when I was 21, on my wedding night
> <Umgawa> I was 16.

<Powerhaus> my old roommate was 11
<BigRob> I lost mine at 17
<blue21> mine at 18
<Umgawa> well . . . does jacking off with a friend count? or are we talk-
ing full oral/anal here?
<Powerhaus> penetrations, top or bottom
<Umgawa> If so, then its more like 13. . . . if not, then its 16. . . .
<Umgawa> ok . . . I was jacking off with friends at 13, so I'll say 16 for
the full penetration event
<blue21> still 18
*** jacker16 has quit IRC

This segment of online discourse, though originating on #gaymuscle, is indicative of the open and sometimes chaotic nature of discussions appearing on the main windows of the channels examined in this study. In addition to the actual typed dialogue of interactants, the text appearing (and often swiftly scrolling by) on the main window includes automated announcements indicating the arrival and departure of interactants (e.g., "*** wrkmynips has joined #gaymuscle") as well as the individual postings or posted messages of interactants on the channel (e.g., "* NJbulge NNJ 4 same"). Though confusing to the reader as a printed transcript, the use of various colors to denote different activities (dialogue, automated channel announcements, interactants' postings) makes it much easier to follow on the computer screen.

This small segment also illustrates the centrality of sex as a theme of conversations on these channels. When I entered the channel, I stumbled into a fairly typical sexually explicit exchange in which several channel interactants not only discuss their sexual experiences and express their sexual desires but also engage in a certain masculine sexual posturing. **Umgawa, Powerhaus, BigRob, puppydog,** and **blue21** all compete with one another in comparing the age at which they lost their virginities. Notably, **Umgawa** also boasts of his virility ("I am now 33, and can't do it any more than nine times a night or so . . .") before commenting on the young age at which he became sexually active. In many respects, the online discourse produced on these channels enacts what Connell (1995) identifies as a "hegemonic masculinity." However, intertwined with these hypermasculine discourses are the ironic undertones of camp, which complicates the mode of masculinity performed on these channels.

What proves uncomplicated is a clear expectation on the part of channel patrons that these are distinctly male spaces, a social expectation so pervasive that it remains implicit in every interaction. This was reflected in the individual interviews I conducted, especially in the reactions of interactants when I made this assumption explicit by simply asking them how they identified their gender online. For instance, **Msclfreak,** a thirty-year-old Danish bodybuilder living in England, appeared confused by my question of *how* he identifies his gender online:

> **John:** How do you identify your gender on IRC?
> **Msclfreak:** what do you mean?
> **John:** well, if asked, would you say your male or female or something else?
> **Msclfreak:** hehe, I am definatley male. that is a silly question!
> **John:** Sorry, this is very basic descriptive data. :)
> **Msclfreak:** obviously!

It is possible **Msclfreak** may have misunderstood my query as one of questioning his masculinity. For **Msclfreak,** any question of his gender may be construed as a question of his masculine self-image and therefore read as threatening: "hehe, I am definatley male. that is a silly question!" To a degree, **Msclfreak**'s confusion is understandable. As Yvonne Wiegers (1998) notes in her discussion of the growing popularity of modern bodybuilding, historically "the gendered nature of men's lives has been denied; generally, gender has been synonymous with 'woman'" (p. 152). Thus, **Msclfreak** and other interactants may be disconcerted by or even defensive about questions concerning their gender identification, as is demonstrated by these responses from participants on all three channels:

> **John:** How do you identify your gender on IRC?
> **WorkOut:** gay
> **John:** Oh, I meant, do you identify yourself as male, female, other?
> **WorkOut:** what???
>
> **John:** How do you identify your gender online?
> **Masculin:** masculine, male, definitely male!!
>
> **John:** How do you identify your gender on IRC?
> **SFBigCub:** I never actually formally identify my gender, unless there is some sort of question

John: Do people normally ask you to identify your gender?
SFBigCub: no.
SFBigCub: Big Cub . . . it's pretty masculine
John: OK
SFBigCub: there are not a whole lot of women cubs out there ;)

Particularly of interest are the latter two responses, in which both **Masculin** and **SFBigCub** identify themselves not merely as male but as "masculine." Such responses fit well within conventional social understandings that see gender encompassing prescribed social roles: to be male is to enact a masculine identity. Getting at an individual patron's understanding of his own gendered identity on these channels involves not only determining how individuals perceive their own biological sex within the dominant categories available (i.e., male/female) but also what they perceive as appropriate behavioral roles based on their biological sex. Inverting or complicating this relationship of biological sex and gender roles is viewed as deviant by some even on these channels. Based on the responses of those interviewed and on the general conversations appearing on these channels, despite the occasional antics intended to play on gender stereotypes, little space is afforded those self-consciously interested in subverting conventional notions of masculinity. This was well demonstrated in a conversation with **TechnoBear,** one of the principal members of the channel #gaymusclebears:

John: what do you think of effeminate acting men?
TechnoBear: I never understood something. . . . . .
TechnoBear: How can a man who likes men (masculine by definition), like a man that is "watered down" or feminized.
TechnoBear: A man is a man. If you like men you want the deep voice, the body hair, the muscles, etc.
TechnoBear: I don't understand the flowers/chiffon coming out of the mouth, the earrings, the jewelry, the limp wrists, the cross dressers, etc.
John: have you encountered a lot of effeminate acting men on #gaymusclebears?
TechnoBear: Few of the "regulars." Lots of visitors.
John: here's a question I have, how can you tell an effeminate acting man on IRC?
TechnoBear: You often can't.
TechnoBear: But if they use phrases like "dear" and "darling" and "hon," there's a good chance.
TechnoBear: Even had someone called "SheMale" drop in.

> **John:** some of the earlier scholarship on cyberspace claims people go online to play with gender. Do you think people come to channels like #gaymuscle or #gaymusclebears to play around with gender?
> **TechnoBear:** No one plays with gender on #gaymusclebears.
> **TechnoBear:** It's male-only.

TechnoBear's comments suggest that on channels such as #gaymusclebears, the regulars have clear expectations concerning appropriate gender behavior. In these virtual spaces, gender roles are monitored, as **TechnoBear** indicates, through the terms or expressions individuals employ in their textual interactions (such as "dear" or "darling") and in the nicknames individuals select to identify themselves online (such as "**SheMale**"). **TechnoBear**'s demeanor toward men perceived as being effeminate was echoed in a comment made by **Umgawa,** a channel monitor on #gaymuscle:

> **Umgawa:** as a channel Op, I am sometimes asked to kickban someone because someone thinks they are being irritating (read effeminate)

Umgawa's note that he, as a channel moderator, is occasionally asked to remove those individuals from the channel that are perceived as being disruptive to the group dynamics by behaving inappropriately in regard to their gender indicates a level of policing surrounding gender roles on these channels. Far from being spaces of experimentation, exploration, and play in regard to gender, these online collectives maintain many of the dominant and oppressive notions of how individuals should act based on their biological sex. Of interest is how **TechnoBear**'s comment on suspect online handles (such as "**SheMale**") and **SFBigCub**'s response regarding why he does not need to explicitly identify his gender on IRC—**SFBigCub:** "Big Cub . . . it's pretty masculine"—reveal the ways in which gender is inscribed into the very nicknames appearing on these channels.

In her discussion of online cross-dressing play, Danet (1998) examines a corpus of some 260 online handles gathered from four unidentified IRC channels and finds "that *less than one-fifth* invite inference with respect to gender" (p. 137, emphasis original). However, observations of the nicknames used on #gaymuscle, #gaychub, and #gaymusclebears suggests that the majority of online handles on these channels possess some direct reference to gender either in terms of physiognomy (e.g., **HairyPECS** or **Big_meat**) or in terms of some secondary gender characteristic culturally understood as male (e.g., **Tuffmuscle** or **ButchBeef**). For instance, of the core group interviewed in this study, arguably half employ nicknames that directly indicate a male ("masculine") identity (e.g., **BIGrGUY, PHLguy, Younghung**). Included in this category of explicitly male handles are nicknames incorporating the terms *bear, wolf,* and *cub,* all of which circulate within the argots of gay male subcultures denoting a male identity. Even of those nicknames that do not directly *denote* a male identity, several *connote* a male identity, including **Mad_Hatter** (a fictional male character derived from Western literature), **Britannic** (a male superhero from Marvel comic books), **Mage78** (derived from "magi," the term mage generally refers to a male wizard), **Quixote** (after the antihero Don Quixote in Miguel de Cervantes's satirical chivalric romance), **Umgawa** (a word associated with the hyper-masculine image of Tarzan), and even **Msclfreak** (which connotes the subcultural world of bodybuilding, a world still very much male dominated). With the increasing prevalence of female weight lifters and bodybuilders, such online handles as **WorkOut** and **TexMuscle** do not explicitly denote a gendered identity, though an argument can be made that their owners perceive them as denoting masculine traits. Assuming my sample is representative, I would contend that *less than one-fifth* of the handles on these channels *do not* indicate a gendered identity, the inverse of Danet's findings. This again demonstrates the importance of specificity in discussions of online communities, as it is most likely, though not acknowledged, that Danet focused her studies on channels governed by heteronormative presumptions.

Clearly the online nickname is one of the means by which gender is enacted or performed in these virtual spaces. In her interrogation of gender relations, Judith Butler introduces the idea of "performativity," which reconceptualizes gender as a social invention that is culturally inscribed onto the physical body as opposed to some "natural" state of being. For Butler, rather than a mere expression of some biological "truth," gender is in fact a human construct that is made to appear natural through its continuous performance, a performance concealing the fact that there is no essential condition outside the act itself; gender exists only in the doing. As Butler (1990a) contends, gender is "the repeated stylization of the body, a set of repeated acts within a highly rigid regulatory frame that congeal over time to produce the appearance of substance, of a natural sort of being" (p. 33). Ultimately, the performance constitutes that very thing it is thought to originate from, transfiguring the individual human being into the gendered subject. It is through this performance that what I identify as the discursive body is constructed, and this discursive body is what renders the physical body meaningful in social relations. This discursive body is not static; rather, it is continuously inscribed onto the physical through this process of performativity. Hence, the physical never exists outside of cultural inscription or social performance.

A key method of exposing the constructedness or artificiality of gender is to, as Butler (1990a) holds, "locate and account for those acts within the compulsory frames set by the various forces that police the social appearance of gender" (p. 33). Arguably, one of those acts functioning to maintain the artifice of gender on IRC is the selection and use of online nicknames. Unlike given names in the physical world, IRC handles are actively constructed with the intent of projecting a particular image of the self into social relations online. Each time an individual logs on to IRC, that individual is given the opportunity to change his or her online handle. Therefore, the decision to maintain a particular nickname is an active process, which on these channels generally encompasses some signification of gender. In continuously electing to maintain an online handle that projects a particular gendered identity the individual is "performing" and reinscribing gender norms in these environments.

Returning to how interactants identified their gender online, **PECS,** a forty-year-old competitive bodybuilder and breeder of exotic birds, provided one of the more revealing responses to the question of gender identification:

> **John:** How do you identify your gender on the channel?
> **PECS:** my dick

The response provided by **PECS** collapses gender and sex; for him, gender is not performative, it is simply his reproductive organ. **PECS**'s comment certainly affirms Butler's (1990b) observation that "gender appears to the popular imagination as a substantial core which might well be understood as the spiritual or psychological correlate of biological sex" (p. 279). Although feminist thought may have complicated some dimensions of gender roles in the popular consciousness of Western nations, the general consensus of sex as biologically determined and "natural" remains primarily intact. Butler, however, questions this "compulsory order" among sex, gender, and desire, in which one's biological sex (male/female) is understood as determining one's gendered identity (masculine/feminine), which ultimately governs one's "appropriate" sexual desires (males desire females/females desire males). For Butler (1990b), the failure to interrogate biological sex itself serves only to reify sexual difference and preserve a "binary restriction on gender identity and an implicitly heterosexual framework for the description of gender, gender identity, and sexuality" (p. 281). Thus Butler challenges this understanding of sex as natural, questioning the location of sexual difference: Is a person's sex found in his or her anatomy, chromosomes, or hormones? Schaap (2002) usefully discusses the ways in which the biological body—that supposedly undeniable determinant of sexual difference—in fact often fails to lend itself to those social dichotomies constructed around sex:

> While the discovery of the "sex chromosomes" was thought to be a unique and definite indicator of someone's sex, the sex chromosomes turned out to be less definite indicators than originally had seemed the case. When you are born, and lately often even before you are born, your sex is determined and of course you're either a man or a woman, because you had a penis or vagina. In those cases where the genitals don't provide a clear answer right away, other ways are available to determine the newborn's sex: most commonly a chromosome test, if the baby has an XX chromosome pair it's a girl, if it's got an XY chromosome pair it's a boy. But even the chromosomes, often deemed to be the defining principle of the human constitution, will not always act in a clearly dichotomous way. There are people with XXX, XXY, XYY and XO chromosome "pair" combinations and even within one individual a mix of for example XO and XXY cells can exist. (p. 33)

In light of this, the responses of **PECS** and **Msclfreak** prove particularly noteworthy when one considers that, as competitive bodybuilders, each commits tremendous amounts of effort and finances to chemically altering his body through the administration of synthetic hormones. As individuals pushing the very pliability of the body, one may well expect them to view conventional understandings of the "natural" more critically. Yet this readiness to ascribe gender to biological fact should not be surprising according to Anne Balsamo (1995), for, as she argues, "the gendered boundary between male and female is one border that remains heavily guarded despite new technologized ways to rewrite the physical body in the flesh" (p. 217). Balsamo draws upon the media's treatment of female body-builders to support her assertion, demonstrating that although male bodybuilders—such as **Msclfreak** and **PECS**—are "treated as ath-letes" and even admired, "female bodybuilders who develop big mus-cles, and consequently greater strength, are considered transgressive of the natural 'order' of things" (p. 217).

Similarly, in his examination of elite bodybuilding culture, Alan Klein (1993) notes the extreme hypermasculinity—what he terms "comic-book masculinity"—of male bodybuilders which necessi-tates the rejection of any behavior perceived as feminine or feminizing and the (physical) exaggeration of a male gender identity. As Klein (1993) indicates, by "emphasizing gender separation based on sexual dimorphism, bodybuilding winds up fueling some of the more anach-ronistic views of gender relations; and in some respects bodybuilding and bodybuilders represent the most extreme view of masculinity our society has" (p. 18). Notably, the bodybuilding culture Klein examines is the ostensibly "straight" bodybuilding culture of elite competitors, avoiding any significant discussion of how a nonheterosexual iden-tity may modify, complicate, or contradict these hypermasculine in-vestments. However, we can surmise from Klein's discussion that the physical distinction between what is culturally accepted as the mas-culine form and that understood as the feminine form is central to the bodybuilder, gay or straight. As Klein contends, the "bodybuilder naturalizes the cultural claim that masculinity is bound up with large muscles" (p. 246). Although **Msclfreak** and **PECS** are both gay iden-tified, as bodybuilders they remain invested in the notion that their bodies must be made to conform to this (sub)cultural image of the idealized masculine form. Certainly the responses of **Msclfreak** and **PECS** can both be read as suggesting that even in a virtual space in which their bodies cannot be physically seen, as self-identifying body-builders their masculine identity should be unquestionably apparent.

Though the majority of interactants on these channels do not iden-tify themselves as bodybuilders, most interviewed indicated that they simply do not find it necessary to identify their gender online. This was clear in the responses of **BIGrGUY,** a thirty-year-old industrial relations professional from Toronto, Canada, and **Mage78,** a twenty-one-year-old undergraduate student in Kentucky:

> **John:** How do you identify your gender on IRC?
> **BIGrGUY:** I don't
> **John:** why?
> **BIGrGUY:** because it's not necessary

> **John:** When interacting online, how do you identify your gender?
> **Mage78:** I generally don't . . . I think it is pretty much assumed

Responses of this sort proved to be the norm in my interviews. Thus, interactants implicitly conceptualize these channels as not only dedicated to the erotic exploration of various forms of the male body but also as spaces intended for the eroticism of the male body exclusively by other males. In general, on these channels the conventional understanding that to have a penis is to be male and to be male is to be masculine remains unquestioned. However, this dominant narrative also encompasses a particular model of sexual desire, holding that one's biological sex determines one's gender and one's gender determines one's object of sexual attraction. Therefore, within this dominant social paradigm, to have a penis is to be male and to be male is to be masculine and to be masculine is to desire that which is feminine. Yet this cultural equation does not hold up on these channels, where to be masculine is to desire that which is also masculine. Arguably, because this sexual dynamic is not so easily naturalized within the dominant social discourses, discussions of sexuality on these channels occasionally initiate instances of controversy, contention, and policing.

WHO ELSE WOULD GO TO A GAY BAR?

As Shaw (1997) notes, whatever "the reason one goes to a gay bar, there is a common solace and excitement in the fact that it is one of the few places in society where by their mere presence all patrons can be assumed gay" (p. 137). As in physical-world gay bars, patrons need not explicitly identify their sexuality when entering these channels—the use of the word *gay* in each channel's designation denotes it as a place for queer interaction. However, as I will demonstrate, a channel's designation alone is not necessarily sufficient to construct a

safe and affirming queer virtual space. This becomes evident when
the sexual identification of patrons conflicts with the presumed sexual identity of the channel, rendering the implicit sexual character of
the space explicit and contested. Examining how individuals negotiate their sexual identity in these spaces, as well as how the presumption of sexuality is policed, reveals both how these channels are rendered queer spaces and how problematic notions of sexuality arise
even within particular gay populations.

In general, channel designations incorporating the word *gay* signal
a presumption that those interacting within the confines of such a virtual space identify themselves as gay. The prevalence of this presumption was apparent in the responses of interactants to the question
of how they identify their sexuality online:

> **Britannic:** Well, I don't identify it . . . I just assume everyone assumes
> I'm a gay male.

> **Younghung:** . . . when talking with someone from that channel or most
> gay channels on IRC it is generally understood you are gay

> **PECS:** I guess by entering a gay room . . . ;)

> **SFBigCub:** it's an assumption about the channels I am in . . . if they be-
> gin with "gay" I don't feel the need to state that I am gay

This implicit understanding that interactants on these channels are
gay, the reverse of the presumption of heterosexuality in most offline
spaces, establishes both a sense of safety in engaging in particular
erotic discussions and an immediate sense of commonality among
interactants. A notable response provided by **BluCollar,** a regular on
the channels #gaymusclebears and #gaychub, further attested to this
presumed gay identity:

> **John:** How do you identify your sexuality online?
> **BluCollar:** After contact is made and the questions start back and
> forth, usually.
> **BluCollar:** Like I am a chub looking for LTR with an in-shape, muscu-
> lar chaser.
> **BluCollar:** Is that what you are asking for?
> **John:** well, I was interested if you identify yourself as "gay" or "bi" or
> what online? But I am interested in your identification as a "chub"

> **BluCollar:** No, I do not identify myself as gay on line. I figure that 99% of the guys in a gay channel just normally assume that.

For **BluCollar,** the presumption of a gay identity is so pervasive that he identifies his sexuality in terms of his actual sexual interests. Notably, the very pervasiveness of this presumption of a gay identity allows interactants on these channels to focus on their particular sexual interests, complicating notions that sexual identity can be easily encapsulated by the gay/straight binary, as if those two categories alone account for the entire constellation of erotic desires. As **BluCollar**'s comments suggest, not all of those on these channels necessarily share the same sexual desires even if they share the same sexual identity. However, despite the pervasiveness of the presumption of shared (homo)sexuality, some expressed an awareness that others patronizing these channels do not classify their sexuality in such uncomplicated terms:

> **John:** How do you identify your sexuality on IRC?
> **GremlinBear:** openly gay
> **John:** are others not openly gay?
> **GremlinBear:** some beat around the bush
> **GremlinBear:** some say they are bi curious

In commenting that "some beat around the bush," **GremlinBear** implies that those interacting on the channel not identifying themselves as openly gay are being less than genuine. Despite the generally shared presumption of a gay identity, not everyone entering these virtual spaces lays claim to such an identity, and for some, their sexual identity is negotiated in terms other than gay or straight. This became apparent in a discussion with **Masculin,** a thirty-five-year-old computer professional from Toronto, Canada. As his comments indicate, it is possible to make a distinction between sexual practices and sexual identity:

> **John:** How do you identify your sexuality online?
> **Masculin:** mostly homosexual
> **John:** Do people generally ask you about your sexuality?
> **Masculin:** sometimes. . . . the standard question is usually "you bi/gay ?"
> **Masculin:** if i get asked that question, i always indentify as bi—don't identify as gay
> **John:** Why not?
> **Masculin:** just making a distinction between homosexual and gay

Masculin: gay seems to imply an all encompassing lifestyle choice
Masculin: whereas homosexual seems to be limited to the sex act it-
    self
John: Do you identify with this "gay" lifestyle?
Masculin: no . . . i live a fairly str8 life
John: Are you "out" offline?
Masculin: no
Masculin: but i will go to a place if it is discreet and i feel safe about not
    revealing my identity

Masculin's distinction suggests an understanding of the difference
between engaging in sexual activities and assuming an entire identity
based on those activities. This distinction is discussed by Chauncey
(1994) in his argument that the gay/straight binary central to organizing sexual identities in contemporary American culture "is a stun-
ningly recent creation" (p. 13). As Chauncey demonstrates, "in working-class culture, homosexual behavior per se became the primary
basis for the labeling and self-identification of men as 'queer' only
around the middle of the twentieth century; before then, most men
were so labeled only if they displayed a much broader inversion of
their ascribed gender status by assuming the sexual and other cultural
roles ascribed to women" (1994, p. 13). Though this gay/straight binary has become pervasive enough that most individuals in North
America base their sexual identity *on* their sexual preferences and
practices, **Masculin** believes it is possible to engage in same-sex sexual activities without having to identify with a particular model of
self or lifestyle.

However, such a distinction is not without its critics on these channels. For instance, **IrishCrop,** a twenty-six-year-old university administrator in Minnesota, is circumspect about the motives underlying an individual's claim to a "bisexual" as opposed to a "gay"
identity:

John: Are you usually asked to identify your sexuality?
IrishCrop: There are definitely certain people who seem concerned
    with a bisexual versus gay identification.
John: Are you concerned with the difference of a bisexual identifica-
    tion as opposed to gay?
IrishCrop: Essentially, I am very skeptical about the existance of bi-
    sexuality. I feel like there are very few real bisexuals, and to most
    guys "bisexuality" is a mode of thought that is some haven for their
    sense of masculinity.

IrishCrop: A kind of masculinity that is fundamentally incompatible with the "gay" designation.
IrishCrop: But for myself, no. It doesn't concern me.

Like **GremlinBear, IrishCrop**'s comments—"I am very skeptical about the existance of bisexuality"—reflect his belief that those identifying themselves as bisexual are somehow being disingenuous regarding their sexual identity. Based on my many conversations with him, I gained the sense that **IrishCrop**'s skepticism originates as a reaction to the predominant cultural image of gay men as weak, effeminate pseudowomen—a cultural image that positions "masculine" and "gay" as mutually exclusive terms. For some on these channels, discrediting this demeaning stereotype of gay men constitutes a critical means of reconciling a sexual-minority identity with their desired self-image. **IrishCrop,** for instance, appears to respond to this stereotype by investing in the gay/straight binary while rejecting the gay/masculine exclusion, discrediting those not identifying themselves as gay on these channels as being unable to resolve their sexuality with their masculine self-image.

Despite the criticism some may encounter for not identifying themselves as gay on these channels, **Masculin** was by no means the only individual to lay claim to a "nongay" and/or bisexual identity. **PHLguy** (known as **PHLguy28** at the time of the first interview in the fall of 1997), a Latino man from Philadelphia, also spoke of his sexual identity in terms other than the gay/straight binary:

John: How do you identify your sexuality online?
PHLguy28: not straight . . .I don't identify myself as gay
PHLguy28: when I use bisexual, which is what I am, people start annoying me with many theories and comments . . . I have to explain myself so I use the term 'not straight'

PHLguy's comment that laying claim to a bisexual identification results in discussions in which he feels obliged to explain and possibly justify his sexual identity provides some indication of how the sexual character of these channels is policed. However, as **PHLguy** also indicates, the very pervasiveness of this gay presumption often makes identifying his sexuality unnecessary in his online social relations:

John: Do people on #gaymuscle usually ask you to identify your sexuality?
PHLguy28: nope, I guess it is assumed

PHLguy is not the only interactant whose bisexual identification is made a nonissue by the very presumption of a gay identity on these channels. **Mage78,** for instance, made a similar observation:

> **John:** How do you identify your sexuality online?
> **Mage78:** mostly I don't but, if asked, I would say bisexual
> **John:** Are you generally asked to identify your sexuality?
> **Mage78:** no.
> **Mage78:** by nature of the channels I frequent, I think that is also generally assumed.

Even though some interactants avoided laying claim to same-sex sexual identity, the clear majority of those interviewed readily identified themselves as gay. However, any question of a gay identity precluding a masculine gendered identity appears to be the strongest issue policed on all three channels. This policing of what can be characterized as the masculine identity of #gaymuscle is apparent in the following sample of general discussion from the main window of the channel:[4]

> *** Legal has joined #gaymuscle
> <Legal> hi boys
> <LiftingDude> heh yeah but that is so . . . i dunno . . . egotistical heh
> <cutslover> jus cocky
> <Absdude> Hey legal
> * NJbulge NNJ 4 same
> *** BiGuy28 has joined #gaymuscle
> <BiGuy28> 28y MASCULINE=NONGAY looks=Manly HANDSome guy, Smart fun genuine, succesful . . . I am looking for friendship , love and fun with SAME
> * cutslover likes gay looks
> <HornJock> what is that nongay look all about?
> <VBall37> what's gay looks? someone wearing a feather boa?
> * HornJock is gay and has np with it
> <beefy-boy> Does gay mean not masculine?
> <HornJock> i guess BiGuy28 is very confused with his own sexuality !
> <Legal> naw, just his gender identity
> <beefy-boy> maybe he's just confused with the english language
> <HornJock> maybe all of the above
> <BiGuy28> quite offensive for pussies
> <LiftingDude> uh oh
> * cutslover luvs that kinda talk!
> <NarkyBark> he has a pussy too?
> <HornJock> actually we know who we are . . . dont you?
> *** LIGWM has joined #gaymuscle

<NarkyBark> . o O (and it's offensive?)
*** Absdude has left #gaymuscle
* VBall37 stays away from the ruckus
<beefy-boy> are we talking cats here?
<VBall37> haha beefy-boy!
<cutslover> there's no ruckus, it's all good
<VBall37> ok
<HornJock> Horn Jock is good tonight

Occasionally, interactants announce their sexual identification in the open conversation of a channel, as **BiGuy28** does here. Of particular interest is the reaction of other interactants on the channel to **BiGuy28**'s posting in the main window. Immediately, other channel interactants begin to challenge **BiGuy28**'s suggestion—"MASCULINE=NONGAY looks=Manly"—that gay does not equate with a masculine identity or manly appearance. Although some affirm that there is nothing wrong with being and/or appearing gay (**cutslover, HornJock**), other interactants directly challenge **BiGuy28**'s distinction between gay and masculine (**VBall37, beefy-boy**), and some even tease **BiGuy28** about his own personal sexual identification (**Legal, NarkyBark**). In essence, these responses to **BiGuy28**'s posting can be read as reassertions of the masculine character of the channel and its function as a space for particular modes of erotic exploration (i.e., the eroticism of the "masculine" male form), a space in which stereotypes associating gay with unmanliness must be discredited. This example also illustrates how patrons police the public discussions appearing on these channels in an effort to maintain an affirming environment for particular, and at times restrictive, understandings of gay male identity. However, despite the obvious teasing and criticism of **BiGuy28** for making such a posting, **cutslover** is also careful to point out this is not an online fight—"<cutslover> there's no ruckus, it's all good"—because open hostility may be perceived as threatening by some, undermining the sense of safety essential to this space.

This brief incident usefully illustrates the two dominant presumptions of these channels—that all interactants are both male and gay. Of course, these are by no means the only presumptions permeating these spaces. Another particularly prevalent presumption involves the racial identity of those interacting on these channels, holding that all patrons—unless explicitly marked otherwise—are white. This was indicated in one individual's response to how he identifies his race on IRC:

> **Mad_Hatter:** usually I just tell people I have brown hair/eyes. . . then they can assume I'm white

Notably, the presumption of whiteness is so prevalent that **Mad_Hatter** need not identify himself as white; rather, simply by *not* explicitly describing himself as nonwhite (keep in mind that brown hair and brown eyes in and of themselves do not necessarily denote a body of European extraction) he is *read* as white by others on these channels. Kendall (2002), in her study of a social-oriented MUD, notes similar racial expectations, observing that when "black participants must state that they are black in order to be recognized as such, [online] anonymity carries with it a presumptive identity of whiteness" (p. 210). This online presumption of whiteness was certainly reflected in a discussion with **Big_Wolf,** the only self-identified African American in the core group of study participants:

> **John:** do people often ask you to identify your race online?
> **Big_Wolf:** yes, sometimes . . . sometimes they go on thinking i'm white
> **Big_Wolf:** Questions in order of most asked. . . . Age obviously, Penis Size, Are you a Top Or Bottom. . . . Sexual Orientation Race Gender is almost assumed.
> **Big_Wolf:** but if they suspect or find out you are black MANY immediately go to the penis size thing

Notably, when **Big_Wolf**'s racial identification is correctly surmised, it is articulated with social stereotypes of black masculinity. In general, on these channels one of the key means by which race is signaled is through the online nickname (such as **BlackMuscle** or **asian_cub**), though primarily only when that racial identity is other than white. As a rule, nicknames do not appear that explicitly identify their owners as white, though some online handles do signal "whiteness" indirectly through ethnicity (such as **IrishCrop** or **Italkisser**). This may originate from, as Kendall (2002) contends, dominant perceptions in the United States of whiteness "as bland, empty, and normative," resulting in white people claiming "more specific 'bounded' heritages" in terms of ethnicity rather than race (p. 201). Indeed, as Richard Dyer (1997) notes, white people often fail to recognize the privileges of whiteness in Western societies because of "the sense that whiteness is nothing in particular, that white culture and identity have, as it were, no content" (p. 9).

Although online nicknames sometimes signal racial identities other than white, nicknames can also be *misread* in regard to race. For instance, **Umgawa,** a thirty-three-year-old information security specialist living in New England, indicated that his online nickname often creates confusion over his racial identity:

> **John:** How do you identify your race on IRC? And are you usually asked to identify your race?
>
> **Umgawa:** Hrmmmm, only in terms of my nick—alot of people immediately assume I am african american . . . So when I do my moniker, ie /me is your average run-of-the-mill, seven foot tall,[5] built irish geek in Boston, I do include irish as a necessity of sorts.
>
> **John:** interesting—Irish serves as an indirect way of identifying yourself as white?
>
> **Umgawa:** well . . . yes.
>
> **John:** why do you think people assume you're african american (black) because of your nickname?
>
> **Umgawa:** Well, Umgawa is a swahili word . . . not your average irish guys nick :)

Umgawa's nickname was derived from the black-and-white Tarzan films of the 1930s and 1940s starring Johnny Weissmuller, such as *Tarzan, the Ape Man* (1932), *Tarzan Escapes* (1936), and *Tarzan and the Amazons* (1945), in which "Umgawa!" was a command used by the fictional hero over the animals of the jungle. Without understanding the reference, many online interactants assume that the word signifies **Umgawa**'s racial heritage. As with **Mad_Hatter, Umgawa** avoids identifying himself as white, preferring to claim a particular ethnic identity (Irish) to indirectly denote his racial identity. **Umgawa**'s reluctance to simply identify himself as white may well reflect the "general taboo in U.S. culture against speaking of race as well as the tendency to view 'white' culture as generic, with no racial content" (Kendall, 2002, p. 198). However, the need to mark his racial identity arises only because his name suggests he may be other than white, confirming the dominant understanding that all those interacting on these channels are white unless indicated otherwise. However, the absence of discussions of race in the public conversations on the channel should not be mistaken for the reduced salience of race online. The very fact that individuals such as **Umgawa** feel compelled to signal their race indicates that bodies in cyberspace remain raced bodies and that online spaces remain racially marked spaces. That individuals are assumed to be white unless marked otherwise indicates these channels are implicitly understood to be white spaces rather than raceless spaces; that is, white is viewed as the norm in these particular online communities.

Despite this general presumption of whiteness, the presumed male gender and gay sexual identity of interactants remain the strongest markers of these spaces. Obviously, this is far from the case on many other IRC channels, where individuals may be attacked if their nickname is construed as representing a nonheterosexual identity. Thus, reaffirming the sexual disposition of the channel through policing "negative" or unwelcome images of gay men, especially discourses suggesting that a gay identity is incompatible with a masculine identity, is a key aspect of maintaining the particular sensibilities of these communities in regard to safety and erotic exploration. Unfortunately, many on these channels reiterate dominant social understandings of sexuality as rigid and fixed, dismissing the possibility of a more fluid model of sexuality. For most interacting in these virtual spaces, the claims to both a gay and "masculine" identity are central in their understandings of themselves.

VIRTUAL QUEER HAVENS: ANONYMITY, SAFETY, AND EROTIC EXPLORATION ONLINE

That safety or, more accurately, the perception of safety is an essential component in constructing an affirming queer space should be self-evident. Even at the dawn of the much-touted new millennium, the United States—like many other Western nations—remains a hostile society for queer-identified individuals. Although the June 26, 2003, Supreme Court ruling in the case of *Lawrence v. Texas* found sodomy laws in Texas and twelve other states unconstitutional, only fourteen states and the District of Columbia have any form of legislation prohibiting workplace discrimination based on sexual orientation; currently there is no such protection on the national level. Furthermore, statistical reports issued by the FBI indicate that hate crimes against gays and lesbians have dramatically increased between 1991 and 2001.[6] Sadly, Maxine Wolfe's (1997) contention that for gay men and lesbians "[v]iolence and discrimination occur with little recourse, legal or political" (pp. 314-315) still holds largely true. In light of the overtly homophobic 1996 Defense of Marriage Act, the national venue provided Dr. Laura Schlessinger, and the murders of gay men such as Matthew Shepard, Billy Jack Gaither, Gary Matson, and Winfield Mowder, Pat Califia's (1994) retort to the notion of queers having "achieved legitimacy" at the close of the twentieth century resonates with renewed sobriety:

> What pathetic crap. What we do in bed is illegal in about half of the states. There are only a few tiny parts of the country where we are legally protected from discrimination. Young, working-class gay people who try to escape their families and get a college education by enlisting in the military still have a good chance of being caught in a witch-hunt and dishonorably discharged. In small cities and towns and even in big cities, there are still many, many gay men and lesbians who don't know how to find our community. Most of us can't get a date, much less a domestic partner. (p. 20)

Thus the need for spaces where gay and lesbian individuals can congregate, affirm their identities, and safely explore their sexuality is obvious, spaces I refer to as *queer havens*. As noted previously, authors writing on the historical experiences of lesbians and gay men, particularly in the United States, have identified various physical-world places that functioned (with varying degrees of success) as havens for erotic exploration and queer community formation.

Kennedy and Davis (1997) in their study of lesbian establishments in Buffalo note at the fore that a "lesbian bar by definition was a place where patrons felt relatively safe, otherwise they would not go" (p. 33). Arguably, the same holds true for online spaces dedicated to the interests of queer-identified individuals. In regard to physical-world gay and lesbian bars, multiple strategies have historically been employed in ensuring they are perceived as safe spaces for their patrons. For instance, Roey Thorpe (1997), in her discussion of the changing character of lesbian bars in Detroit during the mid-twentieth century, notes that an increasing number of lesbian bars were "invisible to heterosexuals, and even to lesbians who were unaware of their existence" (p. 179). Another development Thorpe points out is the employment of lesbian bouncers to exclude male, heterosexual, and potentially hostile patrons. However, I would hold that the primary feature making these locations feel safe is the presumption that everyone within the confines of the space claims a similar sexual identity—creating an interior world of affirmation in the face of an external world of hostility. Arguably, this holds equally true of queer-identified channels on IRC. Though the location of these open queer-identified channels is not necessarily concealed (the existence of most channels can be revealed using the appropriate /list command), they do, like physical-world gay bars, employ bouncers (i.e., channel moderators) to expel hostile individuals. All of this, of course, raises questions concerning the role played by online anonymity in creating a perception of safety.

A considerable amount has been written on the sense of safety interactants feel in engaging in erotic exploration on the Internet, generally attributed to online anonymity (notably Reid, 1996b). For instance, Pavel Curtis (1996), in his sociological discussion of MUDing, contends that "the most significant social factor in MUDs is the perfect anonymity provided to players" (p. 357). However, as I have personally come to realize, online anonymity alone is not sufficient to construct a safe space for the expression of queer sexuality and identity. This was made apparent to me during my only visit to the channel #bodybuilding.

An online acquaintance on the channel #gaymuscle, **Gymrat,** who prides himself a dedicated bodybuilder, referred me to the channel #bodybuilding for a more serious discussion of training techniques and dieting. According to this individual, those interacting on #bodybuilding were committed to the sport/lifestyle and could offer more informed and experienced advice on dieting, which remained my central area of confusion. Based on his recommendation, I ventured onto the channel, which was notably smaller than any of the gay channels I was accustomed to chatting on (only about ten interactants). After entering, I engaged in my customary greeting of "Hey guys!" I was shocked, however, when one of the interactants immediately responded with "Hey fag!" Unsure of how this response was to be construed, or even how my sexual identity was in any way marked—my nickname makes no inference as to sexuality—I retorted with "What's that supposed to mean?" Rather than receiving an explanation, I noticed all discussion on the channel had halted. After several minutes of this oppressive (virtual) silence, I left #bodybuilding and have not returned to the channel since. I later surmised that the individual who, in essence, "outed" me must have preformed a /whois command (a function of the IRC interface that indicates what other channels an individual is chatting on) and noted that I was also logged on to a queer-identified channel.

Two important points can be derived from my experience on the channel #bodybuilding. First, an individual's sexuality can be inferred in multiple ways, even in environments that are often identified as anonymous, so anonymity alone is not sufficient in creating a sense of safety for erotic exploration. In contrast to #gaymuscle, the presumption on #bodybuilding was of a heterosexual identity. The policing of this straight identity and the very clear hostility directed toward anyone suspected to be "other" is congruent with Klein's (1993) identification of homophobia as a predominant aspect of elite bodybuilding culture: "If narcissism works as an institutional backdrop for the bodybuilder's psychologically unaddressed issues and needs, homophobia (and its accompanying sense of hypermasculinity) is the central pillar around which the individual seeks to overcome poorly articulated issues of masculinity" (p. 218). Because, as Klein notes, bodybuilders engage in many activities conventionally perceived as either feminizing (such as the shaving of body hair) or homoerotic (such as the display of the seminude body for members of the same sex), bodybuilding becomes marked by a "hypersensitivity around homosexuality" (p. 220). Arguably, this results in the careful policing of online spaces where male (and presumably straight) bodybuilders congregate. A later discussion with the individual on #gaymuscle who referred me to #bodybuilding revealed that he was careful to conceal his sexual identity on that channel, arguing that it simply was not important to talk about sexual matters there. However, this individual's perceived need to conceal his sexual identity—one which he openly expresses on channels such as #gaymuscle—bespeaks the investment of individuals on #bodybuilding in maintaining that channel as an ostensibly straight space.

This leads to my second point: those channels on IRC lacking any reference to sexuality in their designation are not necessarily *un*marked in terms of sexual identity. Rather, as my experience on the channel #bodybuilding demonstrates, unless specifically identified as queer, virtual spaces encompass a naturalized presumption of heteronormativity. Arguably, it was only the presence of an individual who was possibly *not* heterosexual (myself) that made this presumption evident in the policing of that space. Bell and Valentine (1995) discuss how the visibility of gays and lesbians in public spaces exposes the artifice of sexual identity defining those spaces: "the presence of queer bodies in particular locations forces people to realise (by the juxtaposition 'queer' and 'street' or 'queer' and 'city') that the space around them . . . [has] been produced as (ambiently) heterosexual, heterosexist, and heteronormative" (p. 18). Thus, who is permitted entry, what discussions are tolerated in the main window, and the very presumptions of interactants' sexualities (as sometimes indicated by the designation of a channel) are all means of producing the sexual identity of a particular channel on IRC.

However, when a space is explicitly marked as something other than heteronormative, it also becomes a potential target of homophobic hostility. This is reflected in the occasional attack of antigay sentiment on queer-identified channels through what I refer to as "online gay bashing." As Reid (1999) notes, the "disinhibiting effects of relative anonymity and physical safety in the virtual environment can encourage the enactment of aggressive and abusive behaviors" (p. 114). Arguably, the disinhibition Reid discusses is a central component in the online basher's sense of license in attacking queer-identified channels such as #gaymuscle or #gaychub. It is far less likely that an individual would enter a heavily populated gay bar and begin verbally assaulting patrons in the physical world; yet this is precisely what occurs in online gay bashing, as revealed in a conversation with **TechnoBear,** a thirty-seven-year-old network engineer living in New York City:

> **John:** have you ever seen someone enter a gay channel to bash (attack) people there for being gay?
> **TechnoBear:** Yes.
> **John:** Can you describe generally what happens?
> **TechnoBear:** Either of two things:
> **TechnoBear:** There are no human ops in the channel and the basher has his way until a bot bans him for flooding or he gets bored.
> **TechnoBear:** There are human ops who ban and kick him.
> **TechnoBear:** A basher will often return under a slightly altered host id and continue.
> **John:** How do people on the channel react to the basher?
> **TechnoBear:** Depends.
> **TechnoBear:** Usually shrug him off.
> **TechnoBear:** Sometimes tease him (I do that).
> **TechnoBear:** Few let it bother them for any length of time.
> **John:** How frequent, in your experience, is this "online" bashing?
> **TechnoBear:** Once a month on average, I would say.
> **TechnoBear:** More or less.

TechnoBear: The more channels you're in, the more you see it.
John: Do you think online bashing frightens people away from gay channels?
TechnoBear: Nope.
TechnoBear: I think not being comfortable with being gay or with IRC keeps people away.

To illustrate his comments, **TechnoBear** sent me (via electronic mail) an IRC log of the activities on the channel #gaywrestle which transcribed an incident of online bashing. Like #gaymuscle, #gaychub, and #gaymusclebears, #gaywrestle is a queer-identified online space dedicated to those gay men interested in, as the name suggests, wrestling. Also like the other channels, the general presumptions underlying social interaction on #gaywrestle are that interactants are both male and gay. This segment of the IRC log **TechnoBear** provided demonstrates how a single hostile interloper can disrupt the sexual sensibility of an online space:

> <petenorth> u fucking faggots make me wanna puke, u should all be killed execution style god damn pole smokers, u fuckers are freaks of nature, kill all the queers jews faggats and dagos, kill all the queers jews faggats and dagos,kill all the queers jews faggats and dagos,kill all the queers jews faggats and dagos,kill all the queers jews faggats and dagos,kill all the queers jews faggats and dagos,kill all the queers jews faggats and dagos,kill all t
> *** cwilbur has kicked petenorth
> <TechnoBear> bashers should learn to spell.
> <spiky1> what is a dago?
> <cwilbur> it's a derogatory term for a person of Italian descent.
> <WRSL-N-IL> wow what an asshole
> *** BeefyWrsler has joined #gaywrestle
> <mabbz> Adam =)
> <Pittypat> Thank you cwilbur for kicking that unpleasant person out of here.
> <BeefyWrsler> mabbzles :)
> <TechnoBear> Unpleasant? He needs a good few hours on the mat with a few of us!

Notably, **cwilbur,** who possesses both operator privileges and responsibility for policing the channel, kicks (removes) the basher from the channel before he has the opportunity to complete his attack. Of particular interest, however, is the discussion ensuing after the basher is kicked out. Far from expressing fear at the hostility of the basher, interactants express momentary (and ironic) annoyance (**TechnoBear:**

"bashers should learn to spell") and outrage (**WRSL-N-IL:** "wow what an asshole") before discussions appear to return to normal. Furthermore, **TechnoBear**'s campy humor ("He needs a good few hours on the [wrestling] mat with a few of us!") helps to restore the queer sensibility of the space.

The strategic use of camp to undermine the hostile discourse of a basher is even more apparent in this transcript of an instance of gay bashing on the channel #gaymuscle that occurred during the fall of 1999:

> *** ironchest has joined #gaymuscle
> <ironchest> hi all.
> <ironchest> anyone seen johnred?
> <Brutus> ironchest: I last saw johnred 36 minutes 5 seconds ago.
> <LaceEmUp> hola ironchest
> <ironchest> hola Lace.
> *** prime-evil has joined #gaymuscle
> <LaceEmUp> como estas?
> <prime-evil> fuck all u faggots! You cocksuckers, u all going to fuckin die! We r going to kill all you fucking cocksuckers!!!! fucken die all you faggots!
> <ironchest> oh please
> <lifter_NC> whatever like we haven't heard that before
> <LaceEmUp> bend over prime
> *** Brutus has kicked prime-evil
> <LaceEmUp> sounds like prime needs a good fuck!
> <BeefyBoy> sounds like penis envy to me
> <patrick> that's what happens to straight boys when they don't get enough sex ;)
> <LaceEmUp> anyway how ya doing iron?
> <ironchest> bien gracias. un poco cansado
> <LaceEmUp> that means . . . a bit tired?

Even before **Brutus** employs his operator privileges to kick **prime-evil** from the channel, other interactants respond to the basher's initial assaults with campy retorts. Arguably this is intended to frustrate the basher and demonstrate the futility of his verbal (textual) attack. After the basher has been removed from the channel, camp humor is further utilized to restore the channel's queer sensibility. There is also, of course, a certain degree of typing agility at hand here. Those responding to the basher must compose their retorts quickly to be able to insert them into the main window of the channel before the basher has the opportunity to unleash another attack. Even individuals who were not participating in the discussion on the main window (such as **BeefyBoy** and **patrick**) jump in to add to the sense of camaraderie in policing/restoring the sensibility of the channel. This attests to the degree of emotional investment these interactants experience in maintaining this channel as an affirming queer space.

Chauncey (1994) points out that camp represents an important cultural strategy for negotiating a marginalized sexual identity in a hostile world, noting that by engaging in camp, gay men "affirmed their cultural distinctiveness and solidarity" (p. 286). Camp can also represent a powerful cultural device in undermining the heteronormative presumption of a space and redefining a space (even if temporarily) as queer. As Jean-Ulrick Désert (1997) argues, camp, that "mainstay of 'gay' stereotyping and the domain of the 'homosexual,' serves as one of a myriad of implicit gestures to redefine place and even history" as queer (p. 25). Thus when the queer sensibility of these channels is threatened by hostility, interactants (re)define and (re)produce these spaces as a queer spaces by conspicuously contributing campy remarks:

> **TechnoBear:** Unpleasant? He needs a good few hours on the mat with a few of us!
>
> **Patrick:** that's what happens to straight boys when they don't get enough sex ;)

Such online bashing should not be confused with the online social phenomenon of "flaming." Flaming, as described by Mark Dery (1994), is a compuslang term for "vitriolic online exchanges" which may be "conducted publicly, in discussion groups clustered under thematic headings on electronic bulletin boards, or—less frequently— in the form of poison pen letters sent via E-mail" (p. 1). Flaming and so-called flame wars are not confined to asynchronistic forms of computer-mediated communication, equally appearing in IRC chat rooms and MUDs. Nancy Baym (1995) suggests that this proclaimed "antisocial" online practice may be misunderstood by many Internet researchers, commenting that "flaming can be reinterpreted as a kind of sporting relationship" (p. 157). As Baym (1995) concludes, "flaming might be compared to forms of ritual insults that are popular in children's peer groups and serve to define them as members of that group" (pp. 157-158). Indeed, it not inconceivable to compare the witty insults and snappy posturing of online flaming to the queer practice of camp. The use of the term *flaming* has a long history within American queer society that precedes the advent of the Internet, referring to a defiant and flamboyant behavior playing on predominant stereotypes of gay men (a behavior associated with "flaming faggots," according to Chauncey). Unlike flaming, however, there is no wit or camp value to online bashing. Online bashing is the cyberspace equivalent of being physically assaulted on a street corner, and despite the fact that such attacks do not appear to have prolonged detrimental effects on the social dynamics of a channel, they can serve as painful reminders that for many members of sexual minorities the offline world remains an unwelcoming environment.

Clearly online anonymity alone is not sufficient in creating a safe and affirming space in which interactants can express and explore their sexual desires. Arguably, it is online anonymity that fosters the sense of license bashers exhibit when attacking these queer-identified channels. Rather, I would suggest it is the presumption of a shared sexual identity based on the use of the word *gay* in the channel designation that engenders the vital senses of safety and trust underlining social relations in these virtual spaces. Furthermore, the communal effort to exclude hostile discourses by kicking online bashers out and recuperating public discussions assures individuals of the continued sexual identity of the space.

CHATTING IN PRIVATE

In addition to public activities on the main window of a channel, a perception of safety is equally critical in private exchanges between individuals. In private chat rooms in which moderators are not present and therefore unable to intervene, an ethos is maintained which presumes that others online will interact in good faith. Thus, beyond a sense of commonality, the perception of safety so central to online community formation necessitates a sense of accountability toward other members of the potential community. My observations lead me to conclude that such accountability emerges from the emotional investment interactants experience toward their online identities as represented by their nicknames.

Chris Bradshaw, director of Ottawa Freenet, suggests the allure of the Internet is one of people getting hooked on anonymity (as quoted in Nguyen and Alexander, 1996, p. 102). Indeed, a considerable amount has been written about anonymity as the primary characteristic of interaction in online chat rooms or MUDs. However, anonymity, though applicable to the physical self sitting before computer, is not necessarily true of the self socializing in cyberspace. Even though offline identities are rarely revealed in public discussions on #gaymuscle, #gaymusclebears, or #gaychub (except in the occasional use of an offline given name), individual personalities can become well known on these channels. As one patron (**JB26**) responded when asked why he comes to #gaymuscle, "I've gotten use to the bozos on this channel and we all 'know' each other."

When **JB26** comments on *knowing* other interactants on #gaymuscle, he is not necessarily referring to their offline identities (though this may well be the case) but to their online personae. In this virtual environment in which interactants can be neither seen nor heard, there is only one means of identifying individuals—their online nickname. Reid (1996a) describes how interactants are ensured of a unique nickname, or handle, when entering online chat rooms, noting that the "program design is so structured as to refuse a user access to the system should he or she attempt to use the nickname of another user who is online" (p. 402). In these virtual spaces, the nickname is the face of the other interactant that not only functions as the primary identifier but also is the source of initial impressions. This online nickname, in turn, is central to both the establishment of the online persona and in developing a sense of community on these channels. On these channels, nicknames—commonly referred to as simply "nicks"—do not necessarily functions as disguises as Danet and colleagues suggest. If one understands a disguise as a device used to conceal identity, then the nickname functions quite to the contrary, expressing some aspect of one's identity in virtual space. The emotional investment interactants experience toward their online handles became apparent during a discussion with **PECS:**

> **John:** Have you ever gotten on-line and someone else was using your nick?
> **PECS:** yes
> **PECS:** but not for long!
> **John:** How did you feel when that happened?
> **PECS:** I messaged them and ask them to change it
> **PECS:** pisses me off!
> **John:** So it pisses you off when someone else is using your nick?
> **PECS:** yes, big time!

John: Why?
PECS: I'm PECS and everyone knows I'm the PECS of IRC

For individuals such as **PECS,** the nick not only represents their on-line persona (their self in cyberspace) but also identifies their presence in cyberspace to others. When #gaymuscle regulars greet or gossip about **PECS,** they have a particular online persona in mind (". . . everyone knows I'm the **PECS** of IRC"). Another #gaymuscle patron, **PHLguy,** discussed the significance his nickname has in regard to his interactions with others online:

> **John:** Would it bother you if someone else on IRC used your nick?
> **PHLguy28:** yes
> **PHLguy28:** my nick is well known
> **John:** Why would it bother you?
> **PHLguy28:** cause my nick is known, and I pride myself to be a decent guy, and if someone used my nick, I would not know if they would use it for good or evil, and then others would think that I was doing them wrong

PHLguy used the online nick **PHLguy28** for approximately a year before dropping the number that indicated his age from the handle. In a brief discussion a year after this initial interview, **PHLguy** commented on why he stopped incorporating his age into his online handle: "cause I dont want to be reminded all the time of how old I'm getting!" During a more serious discussion, however, **PHLguy** indicated that the primary reason he changed his online handle was to avoid the confusion engendered by the annual updating of his nick. Despite the alteration of his online handle, **PHLguy**'s identity remained recognizable to others on these channels, and therefore his online persona remained essentially intact. What is truly critical is the sense of accountability **PHLguy** attributes to his online nickname— "I pride myself to be a decent guy, and if someone used my nick, I would not know if they would use it for good or evil"—and his investment in his reputation on these channels. **GremlinBear,** who chats primarily on #gaymusclebears, expressed similar concerns regarding the use of his online nickname:

> **John:** Have you ever gotten online and someone else was using your nick?
> **GremlinBear:** no but I did hear that someone did
> **GremlinBear:** but that was all I heard

John: How would you feel about someone else using your nickname?
GremlinBear: depends on how they use it
GremlinBear: wrongfully is not good for you when you return
John: What do you mean by "wrongfully"?
GremlinBear: well making bad comments to other people and making trouble
John: And what does that do to you when you return
GremlinBear: well people think it was you of course
GremlinBear: and they make their comments and make you justify why you did what ever it was that was done and you are on trial proving your inocence

As **GremlinBear** points out, regardless of the degree of accountability an individual invests in his or her online handle, others on these channels will hold patrons answerable for their online actions, or the actions of those using their nicknames: "you are on trial proving your inocence." To assume another interactant's nick is not only to attempt to assume his or her online identity, it is to compromise that person's position within an online collective. For these individuals, the nick carries with it an ethical accountability much like a face does offline. Thus interactants on these channels demonstrated a keen protectiveness of their nicks. However, **Top_Bear,** who chats primarily on #gaychub, made the important distinction between the accidental use of another's online nick and an attempt to assume another's online identity:

John: Do you always use the same nickname on IRC?
Top_Bear: yes
John: Have you ever gotten online and someone else was using your nick?
Top_Bear: yes
John: How did you feel when that happened?
Top_Bear: depends on the situation . . . if it was another person just coincidentally using the same name not upset. however, if it is someone using mine to be me pissed

For **Top_Bear,** only when someone actually attempts to assume his online identity is there a cause for concern and resentment. Otherwise, **Top_Bear** acknowledges that in a medium where there is no uniform technical means of ensuring others do not use a person's nickname when he or she is absent, there is always the possibility of innocently assuming another individual's handle. However, not all patrons professed a significant emotional investment in their online handles. **Bennoe,** for instance, expressed apparent indifference to the use of a particular online nickname:

> **John:** How long have you been using your current nickname?
> **Bennoe:** 2 years
> **Bennoe:** it may change with an extra "n" or drop the "e" off the end
> **John:** Have you ever gotten online and someone else was using your nickname?
> **Bennoe:** sure
> **John:** How did you feel when someone else was using your nickname?
> **Bennoe:** i have even been msg'd and then abused quite badly for having the same nick
> **Bennoe:** i didn't care . . .i don't own it . . .it's just a name
> **Bennoe:** the other fool however was furious and called me some nasty names
> **John:** he was upset that you were using the same nickname?
> **Bennoe:** he sure was
> **Bennoe:** he was swearing at me and called a cunt and other stuff
> **John:** Why do you think he was so upset?
> **Bennoe:** i looked him up and msg'd him back and warned him that it is an offence to use telecommunication lines to make offences calls and quoted him the sections of the criems act and he shit himself . . . never heard from him again
> **John:** well, it pays to be a police officer I guess ;)
> **Bennoe:** i think he thought he "owned" the nick and it was like taking something from him

Even though **Bennoe** makes no claim to having an emotional investment in his nickname—"i don't own it . . . it's just a name"—the other individual he discusses evidently held a significant attachment to the name. **Bennoe**'s account demonstrates the emotional intensity individuals may experience toward their online handles, at times manifesting in impassioned textual assaults on those perceived as purloining a name, an emotional attachment **Bennoe** contends he neither shares nor understands: "i think he thought he 'owned' the nick and it was like taking something from him." Despite his proclaimed non-investment in his nickname, the fact that **Bennoe** has been using the same handle for over two years with only slight variations suggests some sentimental identification with the nick. Even if **Bennoe**'s attachment to his online handle emerges solely from the convenience of being *recognized* on the channel, the desire of recognition suggests an emotional investment in the particular online persona represented by the nickname.

The fact that these individuals experience both notability in these virtual environments and accountability to their online identities suggests that these channels hold a sense of community for those interacting there. Inversely, it is arguably this very sense of community that instills in these patrons such a strong emotional investment in their online personae. As Reid argues (1996a), the "uniqueness of names, their consistent use, and respect for—and expectation of—their integrity, is crucial to the development of online communities" (p. 403). Appreciating the critical role consistent identities play in these online communities, established patrons will sanction those attempting to appropriate their nicks, often messaging them until they stop. Channel moderators may even kick off individuals who repeatedly attempt to assume the handle of an established channel personality. However, the possibility that individuals can become well known in these virtual spaces raises a critical question: What precise role does online anonymity play in disinhibiting interactants in exploring their erotic desires?

In her study of MUDs, Reid contends that the "immediate effect of this anonymity is to provide users with a feeling of safety" (1995, p. 174). However, in her study of online bulletin boards, Baym (1995) contends that though the offline self remains anonymous to other online interactants, "participants are able to interactively create identifiable personalities for themselves in this potentially anonymous terrain" (p. 156). Therefore, online anonymity must be understood as the (at least partial) concealment of the identity of the physical body sitting at the computer and not as nonidentity in cyberspace. Such understandings of anonymity are even further complicated when one considers that some of those patronizing these channels meet offline (as I have with **PECS** and **Umgawa**). Furthermore, as I have experienced, the process of getting to know other patrons of these channels generally involves revealing information surrounding offline lives, including details regarding occupations, offline hobbies and interests, and even religious beliefs and family backgrounds. Thus, online anonymity for these individuals must be understood as a relative rather than absolute characteristic of their experiences in cyberspace.

The relationship of the online persona and the offline self in regard to anonymity holds certain parallels to the negotiation of identity for lesbians and gay men living in American urban centers during the first half of the twentieth century. In his discussion of gay men in pre-

Stonewall New York City, for instance, Chauncey (1994) indicates how "the relative anonymity enjoyed in Manhattan by gay tourists from the heartland—and even from the outer boroughs—was one reason they felt freer there than they would have at home to seek out gay locals and behave openly as homosexuals" (p. 133). However, by use of the term *anonymity*, Chauncey is not implying that "gay men remained isolated from (or 'anonymous' to) one another" or that they engaged in only "anonymous, furtive encounters between strangers" (p. 133). Rather, the "complexity of the city's social and spatial organization made it possible for gay men to construct the multiple public identities necessary for them to participate in the gay world without losing the privileges of the straight" (pp. 133-134).

Similarly, it is the *physical-world* anonymity found in virtual environments such as #gaymuscle and #gaychub that affords patrons the freedom to explore sexual desires they may not be able to explore as easily (or as safely) offline. As with Chauncey's discussion of pre-Stonewall New York City, this anonymity does not suggest that interactants engage in only furtive virtual sexual encounters, remaining strangers to one another online. Rather, the nature of virtual environments permits individuals to construct online identities and engage in erotic interactions without physical, social, or economic risk to their offline selves. Reid (1996b) made a similar finding in her study of "cross-gendered playing" on MUDs, noting that "the anonymous virtual environment allows this kind of exploration a safety that could only make it all the more attractive a site for it" (p. 333).

During discussions with **PHLguy,** it became clear how the online anonymity of his physical self in virtual environments provided him a freedom not found offline. When asked how #gaymuscle compares to a physical-world gay bar, **PHLguy** responded:

> **PHLguy28:** I don't run the risk of being spotted by a family friend, my boss, coworkers
> **PHLguy28:** I am not out

For **PHLguy,** the anonymity of #gaymuscle allows him to overcome very real fears of being "outed" in the physical world, which could jeopardize his employment and his familial relations. Indeed, for many gay men and lesbians, even those living in major cities, there are legitimate concerns of being seen going into a gay bar or club or of being attacked ("bashed") when leaving a recognized gay or lesbian establishment. However, many of these physical-world misgivings do not apply to interactions in cyberspace.[7] Even though, as demonstrated, a form of textual bashing can occur on queer-identified channels, the structure of IRC does not allow potential antagonists to see or enter private discussions between individuals. Thus, online bashing can occur only on a channel where the queer-identified individual benefits from the sense of solidarity rather than solitude in facing his or her attacker.

This anonymity or concealment of the physical-world self provides another key attribute positioning these environments as safe spaces for erotic exploration: control. In addition to the anxiety engendered by fears of losing one's livelihood or of being bashed, for some gay men there is also the unease of openly expressing their sexual desires in a "public" space. This fear of erotic expression is at times intertwined with nervousness regarding physical appearance. Thus, the relative anonymity of these channels, combined with the textual basis of online interaction, offers some individuals a strong sense of control over their online appearance. Markham (1998) discusses this sense of control in cyberspace: "In an online context, if I control the text, I have control over presentation of self, provided we have never had face-to-face contact" (p. 123). This perception of control, Markham argues, provides many online interactants with an intense experience of empowerment: "All the participants see control as a considerable benefit of, if not the very reason for, being online" (p. 124).

Although both the medium and those social conventions arising within these channels restrict the actual agency individuals have in cyberspace, the *perception* of control over the presentation of self seems to foster in some individuals a confidence in expressing their erotic desires online. The sense of empowerment this perception of control engenders was noted during an interview with **Younghung**. Though **Younghung** is out to his immediate family and does not fear being "outed" by visiting a known gay establishment, he still expressed particular anxieties related to patronizing a gay bar. When asked to compare a physical-world gay bar to #gaymuscle, he made the following observation:

> **Younghung:** well in #gaymuscle you can talk, I mean really talk if you want to, you get past alot of the nervousness, it is a liberating forum, in a bar you have more nervousness, and the noise and other peo-

ple, in #gaymuscle if you like a person and want to talk more, you
can go and have a private, one to one conversation

John: do you feel as safe going to a gay bar as you do #gaymuscle?

Younghung: not alone

Younghung: alone I feel safer in #gaymuscle

John: Does #gaymuscle offer you anything you can't get from a gay
bar in the real world?

Younghung: well it does offer a place where you can be open, removes the nervousness, it's more freeing you don't have to be shy, it
removes alot of the inhibitions

Younghung: in real life I am very shy, on #gaymuscle I don't have to be

John: And what does that give you?

Younghung: freedom of expression of things I'd probably not be able
to express with someone until I had known them for a very very long
time

Living, as he notes, "in the heart of the Bible belt," there is an awareness of a generalized cultural homophobia causing **Younghung** to be
concerned for his physical safety in going to a gay bar or club alone.
However, it appears that **Younghung** equally experiences distress
over his self-presentation, which, in turn, creates a constraining degree of apprehension in visiting physical-world gay establishments.
Arguably, it is this sense of control over the presentation of his online
self that enables **Younghung** to overcome the very self-conscious-
ness inhibiting his ability to express his desires to other gay men
offline. **Mage78,** who is also located in the southern United States
and is approximately the same age as **Younghung,** expressed similar
apprehensions about locating and entering gay bars:

John: May I ask where you're located?

Mage78: Louisville, Kentucky

John: Do you have a lot of access to gay communities there?

Mage78: No . . . not that there isn't much, I know there are gay bars,
etc, I just don't get into it much

John: Why is that?

Mage78: I have limited time because of my studies and work, but also
because, despite my openness online, I am quite a bit more shy in
person . . . I react with individuals, but have a hard time in large
groups.

John: How do you feel then when you go into a gay bar?

Mage78: Like I do when I go into any large group . . . self concious, a bit
out of place, and slightly overwhelmed.

Arguably, the qualities permitting individuals to explore their sexual desires on these channels are an allied sense of safety in regard to the physical self and control over the presentation of the online self. In essence, entering these channels is a chance to reinvent the self without some of the constraints of the offline world but still within the social dictates of these online collectives (most notably those surrounding gender, sexuality, and race). Though physical-world anonymity fulfills a vital function in this online erotic exploration, it is accompanied and tempered by such other social attributes as commonality among interactants, the accountability individuals feel toward their online identities, and the control individuals experience regarding their presentation of self. All of these characteristics—anonymity, commonality, accountability, and control—work in concert to produce the vital sense of safety fundamental to the formation of affirming spaces which serve as the locus of queer communities in cyberspace. These characteristics also demonstrate the ways in which offline needs inform online practices: while the physical world remains a hostile space for many queer-identified individuals, perceptions of safety and mutual trust function as the cornerstones in the construction of online gay communities—communities in which individuals can explore their erotic desires without fear of stigmatization.

VIRTUAL HAVENS AS REAL COMMUNITIES

Two topics central to scholarly discussions of computer-mediated communication are online anonymity and the formation of online communities. Based on the current literature, the existence of the former does not appear to preclude the formation of the latter (Baym, 1995; Bromberg, 1996; Kollock and Smith, 1999; Reid, 1991; Rheingold, 1993; Watson, 1997; Wellman and Gulia, 1999). In this section, I move beyond discussing either those defining characteristics of the individuals patronizing these channels (in terms of gender, sexuality, or race) or those attributes central to interaction in virtual spaces (in terms of anonymity, safety, or control). Instead, I focus on *why* these individuals socialize on these particular channels, their motives for first logging on to IRC, and, finally, what role these virtual environments play in how participants conceptualize their own sexual identity.

In doing this, I endeavor to illustrate some of the complex ways in which offline experiences and needs shape online practices. Many of the earlier writings on computer-mediated communication focused on how online interaction impinged on perceptions of offline life, envisioning a unidirectional relationship in which cyberspace was transforming our understanding of social relations in the physical universe (e.g., Turkle, 1995). The authors of these works, however, appeared to give little thought to the ways in which a person's offline circumstances figured into their online activities. As Kendall (2002) points out, much of the sociological work on cyberspace has characterized "social effects as flowing mostly from cyberspace to the offline world, rather than the other way around" (p. 10). This sociological view has an implicit technologically deterministic bias, denying the ways in which people incorporate communication technologies into their lives to meet existing needs or desires. By examining what transforms these online spaces into meaningful communities for their members, I hope to make explicit some of the ways in which online and offline experiences blend into a single, albeit multifaceted, narrative of life. In essence, I seek to show how these channels become consequential social scenes in the everyday lives of at least some of their participants. Certainly looking more closely at the offline reasons individuals cite for interacting online complicates the notion that there is a radical disjuncture between cyberspace and the physical world.

An important means of understanding what transforms these channels—#gaymuscle, #gaychub, and #gaymusclebears—into communities is examining what motivates individuals to seek out these particular queer-identified sites. One reason interactants often alluded to for initially venturing onto IRC and even into these particular channels was, quite simply, curiosity:

> **John:** Why did you start chatting on IRC?
> **Msclfreak:** out of curiousity, and then I was hooked

> **John:** What made you want to start chatting on IRC?
> **Masculin:** curiosity. . . . some experiences others have had (other str8 friends)

> **John:** Why did you first start chatting on IRC?

TexMuscle: started just as a curiosity
TexMuscle: then to get information
TexMuscle: then i started making friends

Although curiosity was a central motivation for me when I started chatting online, I was equally motivated by the desire to expand my (gay) social networks. Based on discussions with those interacting on these channels, my motives were far from unique. Indeed, the most commonly identified reason interactants gave for venturing onto IRC was to meet other people who share important dimensions of their identity, especially in regard to their sexual identity. This desire to expand social circles was touched on in interviews with **Younghung** and **BluCollar:**

> **John:** why did you start chatting on IRC?
> **Younghung:** somewhat out of curiocity . . .
> **Younghung:** but really I think to meet other gay men . . . to have someone to talk to about gay stuff
>
> **John:** what made you want to start chatting online?
> **BluCollar:** I think it was the feel of comradarie. Knowing that there are other guys out there like me.

Whatever reason given for initially venturing into IRC, the fashioning of online friendships was the universally cited explanation for continuing to chat on these particular channels. Many participants indicated that they had chatted on several different gay-identified channels before coming across one of the three channels studied here. Repeatedly, interactants noted that what drew them back to these specific spaces was a sense of shared identity, and this shared identity, in turn, served as the basis for establishing long-term social relationships with others online. Ultimately, these friendships provided the individuals discussed here with a sense of "belonging" or "acceptance" not necessarily found in other virtual spaces. This was indicated in discussions with **Msclfreak** and **Britannic:**

> **John:** When on IRC, what channels do you usually chat on?
> **Msclfreak:** bodybuild and gaymuscle
> **John:** Why those channels in particular?
> **Msclfreak:** thats where I first met friends, continued chatting there ever since

John: What channels do you usually chat on?

Britannic: #gayboston, #gaymuscle, #gaynj, #gaybigcocks, #gayselfpix, and #gayfisting are the channels I chat in the most

Britannic: Out of those, I'm in #gaymuscle the most

John: why do you chat on #gaymuscle?

Britannic: Because there are a lot of nice people there who are full of good advice and support in my efforts to get in shape.

Britannic: That's also where most my friends are

Discussions with members of these channels suggest that the formation of online friendships were not instantaneous. Rather, individuals related how they had to first locate an online collective where there was some underlying interest that united participants, where, in essence, they felt like they "fit in." Only at that point did many individuals feel they had some foundation on which they could construct meaningful online relationships. What makes friendships possible on these channels is a set of converging attributes in relation to participants' offline identities—a shared sexual identity as well as mutual interests or desires—that serve to unite those drawn to these particular virtual spaces. Indeed, it was a set of converging offline interests that led **Umgawa** and a group of his friends to found the #gaymuscle channel in 1994:

John: when on IRC, what channels do you usually chat on? And why?

Umgawa: today, only #gaymuscle

Umgawa: more or less because it was a channel I founded with five other friends back in 94 or so, so I have a bit of "ownership" rights . . .

Umgawa: and that's where friends I know from past lives and here in Boston hang out

Umgawa: every now and then I'll head over to #macos for geek talk, but that's rare

John: really, you helped to found #gaymuscle?

Umgawa: Yep . . . Me, Jim (Phooey) and a few people not here any more . . . Tony (muscleboy), Jay (bdybldr), Ummm . . . Mike (Nomad) . . . [8]

Umgawa: we started it because #gaysex had too much sex talk on it and we wanted a channel for bodybuilding talk only . . . sex talk would get you banned from it, as we planned

Umgawa: that rule failed within the first six days of the channel's existence

John: So the point of #gaymuscle was to create a space where gay men could explore their interest in bodybuilding and male muscularity?

Umgawa: yeah, but on irc since when does the point of something actually dictate outcome?

John: what would you say the function of #gaymuscle is today?

Umgawa: Indeed, today if there are 60 guys on #gaymuscle at 8pm and if you join and start talking actual lifting and bodybuilding, all but one or two others shut up and don't know what's going on

Umgawa: oh, its a sex shop for alot of guys

John: why do you think some just looking for sexual discussion would talk on #gaymuscle rather than something like #gayboston or #gaysex?

Umgawa: I guess that gay guys go for specific channels for specific fetishes . . .

Umgawa: #gaymuscle, #gaymusclebears, #gaysm

Umgawa: etc.

John: ok, so the "fetish" on gaymuscle is muscle?

Umgawa: guess so . . . I go there to talk lifting

Umgawa: and see old buddies

For **Umgawa,** the original function of IRC was to discuss "really cool things," though clearly the intent was also to establish and maintain social bonds. The very individuals he founded the channel with were friends he had initially met while a student at the University of Arizona and wanted to remain in contact with when he moved to Minnesota, friends who shared his passion for bodybuilding and weight training. **Umgawa**'s characterization of #gaymuscle as now little more than a "sex shop" reflects less the actual reason most people interact on the channel than his frustration that much of the public discussion on the channel is now sexually charged. Perhaps **Umgawa** perceives a shared sexual identity as being reduced to sex alone. (Notably, **Umgawa** exhibits little reluctance in participating in such sexually charged discussions.) However, although sex and sexuality are certainly organizing principles of this channel, the fact that people come to maintain friendships (established both online and off) suggests the site functions as something more than merely a sex shop. **Umgawa**'s reference to going online to "see old buddies" clearly indicates that for some these channels function as a means of sustaining social networks.

In addition to those seeking to expand their social networks, some individuals enter these online spaces in search of a more profound sense of understanding and solace. This was very much the case with **Mad_Hatter,** a twenty-nine-year-old data-entry clerk living in Florida:

John: Why did you start chatting on IRC?

Mad_Hatter: my lover died . . . he used to chat on here . . . so, I thought I'd give it a try

John: Very sorry to learn of your loss

> **Mad_Hatter:** thanks
> **John:** So it was not till after his passing that you started chatting on IRC?
> **Mad_Hatter:** yes, that's correct
> **John:** May I ask what he died of?[9]
> **Mad_Hatter:** a condition know as Lactic Acidous . . . what it boils down to is he ultimately died of complications from HIV
> **John:** I'm very sorry—it must have been very difficult for you
> **Mad_Hatter:** thanks, it was and sometimes still is
> **Mad_Hatter:** but i think coming on here helps
> **John:** How did it help?
> **Mad_Hatter:** it gives me people to chat with. . . . just shoot the shit . . . I've also hooked up with a few guys . . .
> **Mad_Hatter:** it made me feel not so lonely

Painful emotional experiences in the physical world—such as the loss of a partner—can motivate individuals to turn to cyberspace as a means of finding immediate assuagement and companionship. Notably, **Mad_Hatter** came to #gaymuscle in particular because his late partner had already established social ties with others interacting on the channel. In essence, the channel was a means by which **Mad_Hatter** could commune with others who shared emotional bonds with his lost lover. His comments also indicate that he has used the space as a sexual space, meeting new sexual partners to alleviate some of his physical loneliness. The need to overcome some form of physical-world isolation has been cited by other participants as the reason for both entering IRC and frequenting one of these particular channels. Such was the case with **GremlinBear,** who experienced a different form of physical-world isolation than **Mad_Hatter:**

> **John:** Why did you start chatting on IRC?
> **GremlinBear:** I was sick in bed and needed someone to chat with so my old room-mate introduced me to IRC
> **John:** Why do you keep chatting
> **GremlinBear:** I made some friends

Based on discussions with interactants on these channels, a general pattern of motivations emerges: Although some interactants identified curiosity as their primary motive for first venturing onto IRC, or into a particular channel, others identified a more pressing need to overcome some form of physical-world isolation. Whether this isolation resulted from the loss of a loved one (**Mad_Hatter**) or physical illness (**GremlinBear**), these interactants turned to IRC to find others who could offer solace, understanding, or simply some form of companionship (**Mad_Hatter:** "it gives me people to chat with"). However, the incentive for continuing to interact on IRC, and especially for frequenting these particular channels, is the formation of consequential online relationships. These social ties developed out of either shared interests (such as weight training or an attraction to exceptionally muscular men) or shared modes of identification (such as characterizing oneself as a musclebear or a chub). In turn, these online friendships—even if between individuals who have never physically met—arguably constitute the basis of affirming online communities.

Although for some individuals these spaces may be viewed solely as "scenes" for the locating of (cyber)sexual partners, for the core group of participants, these channels represent meaningful communities they can turn to in times of distress, isolation, or loneliness. Arguably, it is for these reasons patrons exhibit such an emotional investment in the channels they frequent, readily policing such spaces against hostile discourses. Though, like physical-world gay bars, there are a number of individuals who will merely pass through these virtual environments, for those individuals constituting the "regulars" of a given channel, tangible social networks in the form of online friendships ensure their continued patronage.

In addition to a means of expanding or maintaining existing social networks, for some these channels function as spaces for the exploration of nonnormative sexual identities. In these virtual environments in which some find camaraderie, comfort, and affirmation, others find opportunities to resolve ambivalences underlying their own understandings of their sexuality. Certainly these channels are not unique in providing a space in which individuals can fashion a nonheterosexual identity. As Chauncey (1994) and Kennedy and Davis (1997) have demonstrated, the gay or lesbian bar has historically provided a physical-world space where individuals could explore their same-sex sexual desires and find entry into some form of queer community. However, important limitations of the physical-world gay and lesbian bar as a site of coming out are found in regard to age and location. Not only must an individual live within proximity of such a place, but also, because most establishments serving gay and lesbian clientele in the United States cannot be entered until the age of twenty-one, younger gay men and women may find themselves ex-

cluded from those communities formed around such locations. This
was apparent in a discussion with **WorkOut:**

> **John:** Why did you start chatting on IRC?
> **WorkOut:** I had just recently come out as a gay at college and found
> chatting online an easy way to talk to others like myself
> **John:** really?
> **WorkOut:** Yep. I wasn't old enough for the bars.
> **WorkOut:** online is actually where I came out.
> **John:** why did you come out online? Did chatting online play a role in
> your coming out?
> **WorkOut:** I came out online because it's where I was easily able to
> find someone who self-identified as gay. When I was questing my-
> self, I logged on and went down the list of people on the single gay
> channel[10] at the time and asked if any of them had a moment to talk.
> One of them did and we talked for a couple hours. The discussion
> reaffirmed my suspicion I was/am gay.
> **WorkOut:** It played a big role in my coming out. Where I went to col-
> lege and came out, there was very little if any of a support network,
> so I found support online through people I chatted with.
> **John:** how do you feel about your sexuality now?
> **WorkOut:** I feel very comfortable with my sexuality

For **WorkOut,** entering a gay-identified IRC channel and speaking at length with one of its members represents not so much an act of
coming *out of* the closet, as coming *out into* a form of gay community
(the pre-Stonewall understanding of the term discussed by Chauncey).
Furthermore, coming out online suggests that some form of community must already by there to come out to. As with **Mad_Hatter** and
GremlinBear, WorkOut experienced a form of physical-world isolation and turned to IRC to find social support and affirmation. By
discussing at length the feelings he was experiencing, **WorkOut** was
able to resolve some of the ambiguity surrounding his sexual identity.

An additional reason online sites such as the channels discussed
here are critical resources for those questioning or exploring their
sexual identity is the low level of initial risk. For an individual such as
WorkOut to actually enter a physical-world gay establishment is
generally read not as exploring one's sexuality but as embracing a
nonheterosexual identity. As such, these physical-world establishments do not necessarily constitute ideal sites for the exploration of
sexual identity. However, the relative anonymity of the offline self
minimizes the risk faced by those individuals probing sexual possibilities in cyberspace. **WorkOut** was not the only participant to indi-

cate that he first reconceived the terms of his sexual identity online. **Big_Wolf,** a well-established member and paternal figure on the channel #gaychub, laid claim to a similar experience:

> **John:** did you come online before you came out offline?
> **John:** Oooops, sorry, I meant, did you come out online before you came out offline?
> **Big_Wolf:** No I came out as a result of speaking to other gay men online back on AOL, . . . my first provider . . . I was victim of a very hate filled fundementalist family . . . it was not till meeting gay folk online and talking that I realized gay men were GOOD people.
> **Big_Wolf:** Oh yes . . . I came out on AOL's gay chat rooms.
> **John:** Did being online help you to understand your sexuality?
> **Big_Wolf:** Thats where I built my strength up to come out offline.
> **Big_Wolf:** Immensely . . . if I had never come online i would have never broke out of the prison of lies my family told me about all gay men.
> **John:** how did you feel about yourself and your sexuality before first chatting online?
> **Big_Wolf:** I saw my first positive role models honest BIG hot men that talked to me like a brother online . . . FINALLY I felt I belonged somewhere . . .
> **John:** when you say "BIG" what do you mean?
> **Big_Wolf:** Oh Gad . . . I was a repressed basketcase . . . I was a frustrated closet queen to the max . . . a semi basher I bashed only those who got too close to my closet door.
> **Big_Wolf:** BIG as in Fat huge men.
> **John:** Is fat desirable to you?
> **Big_Wolf:** Fat huge men have been my love and, sexual ideal since I can remember.
> **Big_Wolf:** Fat men is how I first knew I was gay before I even knew what gay was.

Due to what is referred to online as "lag," the questions and responses constituting this conversation frequently overlap. However, the important role these queer-identified cyberspaces played in **Big_Wolf**'s understanding of his own self-identity remains clear and merits repeating:

> **Big_Wolf:** I saw my first positive role models honest BIG hot men that talked to me like a brother online . . . FINALLY I felt I belonged somewhere . . .

Big_Wolf alludes to possessing some awareness of his particular erotic interests before actually understanding his sexual identity in social terms (**Big_Wolf:** "Fat men is how I first knew I was gay before I even knew what gay was"). **Big_Wolf**'s experiences offer an indication of how erotic exploration online can lead to startling self-discoveries offline. Clearly, some entering these spaces may be irresolute about their sexual identity, or, more accurately, what sexual identity to lay claim to in their daily negotiation of life, yet these individuals are motivated to join queer-identified channels out of a dissatisfaction, frustration, even alienation experienced in their offline social relations. Only after having developed a stronger sense of their erotic interests and some affirmation of those interests—particularly in the form of shared desires—are these interactants comfortable in conceptualizing their own sexual orientation in terms other than heterosexual (**Big_Wolf:** "FINALLY I felt I belonged somewhere"). This strongly suggests a more fluid and constructionist view of sexuality in which nonheterosexual identities are far from fixed at birth but rather are the result of exploring erotic interests that resist conforming to those socially dictated as "normal."

Klein (1993), in his discussion of how competitive bodybuilders become involved with hustling (the solicitation of sex from gay men in exchange for pecuniary or promotional rewards), draws upon David Matza's (1990) notion of "drifting into nonnormative lifestyles" (Klein, 1993, p. 199). As Klein states, "For the hustlers in bodybuilding the 'drift' is more abrupt, not coming from adolescent transgressions, but rather from a combination of adult pragmatism and psychological needs stemming from childhood. Nevertheless, there is a gradual quality about it" (p. 199). The notion of drifting—gradually assuming a particular identity based initially on curiosity and then the discovery of new experiences that meet some long-standing but previously unacknowledged need—describes the experiences of many individuals who come to these channels. As with **WorkOut** and **Big_Wolf,** this drifting was also suggested in a conversation with **PHLguy:**

> **John:** has #gaymuscle given you a place to talk about things that you were not able to do before?
> **PHLGuy28:** yes, definitely so
> **PHLGuy28:** before I didn't talk about sexual things
> **PHLGuy28:** It has been a slow awakening, from just jerking off to straight porn with cool penetration and double penetration scenes, to gay porn, bi porn, to talking on here, to the actual meeting of people and having sex

PHLGuy28: I have met people here that have introduced me to others, thus making my sexual life even more active

In addition to communities of affirmation and solidarity, these are communities of self-discovery. The form of self-discovery exhibited on these channels is possible only within an environment in which patrons feel safe exploring their erotic desires. This vital sense of safety originates as much from the relative anonymity of the offline self that is capable of entering these queer spaces without, in some respects, actually leaving the closet, as it originates from the commitment patrons make toward maintaining these channels as affirming spaces for same-sex sexual activities by excluding hostile discourse (such as those of the online basher). Although each channel has a clear erotic ideal, the relative ease with which individuals can drift in and out of these social scenes positions them as suitable spaces for the investigation of desires that may be viewed as deviant within the larger social context. Of course, this should not be read as suggesting these channels constitute some form of sexual utopia, for these spaces continue to be shaped by repressive understandings of race and gender.

Whereas some participants indicated that they turned to these cyberspaces out of curiosity, others indicated that these channels have served a more critical role in their lives—offering solace in times of crisis, companionship in times of isolation. The stories related by those interacting on these channels speak of how offline and online experiences merge into a single life narrative for their owners—a narrative in which these virtual spaces constitute meaningful social scenes for those frequenting them. This is why I identify these channels as online communities or communities existing in virtual space, rather than referring to them as "virtual communities." As with the term *virtual ethnography,* to qualify the word *community* with the word *virtual* is to suggest that these social scenes and the social relations occurring within them are somehow less real and less vital to their participants. In opening up avenues for erotic exploration, which, in turn, can lead to a significant reconceptualization of an individual's offline sexual identity, these virtual gay bars become loci for communities of material consequence.

Drawing upon the writings of Ray Oldenburg, Howard Rheingold (1993) foresaw the possibility that online spaces could serve as distinctive "third places." In Oldenburg's (1991) schema, there are three essential places in the daily life of people: their place of residence, their place of employment, and the place where they gather solely to socialize. It is in this social space, this third place which Oldenburg identifies as "the great good place," that community life is established and sustained. Like the neighborhood pub or café, Rheingold (1993) suggests that virtual environments could also function as such third places: "Perhaps cyberspace is one of the informal public places where people can rebuild the aspects of community that were lost when the malt shop became a mall" (p. 26). Certainly for gays and lesbians in technologically advanced nations, online spaces such as those examined here can indeed serve as vital third places—virtual gay and lesbian bars—where affirming communities can be forged and maintained. When one considers the hostility members of sexual minorities still face in many societies, the need for such queer third spaces becomes evident. Ideally, such online third places would provide their patrons with a vital sense of connectedness during times of isolation and crisis, as well as a forum in which to explore their erotic identities. Although not free of repressive understandings of race, gender, and even sexuality, I believe these channels constitute such a "great good place" and an important social resource in the lives of at least some of their patrons.

Chapter 4

Singing the Body Cybernetic

> I sing the body electric,
> The armies of those I love engirth me and I engirth
> them,
> They will not let me off till I go with them, respond
> to them,
> And discorrupt them, and charge them full with the
> charge
> of the soul.
>
> Walt Whitman
> *Leaves of Grass,* 1855

As already mentioned, a tremendous amount of discussion has concerned the liberating potential of interacting in a space disencumbered from the physical body (Bruckman, 1996; Reid, 1996b; McRae, 1997; Danet, 1998). For these authors, to enter cyberspace is to transcend the physical and to exist, albeit temporarily through communication technologies, as a disembodied entity emancipated from the burdens society places on the corporeal self—race, gender, age, beauty, and so forth. Ultimately, many of these authors conclude that cyberspace represents a realm where, in radical departure from the dictates of the physical world, the body is inconsequential. Stone (1996), for one, argues that as communication bandwidth—"the amount of information exchanged in unit time" (p. 93)—narrows, the experiencing self becomes increasingly divorced from the restrictions of the physical body. Thus, through computer-mediated communication (which is at present primarily narrow bandwidth), Stone (1996) suggests the individual transcends physical constraints, experiencing and interacting as a being of pure symbolic exchange: "The body in question sits at a computer terminal somewhere, but the locus of sociality that would in an older dispensation be associated with this body goes on in a space which is quite irrelevant to it" (p. 43).

Argyle and Shields (1996), however, are not convinced that online experience is necessarily a bodiless experience. Contesting notions that being online means being disembodied, they see the relationship of the online self and the offline body as one of complex and co-dependent exchange: "bodies and everyday lived experiences are both the content of Internet communication (in the banality of the gossipy postings or the discussions of sex) and contiguous with its use (in the form of users' bodies)" (p. 58). I would further Argyle and Shields's skepticism by problematizing the very distinction between the *online self* experiencing interaction in cyberspace and the *offline body* sitting at the computer terminal. Is the body only that physical manifestation sitting before the screen and typing on the keyboard? Or is the body equally a discursive phenomenon accompanying individuals into virtual terrains?

In this chapter, I examine the vital function the body plays in defining these online communities, thereby problematizing this online disembodiment thesis. As I demonstrate, for interactants on these channels "the body" is both a shared reference for online communication and a principal component of online identity. The very incorporation of the body into online interaction reveals its discursive construction. That is, in addition to being a physical presence, the body is equally a discursive constellation apprehending pleasures, sensations, desires, practices, and erotic impulses fundamental to the conception of *self* in cyberspace. Examining from a Foucauldian perspective how the body is experienced on these channels, I endeavor to complicate essentialist understandings of the body as some "natural" and pre-discursive component of identity. As I will argue, the very multiform and conflicting understandings of not only what constitutes the desirable body but also what constitutes the sexual for those interacting in these online communities effectively undermine naturalized understandings of sex, sexuality, and the sexed body.

Starting with a discussion of what I refer to as a semiotics of the body in cyberspace, I reveal the development of online vernaculars for describing the body. I also demonstrate how this semiotic system is predicated on an understanding of the body as objectifiable, divisible, and, ultimately, quantifiable. I then examine how this conception of the objectified body is incorporated into the holistic notion of idealized sexual "types." Because these types—specifically bodybuilders, musclebears, and chubs—also come to be associated with particular sexual predilections, I examine two interesting sexual practices discussed in these virtual environments: gaining and muscle worship. In doing so, I endeavor to demonstrate how some interactants articulate an understanding of the erotic quite distinct from that presented in mainstream offline discourses.

SEMIOTICS OF THE (CYBER)BODY

Facilitating the incorporation of the physical into online social relations is a distinct vernacular for the body, generally shared across the three channels. This vernacular is comprised of words that, although not necessarily unique to online interaction, carry particular meanings on these channels, allowing patrons to convey a strong image of bodily attributes that cannot be accomplished through quantitative characteristics alone (height, weight, waist size, etc.). Two aspects of this vernacular merit mention at the fore: First, though the terms central to this vernacular are shared across the three channels, they can vary in connotation, and to a lesser extent in denotation, from one channel to another. Generally this connotative shift concerns the desirability of the physical trait the term identifies. For instance, in the context of #gaychub, or even #gaymusclebears, the term *gut* can signal a sexually desirable physical characteristic, while on #gaymuscle, the term often carries negative connotations. The second aspect meriting comment is the interplay between this vernacular and quantifiable information regarding the body. Underlying this vernacular that appears, superficially, to speak of the body holistically, is an understanding of the body as a collection of distinct and measurable components. These components can be assigned quantified values, which, in turn, serve as the basis of symbolic exchange. As I will demonstrate, many of the key terms comprising this online vernacular gain expressive significance only because they connote particular quantified values. Thus, there is not so much a tension as a complementation between discussions of the holistic body and a body understood as an amalgamation of assessable components. On these channels, the body is at once monadic and composite, a unified self and a collection of parts, a desirable person and an object to be desired.

The centrality of the body to discussions on these channels is evident in the multitude of terms patrons employ for speaking of the body, the most common being big, huge, freaky, ripped, and beefy. Obviously, these terms are not unique to these channels, and, as Klein (1993) notes, similar terminologies appear in the cultural vernaculars of professional bodybuilding. However, examining what such terms mean to patrons is arguably an important way of understanding how the body is viewed in these virtual spaces. For instance, two terms frequently appearing in public conversations on the channels #gaymuscle and #gaymusclebears are "big" and "huge." **Britannic** defines these two words relationally:

> **Britannic:** Big means a muscular guy. Huge means a VERY muscular guy!

Based on my interviews, **Britannic**'s understanding of the terms *big* and *huge* is shared by others who chat primarily on either #gaymuscle or #gaymusclebears, such as **Msclfreak:**

> **John:** What does "big" mean to you?
> **Msclfreak:** muscular
> **John:** Do you consider yourself "big"?
> **Msclfreak:** yes, according to some I am huge, but I don't consider myself huge yet

Like **Britannic, Msclfreak**'s responses suggest the understanding of "big" and "huge" as states of being on a continuum of muscularity. In addition, **Msclfreak**'s final comment—"I don't consider myself huge yet"—indicates the possibility that the body's position on this continuum of muscularity is mutable. However, when the context of the discourse is changed to the channel #gaychub, a very different understanding of some of the same terms becomes apparent. **Big_Wolf,** one of the most senior patrons on #gaychub, offered the following understanding for the term big:

> **John:** when you say "BIG" what do you mean?
> **Big_Wolf:** BIG as in Fat huge men.
> **John:** Is fat desirable to you?
> **Big_Wolf:** Fat huge men have been my love and, sexual ideal since I can remember.

Simply by moving from one channel to another, the terms *big* and *huge* stop representing positions on a continuum of muscularity and come to indicate an individual's girth. For **Big_Wolf,** not only does "big" mean "fat," but fatness itself is desirable and erotic. This was apparent in **Big_Wolf**'s response to the question of whether he ever chats on the channel #gaymuscle:

> **Big_Wolf:** Nope . . . I am not into muscle. . . . I am here[1] because I find Adult fat dudes endlessly attractive to the total max . . .

In general, **Big_Wolf**'s understanding of "big" as referring to an obese body and his conceptualization of obesity as a desirable trait is very much in opposition to those interacting on #gaymuscle, where the focus is on the degree of muscular development and where fat is viewed as a hindrance to the display of such muscularity. Thus, these online vernaculars for the body change meaning depending on the orientation of the individual channel, especially in regard to what is understood to be physically desirable. Like any semiotic system, then, that which the sign (e.g., "big") actually signifies (e.g., muscular or fat) is ultimately arbitrary, dependent on the contextual schema within which the sign works.

Returning to the channel #gaymuscle, another term prevalent in public discourse is *freaky,* which appears to represent an extreme on the same continuum encompassing "big" and "huge." This is suggested in **Younghung**'s articulation of the term:

> **Younghung:** Freaky mean outrageously huge, larger than normal, larger than even is common to see, freaky is a man that is super huge, it means that same thing to most on #gaymuscle.
> **John:** Is that a desirable thing—to be freaky?
> **Younghung:** Yes, that is very desirable thing in my eyes, and in most

While in offline social relations the term *freak* generally carries negative connotations and a sense of stigma, on #gaymuscle the term functions as an expression of admiration and desirability. Cecile Lindsay (1996) observes a similar employment of the term in the world of contemporary bodybuilding, noting that bodybuilders often "compliment each other with the term 'freak'" (p. 360). As Lindsay indicates, "freak" functions as an "expression of awe and respect for those who push their physical development beyond current limits," and "freakiness" is conceptualized as a desirable state "most often acquired through drug use in addition to intense workouts" (p. 360). In a discussion with **Umgawa,** he noted the contrast between more mainstream understandings of the term *freak* and those understandings emerging out of the bodybuilding subculture. Of particular interest is how he articulates his self-image in relation to this concept of "freakiness":

> **John:** I was wondering if you would tell me what the word "freak" or "freaky" generally connotes on #gaymuscle?
>
> **Umgawa:** well, freak and freaky are more a term out of the bodybuilding community than the gay, I would think
>
> **Umgawa:** a freak at a gay bar would be someone to avoid due to their mental problems
>
> **John:** what does freak mean within the bodybuilding community?
>
> **Umgawa:** a freak in bodybuilding is someone who has obtained a near-incredible amount of muscle and size
>
> **Umgawa:** the first is a term of avoidance, the second is a term of awe
>
> **John:** so being freaky is a desirable thing?
>
> **Umgawa:** For some guys, yeah . . .
>
> **Umgawa:** for me, absolutely.
>
> **John:** do you want to be freaky? or are you sexually attracted to someone who is freaky?
>
> **Umgawa:** For me?
>
> **Umgawa:** Well, at 17, I hit 7' in height and weighed like 172 or so . . .
>
> **Umgawa:** so all I wanted then was to date/fuck someone who was a freak of muscle
>
> **Umgawa:** as I've bodybuilt, I slowly became attracted to that which is what I was, yet for myself the freak look is still my goal
>
> **Umgawa:** to gain the size I need, at near whatever the cost . . . but the guys I am attracted to (physically) are the lean ones . . .

On the channels #gaymuscle and #gaymusclebears, "freak" functions as both an acknowledgment of unusual physical achievement and an expression of sexual desirability. Arguably, this sexual desirability represents the connotation individuals such as **Msclfreak** seek when they incorporate the term *freak* into their online nickname. Furthermore, because the use of the term *freak* is generally reserved for more exceptional physical conditions, appearing far less frequently than either the terms *big* or *huge,* the use of the term in his online handle provides some indication of how **Msclfreak** wants others online to perceive his body:

> **John:** Let me ask you, how do you view your body?
>
> **Msclfreak:** big and impressive, but want to get even better

John: what do you mean by better?
Msclfreak: bigger, more powerful, more ripped

As **Msclfreak**'s comments suggest, "freaky" refers to both the "freaky" state of an interactant's body in terms of overall musculature and the "freaky" transformation of the interactant's body in terms of increasing muscle mass. In either regard, "freaky" denotes a condition of the body that would likely be viewed as extreme and even unhealthy within more mainstream contexts. This was illustrated in a conversation with another #gaymuscle interactant self-identifying as a bodybuilder, **Lifter-NY**.[2] Discussing his perceived "need" to extensively increase his overall muscle mass and transform his body into a "freakish" state, **Lifter-NY** commented, "I want to get so big I make people puke!" Based on my conversations with **Lifter-NY** and other patrons of #gaymuscle, "freakiness" is achieved when the body becomes so remarkably muscular as to be viewed as monstrous in comparison with those images of the male body presented by the mainstream media as desirable. The same condition of the body that would position it as undesirable, unhealthy, arguably repulsive within the norms of mainstream culture, increases its allure on these channels. This was indicated in **Msclfreak**'s response to the question of why he wants to increase the muscle mass of his body beyond what the dominant society identifies as "healthy": "I like the attention I get!" In fact, it appears that on the channel #gaymuscle, the more extreme the level of muscle mass the body possesses—the more "freaky" it is—the more erotic it becomes. Indeed, for some interactants, "freakiness" becomes, in itself, an erotic state.

To illustrate this eroticism of "freakiness," of being so big as to be repulsive within the context of mainstream culture, #gaymuscle patrons occasionally exchange "morphed" pictures (i.e., graphically modified images) of professional bodybuilders. These pictures are representative of the state of true "freakiness," a state that no human can fully achieve because its very extremity positions it as "superhuman." For instance, Figure 4.1, a morphed image of an unidentified professional bodybuilder, has been exchanged many times on both #gaymuscle and #gaymusclebears. Images of already unusually large bodybuilders enhanced through graphics software such as this one function as a form of erotica on these channels, suggesting a fetishism surrounding extreme, even impossible degrees of muscular development. For patrons on these channels, the "freaky" body becomes—by

FIGURE 4.1. Graphically modified image of an unidentified professional bodybuilder

its very extremity—an object of intense erotic allure, and arguably part of this erotic attraction stems from that body's nonconformity to mainstream conceptions of the healthy and desirable male physique.

In addition to "freaky" and terms that generally describe the size or mass of the body, various terms are employed to characterize the body in regard to the ratio of body fat to muscle mass. "Beefy" and "ripped" are two such terms people use to express this attribute of the body, which, unlike big, huge, and freaky, function as contrasts rather than matters of degree. This was indicated in a conversation with **Younghung:**

> **Younghung:** Beefy to me means a man that is very muscular but isn't "ripped" or in other words to have a low body-fat, they are generally big, thick waisted thick necked and generally big men.
> **John:** Is "beefy" a term a lot of people on #gaymuscle look for?
> **Younghung:** Not necessarily, some of them like the more "ripped" look of men with big chests and smaller waists.

All of these terms—big and beefy, huge and ripped—indicate a holistic condition of the body. If one is characterized as big or ripped, it connotes a state the entire body occupies. This raises two important questions: How do those interacting in virtual spaces, where the physical body is generally not seen, arrive at some consensus, some shared understanding of what these terms actually signify? Furthermore, how do patrons themselves make claim to such terms? These questions indicate the necessity of the compartmentalization and quantification of the body in online textual interaction. In these virtual spaces where the big body or the ripped physique is not apparent, one lays claim to these states (e.g., being big, being ripped) by objectifying his body and relating it as a collection of measured attributes.

By reconceptualizing the body as a composite of quantified and comparable measurements, the body becomes an object of symbolic exchange on these channels. This compartmentalized conception of the body is most apparent in how those identifying themselves online as bodybuilders relate their own bodies in terms of "parts" or "components" (i.e., biceps, triceps, chest, legs, back), ascribing considerable value to the quantitative measurements of each component. **Msclfreak,** for instance, finds the quantitative values for key areas of the male body fundamental to his conceptions of big and small, muscular and nonmuscular, as demonstrated in these excerpts from my discussions with him:

> **Msclfreak:** well, on here some call themselves muscular when they have 13 inch arms . . . when you have muscles that stand out—that make people turn their heads in the street—then you are muscular!

> **Msclfreak:** first of all: many guys on #gaymuscle call themselves muscular if they have 14 inch arms and 38 inch chest.

> **Msclfreak:** I was never really small—my legs were 25 inches before I touched a weight

Msclfreak introduces an interesting means by which the body is rendered into text: quantitative measurements. Unlike the use of terms *big* and *huge* to characterize the body holistically, here the body is communicated as a collection of measurable components—fourteen-inch arms, thirty-eight-inch chest, twenty-five-inch legs. Thus the body becomes an object that can be categorized based on statistical information; if particular regions of the body are identified as having certain numerical values, then the entire body can be characterized as big, huge, or even freaky.

Within this mode of discourse, the body is reproduced as a product of culture and technology. For interactants such as **Msclfreak,** their bodies are perceived by themselves and others online as technobodies, physically developed through cultural practices (e.g., progress weight training and dieting) and pharmacological technologies (e.g., synthetic anabolic hormones) and displayed to others through communication technologies. This conception of the body as a product, the result of a particular regime of social intervention, is apparent in **Msclfreak**'s response to how he became "big":

> **John:** What did you do to get big?
> **Msclfreak:** ate, trained and took steroids

Msclfreak's perception of the body as an object that is somehow other than the self—even when the self wants to be understood or "read" through that body—is fundamental to the performance of the body through compartmentalized and statistical information. This simultaneous objectification and compartmentalization of the body is not unique to online social relations. As Klein (1993) discusses, it is also a central cultural practice within the world of professional bodybuilding:

> If bodybuilding has historically occupied a less than status-filled position in our society, it nevertheless feeds our current cultural view of the body as "partible" and "bounded." The bodybuilder's perception of the body as being made up of parts (chest, abs, back, arms, legs) and subdivided ("traps" [trapezius], front and rear "delts" [deltoids]) fits this partible notion perfectly. It even extends into the psychoperceptual realm, in that bodybuilders view each body part as objectified. The bodybuilder's body is bounded in a series of subcultural perceptions and practices that have to do with absolute control of diet and physical regimen, and viewing it as a system that has to be mastered. (p. 189)

In the realm of professional bodybuilding, the body must be objectified into a collection of distinct parts, if it is to be assessed and assigned a value in competition and as a site of self-mastery. This same principle holds true for many of those interacting on #gaymuscle and #gay-musclebears, though on these channels the assessment of the body is in terms of its desirability and erotic potential.

Klein (1993) also notes the critical role of language in the world of bodybuilding, indicating that language is "the most forthright expression of self-objectification in bodybuilding" (p. 244). Similarly, it is in the online language of these individuals that their understanding of the body as an object of achievement and desirability is most apparent, and it is through this same online language that the body is performed through textual interaction. A desirable arm, for instance, can be understood as being large, large can be assigned a quantifiable value (e.g., 18 inches), and this value can be readily communicated online. Once the body is deconstructed into constituent and quantifiable parts, it becomes a static body, and once it is static, it can be communicated as a fixed set of values. This is the underlying principle of a pervasive online convention known as "stats."

TO SEE SOMEONE ONLINE, JUST ASK FOR HIS "STATS"

In these virtual gay bars, where none of the other patrons can actually be seen or heard or touched, locating a desirable body proves more complicated than it would in a physical-world gay bar. Though patrons can gain some sense of another's bodily attributes from the online handle (**Big_biceps, youngmuscle, Hairybeef**), the limited information available is insufficient for discerning the physically desirable body. So to facilitate the identification of desirable bodies, these individuals have devised the communicative convention of stats. Deriving the term from the world of professional sports in which stats refers to the statistical record of performance for a particular athlete, patrons relate all of the key information regarding their physical body in a single textual message. The pervasiveness of this practice is apparent in **Younghung**'s response to how he discerns the physical attributes of another individual online:

Younghung: normally I just ask for their "stats"
John: What is "stats"?

> **Younghung:** well "stats" is a slang term for asking how someone
> looks, their appearance . . . age, height weight built type eye color
> hair color and measurements of muscle size, like arms chest waist
> and thighs

When an individual messages another requesting stats, the other
party is expected to provide key quantitative information regarding
his body. Occasionally, this quantitative information is supplemented
with qualitative descriptors (beefy, huge, ripped, etc.). Frequently, for
the sake of speed, stats will consist of purely numerical values (e.g.,
"225#, 5'10", 50c, 35w, 18a, 27q, 12%bf" which would be read as
"weight 225 pounds, height five-foot, ten-inches, chest fifty inches in
circumference, waist thirty-five inches, arms eighteen inches, and
thighs or 'quads' twenty-seven inches, all at 12 percent body fat").
Although this convention of asking for one's "stats" may appear
abrupt, even rude to those new to the channel, it not only quickly becomes an accepted practice but also appears to provide a sense of cooperation, openness, and ease of interaction.

In essence, this IRC practice of stats functions much like character
descriptions found in some MUDs (Schaap, 2002), though considerably less formalized and elaborate. More closely, this convention resembles the Muff Diva Index (MDI) on the lesbian Sappho mailing
list discussed by Wakeford (1996), who notes how the "lesbian body
may also be coded in the signature, providing another means of
screening a 'real' body" (p. 101). Using a fairly extensive coding
schema, the participants in the Wakeford studies are able to communicate such dimensions of the lesbian body as hair length, muscle
tone, and "Femme-Butch factor." Indeed, stats accomplish much the
same purpose on these IRC channels, reproducing those dimensions
of the physical body participants deem important to online interaction and, in doing so, adding social weight to those bodily characteristics (such as bicep or chest size).

While facilitating the speed of online communication, stats also
function to institutionalize the quantification of the body. Those new
to #gaymuscle or #gaymusclebears quickly learn the importance of
compiling statistical information regarding their own bodies if they
expect to fully participant on these channels. Failure to provide such
statistical information in these virtual environments is often read un-
favorably as concealing the body, akin in many respects to the online
practice of "lurking." If newcomers are unsure how to compile their

own stats, veteran patrons will instruct them on what areas of the body to measure, how to measure them, and what those measurements connote—big, huge, freaky, ripped. In fact, the mere presentation of stats can position an individual as big, huge, or even freaky on a channel without that individual actually having to lay claim to any such characterization of his own body. This is important, since many of the descriptive terms, such as big or huge, carry different connotations on these channels than they do in more mundane offline interactions. For instance, height, an aspect of the body often considered important in most offline experiences, is considered to be much less important on channels such as #gaymuscle than overall muscle mass is. Thus, an individual such as **Msclfreak,** who is only five-foot-six-inches tall, can lay claim to being big, or even be characterized as huge by other interactants, because his body carries sufficient muscle mass. Inversely, very tall individuals who may be accustomed to characterizing themselves as big offline may be characterized on these channels as thin or even small if their stats are read by other interactants as insufficient in regard to muscle mass. Interestingly, the relational dimension of words changes online, where pairing short and big or tall and small is not contradictory.

Stats become incorporated into an individual's online identity in much the way a face and a particular build becomes representative of a person in physical-world interactions. This is possible because, like a person's face or general build, a patron's stats are expected to remain relatively consistent, even if that person engages in bodybuilding or weight training. Thus, a regular of a channel such as #gaymuscle may be characterized as "having great legs" or "having the biggest arms around" in the public discussions of the main window without having to post his stats or make any reference to his own body. Should an individual's stats change too radically, they are likely to be called into question by others on the channel. At such a point, the individual may have to e-mail electronic images of his body to those on the channel to substantiate his altered stats. While some variation in muscle mass or levels of body fat is acceptable—providing said variation is not "too extreme"—any alteration in terms of gender or race is not.

This online convention of stats and the vernaculars for the body appearing in these channels fundamentally rest on the understanding of the body as an object that can be compartmentalized and assigned quantifiable values. In essence, for these interactants, the body can be rendered into text. Of course, as text, the online body should be easily mutable; effecting a physical change is as simple as altering the numerical values composing an individual's stats. However, considerable policing surrounds the presentation of the body online. This indicates the importance of both the offline body and those social constructs imposed on the body for individuals patronizing these virtual environments. The body performed online through stats and various qualitative descriptors is desirable only as long as it is understood as corresponding to an *actual* physical body. In other words, the erotic potential of discourses appearing in these virtual spaces is predicated on there being a physical reality behind the textual self, even if that reality will never be seen or touched.

Thus, in these online communities, a central ethos exists that interactants are representing their bodies in good faith. Of course, this ethos exists because of the implicit awareness that online and offline bodies can ontologically differ. Violation of this ethos can result in the loss of online friendships, as well as teasing or outright attacks on the main window of a channel. This is not to suggest that interactants do not emphasize what they perceive to be their strongest features online, conceal those features they perceive as deficient, or occasionally lay claim to terms such as *big* or *muscular* that may be contested by others on the channel.

Rather, those who engage in what I identify as "virtual body bending," that is, presenting a body online that does not reasonably correspond to the physical body offline (an activity sometimes accompanied by electronically distributing pictures of little-known bodybuilders and claiming them as self-images), are censured on these channels. This was demonstrated in **Umgawa**'s discussion of his reaction to those perpetrating virtual body bending on #gaymuscle:

> **John:** In general, what do you think of people that present themselves as something other than their offline selves online?
> **Umgawa:** today? Ummm, I get great enjoyment out of fleshing them out :)
> **John:** How do you think people on #gaymuscle feel in general about guys who pose as something they're not?
> **Umgawa:** Well, I dunno what others think . . .
> **Umgawa:** I'm more ambivalent about it, though fleshing some major poser out is enjoyable (such as MAbodybldr right now)

Umgawa: generally, if they show up with attitude and no clue to lifting, we'll have fun taking them apart . . .
John: what does "fleshing" mean?
Umgawa: fleshing . . . uh. . . . :)
Umgawa: as in "fleshing out a topic"
Umgawa: in this case, determining who they really are . . . or their real experience level
John: ah
John: in general, do people on #gaymuscle try to expose people who present themselves as something they are not, or that send pics that are of other people?
Umgawa: only when they become a problem I guess
Umgawa: hugemscl from florida was sending out pics claiming to be Tom . . . oh, forgot the guysw last name
Umgawa: I knew him at the gym in Minnesota while he took his masters in english at UMN
John: Tom Prince?[3]
Umgawa: and the guy, even when not able to answer stuff, still claimed to be him
Umgawa: yes, thanks
John: interesting, how did other members of the channel treat him in public discussions?
Umgawa: some teased him whenever he came on the channel
Umgawa: some more or less set him to /ignore all and didnt do much
Umgawa: the easiest thing to do . . . set an /ignore list and simply never see their presence again

This awareness that some individuals do use IRC as a medium through which to perform constructed personae has led **Umgawa** and other veteran patrons to devise means of ensuring individuals are what they claim to be on these channels, especially when individuals present themselves as bodybuilders of considerable physical development.[4] As illustrated in **Umgawa**'s comments, one means of policing bodily representations is by noting inconsistencies in an individual's knowledge of weight training. This is not to suggest that there is no room for fantasy on these channels but rather to indicate that assuming a fantasy persona is acceptable only within a context explicitly understood by all parties as a fantasy performance, otherwise it is considered deception.[5]

In addition to terms characterizing the condition of the body—big, huge, ripped, beefy—terms exist that signify not only a particular condition or shape of the body but also an accompanying lifestyle and mental disposition. These terms identify what are called "types," which are, in short, discursive configurations combining objectified and compartmentalized understandings of the body with a holistic conception of the person as read through that body.

ONLINE TYPES: BODYBUILDERS, MUSCLEBEARS, AND CHUBS IN CYBERSPACE

Discourses emerging from the three channels often invoke idealized images of the desirable person referred to as "types." A *type* essentially identifies what could be understood as a category of person, and it is common to find patrons on these channels asking one another "What's your type?" On the channel #gaymuscle, for instance, this ideal type is epitomized by the bodybuilder; while on #gaymusclebears, the ideal is, evidently enough, the musclebear; and on #gaychub, it is the chub. Though expressed through particular collections of stats, the reference to a type generally encompasses not only particular images of the body but also equally particular understandings of the social practices, cultural attitudes, and behaviors of an individual. Thus, invocation of a type conjures for participants an all-encompassing model of the idealized person, *including* expected sexual proclivities. The following discussion, however, should not be taken as an exhaustive delineation of either online or gay male types (there are also "cubs," "twinks," and "leather men," to name but a few common ones). Rather, this is a discussion of only those idealized erotic images around which these particular channels have been constructed, starting with #gaymuscle and the image of the bodybuilder.

Although references to bodybuilders and bodybuilding also appear on #gaymusclebears and #gaychub, the bodybuilder as an idealized type remains a principal focus on #gaymuscle, where individuals tend to either identify themselves as bodybuilders or express their sexual attraction to bodybuilders. The existence of the athletic field of professional bodybuilding offers some immediate understanding of what constitutes the "bodybuilder," but some specific erotic associations surrounding the body of the male bodybuilder are more particular to these virtual spaces. For instance, interactants on #gaymuscle invoked similar characteristics as being personified in the body of the male bodybuilder: powerful, virile, disciplined, dominant, and, without doubt, desirable. On this channel, the bodybuilder was primarily understood through his body, a body that defined those social practices and attitudes of value to the bodybuilder. Some interactants, such as

Younghung, described the bodybuilder basically in terms of those activities intended to increase physical size and strength:

> **Younghung:** a bodybuilder is any man that spends great time and effort lifting weights to build a very large very strong body

Many other #gaymuscle patrons understood the body of the bodybuilder as signaling much more elaborate and demanding practices than weight training. Though still conceptualizing the bodybuilder through his body, these individuals viewed that body as indicative of a complex convergence of cultural values and conventions, as was demonstrated in a distinction made by **PECS:**

> **John:** Is bodybuilder the same as a weightlifter?
> **PECS:** No!
> **John:** How are they different?
> **PECS:** Bodybuilder is a person who sculpts their body as in art, most guys are weightlifters basically to stay in shape . . . you understand John??
> **John:** So bodybuilders do more than just lift weights?
> **PECS:** Yes, they turn their bodies into art

While others might define bodybuilders as simply men trying to increase muscle mass (a description that would apply to any man engaging in progressive weight training), **PECS** raises the distinction of the bodybuilder's body as a work of art and bodybuilding itself as an art form. As a bodybuilder who participants in competitive exhibition, this distinction is important in **PECS**'s own sense of self. However, this conception of the bodybuilder's body as an artful achievement was shared by many interactants across all three channels, including those not identifying themselves as bodybuilders, such as **Big_Wolf:**

> **Big_Wolf:** a bodybuilder is an artist and, flesh and, muscle are his pallate.
> **Big_Wolf:** canvas shall I say

For many on these channels, especially those self-identifying as bodybuilders, bodybuilding was articulated not as a solitary cultural practice but rather as an all-encompassing lifestyle. This was evident in discussions with both **Msclfreak** (a competitive bodybuilder) and **TexMuscle** (a self-identified novice bodybuilder):

John: Is being muscular the same thing as being a bodybuilder?
Msclfreak: not necessarily
Msclfreak: bodybuilding is a lifestyle.

John: When you refer to yourself as a bodybuilder, what does that mean?
TexMuscle: i am a bodybuilder
TexMuscle: the diet, exercise, the whole lifestyle

In general, bodybuilding was identified by interactants as a lifestyle predicated on physical practices and signified (as well as validated) by the very body of the bodybuilder. In other words, in spaces in which the body can be seen, the male bodybuilder does not need to identify his distinct lifestyle, as it is made evident by the display of his body. In his discussion of the world of professional bodybuilding, Klein (1993) notes how bodybuilders expect their extreme muscularity to communicate their lifestyle and values tacitly: "Like the cartoon without a caption, the hypermuscular body, too, is supposed to communicate without an act; its presence is its text" (p. 274). On these channels, where the body is not readily visible, the bodybuilder nevertheless displays his body and its corresponding lifestyle through both the incorporation of key terms into his online handle (e.g., **PECS, Msclfreak, TexMuscle**) and the conspicuous posting of stats on the main window. By introducing unusually large stats into the discussions appearing on the main window of a channel (e.g., 5'6", 215#, 50c, 34w, 20a, 32q[6]), the bodybuilder lays claim to a bodybuilding identity and, arguably, the virile and masculine persona expected to accompany such an identity. To be a bodybuilder is to be invested in a lifestyle constructed around and read through the body—a lifestyle of physical discipline and regimentation, and of a certain projected arrogance, even if this outward arrogance, as Klein (1993) argues, is compensating for some inner insecurity: "bodybuilding is a complex of behavior historically premised on the male need for increased size, partially to compensate for feelings of inadequacy," and by engaging in such a lifestyle, the bodybuilder is actually making an "attempt at validating his sense of masculinity" (p. 191).

However, a more complex cultural reading of bodybuilding presents itself within the context of these channels. In virtual spaces in which exaggerated and even "freakish" male muscularity is eroticized, bodybuilding may be viewed as an erotic practice designed to make the body more appealing to other men. Thus, when an extremely large bodybuilder, who has invested considerable effort, time, and resources in building an unusually large body, uses that body to increase his sexual attractiveness to other men, he is implicitly rejecting the collapse of masculine images of the male body with compulsory heterosexuality. In essence, his inflated muscularity and hypermasculine form can be read as a caricaturing of the male body as the virile reproductive heterosexual body. As David Halperin (1995) writes in his discussion of Foucault, the gay male bodybuilder should *not* necessarily be read as an internalization of heterosexual masculine dictates:

> On the contrary, the exaggerated, arcane, highly defined, elaborately sculpted muscles of the gay male gym body derive from no useful pursuit and serve no practical function: they are the sort of muscles that could only have been developed in a gym. They are explicitly designed to be an erotic turn-on, and in their very solicitation of desire they deliberately flaunt the visual norms of straight masculinity, which impose discretion on masculine self-display and require that straight male beauty exhibit itself only casually or inadvertently, that it refuses to acknowledge its own strategies. (p. 117)

As Halperin concludes, gay male bodybuilders, such as **Msclfreak** or **PECS,** are "visibly inscribing their erotic desires on the surfaces of their bodies" (p. 117). Thus, when interactants identify themselves as bodybuilders and display their built bodies on these channels through stats, they do so with the sole intention of attracting same-sex sexual attention. This is evident in **Msclfreak**'s discussion of how bodybuilding has impacted his life:

> **John:** how has your life changed since you became a bodybuilder?
> **Msclfreak:** more self confidence and more attention
> **Msclfreak:** much more sex

As his comments suggest, **Msclfreak**'s body becomes an object of intense erotic attention on these channels because of its extreme and artificially attained muscle mass. Though I would not suggest that these individuals see themselves as parodying or deconstructing truisms surrounding straight masculinity, I would hold that individuals interacting on these channels are aware of the possibility of (re)constructing the body to become a symbolic focus of same-sex sexual attention. Thus, a central aspect of the bodybuilding lifestyle, for these interactants, may be intense (homo)sexual attraction and activity. Indeed, in his discussion of bodybuilders transforming their bodies into art, **PECS** introduces the notion of the body as a work that can be, like other art products, viewed, admired, and consumed.

Turning to the channel #gaymusclebears, a different idealized type emerges as the focus of considerable discussion: the musclebear. As conversations appearing on the main window of the channel suggest, the musclebear represents the complex convergence of the *bodybuilder,* as understood on the channel #gaymuscle, and the *bear,* as emerging out of the gay male "bear movement" of the 1980s and 1990s. Unlike bodybuilding, however, there is no offline athletic equivalent to provide some initial understanding of what constitutes a musclebear. Although a "musclebear" is evidently a specific form of bear (the word *muscle* clearly qualifies the word *bear*), the question of what a bear is remains, as Les Wright (1997b) indicates, "very much unresolved" (p. 1). Noting the lack of consensus within the mainstream gay male community, Wright discusses how the term *bear* is "applied in a self-defining manner," and thus is often "vaguely defined, sometimes in self-contradicting ways, and is interpreted variously" (1997a, p. 21).

In general, however, the designation of bear connotes, according to Wright, a self-consciously masculine gay man, often polarized against the image of the "twink" (i.e., the propagated image of the young, often blond, mainstream model-like gay man). Though, as Wright discusses, mediated images of men identified as bears within gay subcultures have more recently created some shared sense of which physical attributes may be considered bearlike, the ability of diverse gay men to lay claim to the term undermines its application to only one particular physical or mental disposition. Arguably, this holds equally true for the appellation of musclebear. However, despite the absence of a formulated understanding, interactants generally identified similar key attributes when discussing the musclebear: masculine; muscular, though in contrast to the bodybuilder this muscularity could be either the result of weight training or physical outdoor activity; naturalness, though, again, this notion of "being natural" seemed to be invoked in contrast to the constructed image of the bodybuilder or twink. Commonly, facial and/or body hair was invoked as an identifying trait, and should hair be absent on the body, it was a "natural" condition of the individual and never the result of shaving or waxing. These traits were consistently identified by interactants, particularly those on the channel #gaymusclebears, when characterizing a musclebear:

> **Bennoe:** muscles and hair or muscles and no hair but thats from not being waxed
> **Bennoe:** a beefy natural man i think
>
> **SFBigCub:** a musclebear would, In my opinion, be a muscular man with body and facial hair. . . . or a man with body/facial hair who was building his body.
>
> **WorkOut:** Musclebear, as far as my definition goes, fits between chub and bodybuilder insofar as bodyfat content and also tends to leave body hair as-is instead of, as a bodybuilder might tend, shaving it often for posing competitions.
>
> **Mad_Hatter:** a big buff fuzzy dude

Frequently accompanying discussions of those physical traits identifying the musclebear were references to expected personality traits, as well as a predisposition to a particular lifestyle. This was apparent in **Mage78**'s discussion of a musclebear:

> **John:** what do you think makes a person a musclebear?
> **Mage78:** That is a bit complex . . .it is a combination of many physical features, not least of which is body hair and muscle mass/size, as well as other lifestyle traits, even as identifying oneself with other musclebears.
> **John:** do you consider musclebears desirable?
> **Mage78:** I am physically attracted to that style of man, as well as many of the personality traits that numerous musclebears exibit, such as forwardness, intelligence, and humor . . .but definitely the fur!

As participants indicated, like the bodybuilder, the musclebear is an individual largely identified through his body—a body marked by the presence of greater than normal muscle mass, facial and/or body hair, and arguably a more functional or "natural" appearance in comparison to the fabricated image of the bodybuilder. This latter distinction was most apparent when patrons explicitly compared musclebears and bodybuilders:

Mage78: Muscle bears have that body hair, though bodybuilders usually do not, particularly if they compete, also many musclebears enjoy outdoor activities that many bodybuilders I see do not . . .

Younghung: bodybuilder are ripped, little to no fat on their bodies and are typicaly smooth, no hair, musclebears however are more rugged, less refined, normally older in age, hairy, with bigger waists, more natural looking

Though muscle mass is a key component of both the bodybuilder and the musclebear, and both may engage in progressive weight training in an effort to increase the musculature of their bodies, the two appear to depart considerably in lifestyle traits. Based on the comments of participants, musclebears were characterized as engaging in certain activities (such as outdoor activities) that bodybuilders were stereotypically seen as avoiding and were described as generally being more "natural" (e.g., "less refined," leaving their body hair intact) than bodybuilders. Arguably, the most pronounced contrast between the bodybuilder and the musclebear seems to center around this notion of naturalness of the body.

However, the natural body of the musclebear was still clearly a labored body achieved through either demanding outdoor activities or, more commonly, through some form of weight training. Implicit in all participants' discussions of the musclebear was the understanding of the body as a physically active and functional body, which differs significantly from the general image of the sedentary body of the chub. Certainly when patrons discussed their understandings of a chub—that erotic ideal identified on the channel #gaychub—the body of the musclebear, in comparison, took on connotations of a constructed or achieved body. Notably, **WorkOut,** in his prior comments on the musclebear, suggested a continuum of body fat, with the bodybuilder and the chub occupying extreme opposite positions. It may be equally possible, however, to understand these three ideal types as positions on an abstract continuum of "naturalness" in regard to the condition of the body. Again, the chub would, as often suggested in conversations with participants, be situated in extreme opposition to the bodybuilder, representing the unachieved, untrained body. This is apparent in a comment made by **Masculin** regarding the importance he places on distinguishing the big muscular body (i.e., the body of the bodybuilder) from the big corpulent body (i.e., the body of the chub):

Masculin: if a guy is big because he's fat. . . . well it's just not as impressive. . . . it doesn't inspire

Masculin: a bodybuilder's size is admired usually because it is the result of many years of consistent hard work. . . . considered an achievement

Masculin's response reflects the dominant Western conceptions of the "fat body." As Laurence Brown (2001) notes in his discussion of fat desirability, fat and muscle are socially coded in opposition: "muscle is taken as a sign of power, an enhancement of masculinity, fat is considered a signifier of ridicule, asexuality, and lack of self-discipline and self-respect" (p. 45). In general, those interacting on the channels #gaymuscle and #gaymusclebears subscribe to this view of the fat body, seeing the chub as simply an obese male who may be characterized as lazy or undisciplined. Usually, in contrast to the muscles of the bodybuilder and the hair of the musclebears, the chub was primarily identified by the presence of a pronounced distended abdomen, commonly referred to as a belly or gut:

John: What does "chub" mean to you?
Msclfreak: having a bit of a belly

John: what is a chub?
GremlinBear: a large person with a gut
GremlinBear: a weighty person
GremlinBear: in the weight range of 230 and up

Some participants, however, made an important distinction between an individual with a distended abdomen and a chub, suggesting that the chub was more specifically an exceptionally obese male. Because many of these same individuals had indicated that the musclebear could well possess a gut or belly, a more precise understanding of the chub was necessary:

John: What does "chub" mean to you?
Britannic: To me, "Chub" means overweight. . . . anything more that 101lbs overweight to me, would be chubby.

John: What is a "chub"?
SFBigCub: a chub is any person who is chubby—which is, more than just a little overweight.

> **John:** how would you identify yourself online in terms of body "type"?
> **BluCollar:** Chub, chubby, chubbear.
> **John:** What's a "chub"?
> **BluCollar:** Anything from 40 to 50 pounds over the ideal height/weight norm to obese, 300, 400, 500 pounds.

On all three channels, those discussing the chub demonstrated some consensus that this type is chiefly constituted by the presence of greater than normal body fat, with some specifying (especially those interacting on #gaymusclebears and #gaychub) the necessity of extreme obesity. There was no indication that secondary male attributes—such as facial or body hair—were important in identifying the chub, thereby emphasizing the centrality of body fat in distinguishing this type. For most participants, the body of the chub represented, in furthest departure from the body of the bodybuilder, an idle, un-labored, and natural body, signifying a person consciously avoiding physical activity.

What varied dramatically was whether the chub represented a desirable image of the male body. This striking variation in how the chub is perceived across these channels becomes apparent in comparing the comments of three different patrons: **Masculin** (who chats primarily on #gaymuscle), **WorkOut** (who chats on both #gaymuscle and #gaymusclebears), and **Big_Wolf** (who chats primarily on #gaychub as a self-identified "chubby chaser"):

> **John:** Have you ever chatted on #gaychub?
> **Masculin:** never
> **Masculin:** nothing against chubby people, but generally not attracted to people because of obesity
> **John:** so for you, is fat attractive?
> **Masculin:** no because in our society it is too easy to be fat . . . it is difficult to not be fat

> **John:** Do you find either chubs or bodybuilders attractive?
> **WorkOut:** Bodybuilders, yes, for the most part. Chub . . . it's rare but every once in a while I do find them attractive.
> **John:** Are you attracted to the low levels of bodyfat on bodybuilders?
> **WorkOut:** I like it but it's not really the main thing I find attractive about bodybuilders but it's the musculature. It's something you tend to still find a lot in "musclebears" but in "chubs" it's much harder to see, if not ever.

John: Why do you chat on #gaychub?
Big_Wolf: I enjoy the company of truly big men, . . . the fact that I can chat with fat natural guys online offers me hope that someday I might meet a really big chap in my life

In the comments of both **Masculin** and **Big_Wolf,** there are references to the unlabored and natural condition of the body of the chub. The chub is fat, **Masculin** suggests, because it is "easy to be fat," whereas, implicitly, the bodybuilder's body is marked by the difficulty of its achievement. However, in a conversation with **IrishCrop,** this understanding of the chubby body as natural and unlabored was problematized:

John: What does "chub" mean to you?
IrishCrop: Stocky is a good word, husky a little less so. A stocky guy could also be chubby, but "chubby" just doesn't seem manly at all.
IrishCrop: "Chub" evokes someone who is obese, soft, where being fat is their predominant feature. It suggests to me some kind of fetish about "feeding" and "growing," and I don't identify with that.

In his identification of chub, **IrishCrop** alludes to one of the more distinctive and interesting erotic practices discussed on these channels: "gaining." By identifying a practice (i.e., "gaining" or "feeding" and "growing") actively imposed on the body of the chub to increase its girth, **IrishCrop** complicates the understanding of the natural and unlabored body of the chub. Arguably, like the bodybuilder, the extremity of the chub's body may, in fact, indicate some purposeful endeavor intended to push the body beyond normal limits of mass, even if this mass is composed of fat tissue. Thus, the chub also can be conceptualized as possessing a constructed body—a body made to conform to the erotic desires of the individual, a body on which certain cultural practices (e.g., gaining) are inscribed. This undermines any notion of a continuum of naturalness of the desirable body unless naturalness is understood as a relative and culturally constructed attribute.

EROTIC BODIES, EROTIC PRACTICES

In his discussion of the chub, **IrishCrop** links this particular body image to one of the distinct erotic formations discussed on these channels—gaining. Gaining is one of the two noteworthy sexual practices I will examine in this chapter (the other being "muscle worship") with the intent of unsettling conventional understandings of the sexual. Unlike erotic acts performed to elicit a particular physical sensation within the context of a sexual encounter, gaining and muscle worship are characterized by the patrons of these channels as comprehensive sexual experiences. Of particular interest is how these sexual acts appear to form new sexual paradigms for those engaging in them, effectively redefining the sexed body. In this respect, these sexual practices support Foucault's (1978) contention that sex is, in fact, a culturally constructed and historically specific discursive figuration within the historical deployment of sexuality. Informed by the thought of both Foucault and Butler, I will demonstrate how, for those engaging in either gaining or muscle worship, there is a focal shift in the erogenous zones of the body, a reconceptualization of what constitutes the erotic, and, finally, at least a momentary redefining of sex roles.

Primarily on the channel #gaychub, within the context of the main window, postings will frequently appear containing the words "gaining" or identifying the poster as a "gainer." Occasionally, these postings will explicitly indicate the poster's search for an "encourager" or "feeder" (i.e., an individual facilitating the gaining process), though generally the mere identification of oneself as a gainer is sufficient to draw the attention of those interested in the activity. This sexual practice of gaining is never actually described or articulated within the context of the main window. Rather, there is some implicit understanding that many of those frequenting the channel are interested not only in chubs but also in the associated practice of gaining. The implicitness of understandings surrounding this practice, as with muscle worship, may explain why most participants were familiar with the practice but unable to articulate a concise description. This inarticulateness may also reflect a discomfort with discussing erotic practices outside the context of a sexual conversation, especially practices viewed as aberrant even within the broader gay male subculture. In general, those not patronizing #gaychub, and especially those interacting solely on #gaymuscle, characterized gaining simply as a fetish of no real interest to them. However, those frequenting all three channels, such as **Younghung,** were able to offer a more insightful discussion of the practice:

> **John:** what's gaining?
> **Younghung:** gaining more weight

John: More weight? Are people on #gaymuscle interested in gaining?
Younghung: gaining more muscle, yes
John: Are people on #gaychub also interested in gaining
Younghung: well, the gaining i was referring to was gaining of fat
Younghung: getting fatter
Younghung: on gay muscle they mean more muscle, they talk about making gains making progress
Younghung: on gay chub they mean gaining fat
Younghung: "gainer" means a guy gaining fat, not muscle
Younghung: "gaining" said by itself is gaining fat

What became apparent in discussions surrounding gaining on all three channels is that it can prove to be an intensely erotic experience for some while being of little interest or incomprehensible to others. In general, as an erotic practice, gaining was associated with the body of the chub, and there seemed to be a wide-ranging expectation that those identifying themselves as chubs were invested in the practice (though this is certainly not always the case). Of note are those men identifying as thin or slim who come to #gaychub seeking "feeders" or "encouragers" to mentally and physically nurture them as they develop their bellies in an effort to transform themselves into chubs. In addition, for some interested in the practice, the parameters surrounding the erotic act may prove to be very specific. This was apparent in **BIGrGUY**'s description of gaining:

John: what is a "gainer"?
BIGrGUY: someone who wants to gain
John: Could you explain what gaining is?
BIGrGUY: it is the act of gaining weight
BIGrGUY: it could be physical or fantasy . . . gaining can be erotic
BIGrGUY: weight could be either fat or muscle
BIGrGUY: one gains physically by eating or bodybuilding
John: does it matter to you if the gaining is fat or muscle?
BIGrGUY: I prefer muscle and fat combined . . . some just like fat though

To help convey his understanding of the practice, **BIGrGUY** introduced me to the large collection of "gainer art" that circulates in online forums such as #gaychub, or on Web sites dedicated to chubs and gaining, such as <www.BellyBuilders.com>, <www.gainrweb.com>, and <www.BiggerCity.com> which identifies itself as a "web community for gay chubs, chasers, and bears." This gainer art generally consists of drawn illustrations depicting either men engaging in the act of gaining (in which one man ostensibly force-feeds another, causing the other man's belly to grow) or the aftermath of such force-feeding (in which the eroticized belly or gut is now proudly displayed and admired). Often known only by their online pseudonymns, the artists that produce these illustrations by and large identify as part of the "gainer community," intending their work to be shared with others who engage in or are aroused by the practice. For instance, **CMBigDog** has contributed illustrations to various online forums dedicated to gaining, including the two shown in Figure 4.2. Through e-mail correspondence, the artist indicated that these two illustrations—"Pig Out" and "Belly Contest"—are his favorites because "they capture the truly mythical belly size that many gainer/encouragers fantasize about." Worthy of note is the distinction **CMBigDog** makes between gainer art and what he classifies as "chub art" in which the obese male body is celebrated and even eroticized, but is not necessarily intended to be associated with the practice of gaining. As **CMBigDog** points out, "not all obese gay men have purposely willed themselves into that condition." **CMBigDog** also informed me of a recent documentary film by Frédéric Moffet, *Hard Fat* (2002), which explores the social world of gaining and features illustrations by the most popular creator of gaining art, Warren Davis. Those illustrations produced by artists such as Warren Davis and **CMBigDog** are considered intensely erotic by individuals such as **BIGrGUY** and effectively function as a form of erotica or what Les Wright (2003) identifies as "erotic folk art."[7]

Although for **BIGrGUY** gaining fulfills its erotic potential only when the bodily growth is composed of both fat and muscle tissue, for all gainers and feeders or encouragers there is an intense sexual focus on the increasing proportions of the male abdomen or gut. Within the context of prevailing (straight) discourse, "gut," much like "freak," carries negative connotations, generally alluding to the failure of a body to be fit and healthy—an image predominantly associated with inactivity. Thus, the understanding of a gut not only as a desirable physical trait and a focus of sexual attention but also as something achieved through the active process of gaining conflicts with accepted understandings in mainstream cultural contexts.

Certainly, the very notion of desiring a fat body unsettles essentialist views of fat identity. Kathleen LeBesco (2001) discusses the controversy surrounding the basis of fat identity within identity politics, a

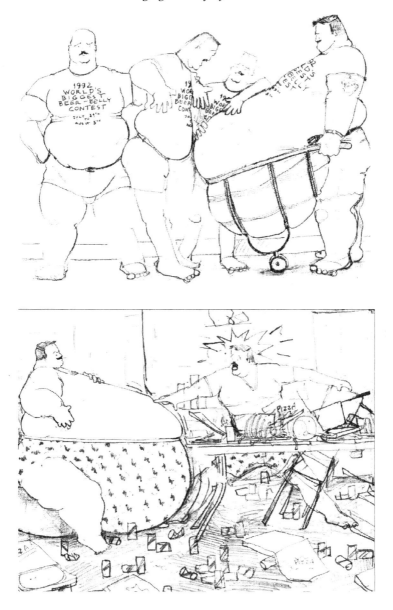

FIGURE 4.2. Illustrations of "gaining" by **CMBigDog** that circulate on online forums and Web sites dedicated to the erotic practice. "Belly Contest" (top) and "Pig Out" (bottom) ©2003 by **CMBigDog** and reprinted with permission.

controversy mirroring the essentialist/constructionist debate in queer politics:

> An essentialist position on fat identity can take a biological or sociocultural perspective; common to both is the theme that the condition of fatness is necessary, could not be otherwise, or has some essential (usually failure-related) cause. Whether they trace a biological path to bad genes or horrible hormones or a social path to traumatic childhood experience, those arguing for essentialist positions view fat identity as the unfortunately unavoidable outcome resulting from some original variable gone awry. (p. 84)

What is evident in these essentialist positions, especially so in the medical discourse surrounding obesity, is that the fat body is always positioned in opposition to the healthy and attractive body, rendering the fat body the deficient or defective body, possibly reflecting a deficient or defective psyche. This dominant view of fat identity may explain why some participants, particularly those on #gaymuscle, were unreceptive to the practice of gaining, as indicated in this conversation with **TechnoBear:**

> **John:** What does the practice of "gaining" refer to?
> **TechnoBear:** Refers to adding weight, whether fat, muscle or both, for some WEIRD sort of self-satisfaction.
> **TechnoBear:** I believe it is sexual
> **TechnoBear:** I knew a gainer online, who was very cute then added pounds and lost his appeal (to me).
> **TechnoBear:** It makes those people more appealing to others who like the same look.
> **TechnoBear:** It's unhealthy and foolish.

TechnoBear's conception of gaining as "unhealthy and foolish" is consistent with mainstream conceptions of the corpulent body. Notably, when participants such as **TechnoBear** do not share an interest in a particular erotic practice, it becomes characterized as an incomprehensible "fetish" or "weird" preoccupation. Indeed, fully one-third of those interviewed indicated that the practice made "no sense" to them and was "silly" or "strange." Telling, however, is how the perspectives of individuals such as **TechnoBear** radically change when the discussion turns to a sexual practice they find personally appealing, such as muscle worship.

While the practice of gaining was generally associated with the channel #gaychub, the sexual practice of muscle worship (often referred to online as simply "worship") was primarily discussed on the channel #gaymuscle. Many of those on #gaymuscle who had characterized gaining as a practice that was "odd," "strange," or simply unintelligible offered very different characterizations of muscle worship. This was apparent in a conversation with **WorkOut:**

> **John:** what do you know about "gaining"?
> **WorkOut:** Very little, apart from the fact I'm definitely not into it. Its about eating and getting fat, and not something I will ever understand.

However, when the conversation shifted to a discussion of muscle worship, **WorkOut** proved more knowledgeable, though he also indicated that he was not personally interested in the practice, commenting, "I like affection/adoration to be a two-way street":

> **John:** what do you think muscle worship is?
> **WorkOut:** Well, I've never "done it" before, but I see it as one guy showing off his body while the other idolizes him . . . dashes off gushing commentary . . . a pretty sexually charged atmosphere. I see it pretty much as a private R-rated porn show with massive ego-boosting involved.
> **John:** ok, do you think people that are into it see it as a sexual act?
> **WorkOut:** Definitely!

For **WorkOut,** the experience of worship is understandably erotic (even if not of personal interest), while the practice of gaining remains incomprehensible. Many of those interviewed indicated that they had never actually engaged in the practice of worship, despite having discussed it extensively online. In fact, several participants admitted that the underlying reason they had originally started chatting on #gaymuscle was to find others receptive to the practice.

It is not uncommon for individuals such as **Msclfreak** to identify themselves as bodybuilders with the intent of attracting suitable partners to engage in this particular sexual activity offline. To be clear, a fundamental resource these channels offer their patrons is an online forum for meeting others who share their erotic desires.[8] This was very much the case with **TechnoBear,** who engaged in a more

lengthy discussion of worship, plainly indicating his desire to participate in this activity:

> **John:** how would you describe muscle worship?
> **TechnoBear:** It's flexing for someone.
> **TechnoBear:** Being felt by that person.
> **TechnoBear:** Maybe massaged.
> **TechnoBear:** Standing over or sitting on that person.
> **TechnoBear:** Posing.
> **John:** do you engage in muscle worship?
> **TechnoBear:** I have never yet had the opportunity.
> **TechnoBear:** I have fantisized about it.

Worship, as described by **TechnoBear,** again demonstrates the centrality of the physical body in social relations on these channels.
Though individuals can engage in intense and erotic discussions of
worship online, full sexual realization of the practice can only be had
offline, in physical copresence, where the body can be "felt by that
person." **TechnoBear** also expounds upon the two fundamental roles
in worship:

> **TechnoBear:** There are two Roles: Worshipper, Worshipee.
> **John:** what's the difference between the two?
> **TechnoBear:** The worshipee is the "muscle man."
> **TechnoBear:** The worshiper is the admirer who lays on hands.
> **TechnoBear:** . . . or takes a subordinate role.
> **John:** what in your opinion makes a person a "muscle man"?
> **TechnoBear:** Visible muscle definition.
> **TechnoBear:** And bulk.
> **John:** do they have do act any particular way to be worshipped?
> **TechnoBear:** Often superior.
> **TechnoBear:** One person takes a subordinate role. The other a supe-
> rior one.
> **TechnoBear:** Might have a commanding attitude.
> **TechnoBear:** Often think of a muscle man as a "top."
> **TechnoBear:** Assertive.
> **John:** ok, does top means he engages in penetration?
> **TechnoBear:** Not during the worship session.
> **TechnoBear:** If all that is being done is worshipping, there will be no
> penetration.
> **TechnoBear:** It can end with mutual j/o [masturbation] or massage or
> sleep or nothing at all.

Like gaining, the practice of worship encompasses engagement
in two distinct but complementary roles—the "worshiper" and the

"worshipee" or "muscle man." Other participants noted that these roles are not necessarily fixed from one experience of "worship" to the next, discussing how the "worshiper" within one dynamic may function as the "worshipee" in a different encounter. As **TechnoBear** specifies, the primary prerequisite (penis notwithstanding) is the possession of conspicuous muscular "bulk" on the body of the "worshipee" or "muscle man."

Concerning the role of the "muscle man," **Britannic** makes a critical observation in his brief reference to muscle worship:

> **John:** could you tell me what you think muscle worship is?
>
> **Britannic:** To me, it means being subjugated by a guy and his muscles. But his muscles are the primary focus of the attention, more so than him. It does not have to have any sex involved, but it is a sexual act to some degree, I think.

Of particular interest in **Britannic**'s description of the practice is the significant shift in erotic focus from the male phallus to the male musculature, complicating conceptions of sexual object choice. Arguably, in this sexual practice, the biological basis on which the body is sexed and on which its sex roles (i.e., "worshipee" or "worshiper"; dominant or subordinate; active or passive) are determined is the convergence of the male phallus (even if concealed) *and* conspicuous muscle mass (or its absence). This is apparent in those erotic images circulating on these channels that function as forms of online pornography (and offline masturbatory aids). For instance, Figure 4.3 is a graphically modified ("morphed") image of an unidentified professional bodybuilder that is considered both erotic and pornographic on the channels #gaymuscle and #gaymusclebears.

In his historical survey of gay male pornographic photography, Tom Waugh (1996) notes the "centrality of the genitals" as a standard in such images (p. 42). However, in many of those erotic images traded on these channels, such as in Figure 4.3, the genitals are concealed (even if only modestly by the posing briefs of a bodybuilder), shifting the focus to the extreme or "freakish" muscularity of the body. This is not to suggest that the penis simply disappears for those consuming these images but rather to indicate that the male genitalia no longer function in themselves as arousing features for those engaging in either worship or gaining. This may be understood as broadening the constellation of the sexed body beyond the simplistic

FIGURE 4.3. Graphically modified image of an unidentified professional bodybuilder

male/female binary, which, in turn, suggests the constructedness of that binary.

Foucault (1978) argues that not only is sexuality a "historical formation" but that sex itself is a particular cultural construct naturalized within the historical deployment of sexuality; in this understanding, sex is an oppressive discursive figuration that grouped together "in an artificial unity, anatomical elements, biological functions, conducts, sensations, and pleasures, and it enabled one to make use of this fictitious unity as a causal principle, an omnipresent meaning" (p. 154). In essence, sex emerged as a cultural tool for socially understanding, organizing, and extending power relations over bodies and life processes. Drawing heavily upon Foucault, Butler (1990a) also argues that sex "imposes an artificial unity on an otherwise discontinuous set of attributes" (p. 114). In her discussion, Butler makes the critical observation that not only is sex a historically contingent regime but also that the very features defining the sexed body are themselves socially informed: "That penis, vagina, breasts, and so forth, are *named* sexual parts is both a restriction of the erogenous body to those parts and a fragmentation of the body as a whole" (p. 114, emphasis original). In other words, no "natural" properties inherent in either the penis or vagina function to make them erotically distinct sites outside of how they are socially apprehended.

Both Foucault's and Butler's theoretical understandings of sex as culturally constructed are supported by the experiences of patrons on these channels. When, for example, the identification of the erogenous areas of the body are reformulated in such erotic practices as muscle worship and gaining, arguably the sex of the body is unsettled. In other words, when the erogenous is expanded to include guts and biceps, the body is artificially united under a different sexual regime, accompanied by a different understanding of bodily functions and pleasures. Clearly these practices—intensely discussed online and enacted offline—complicate not only any universal signifier of the sex of the body but also any universalized understanding of what constitutes the sexual. For instance, what may in fact appear "naturally" erotic to someone interacting on #gaymuscle may prove uninteresting, even repugnant, to someone frequenting #gaychub. Furthermore, what may be considered an intensely sexual act by some participants—such as the force-feeding of another man with the intent of increasing his girth—may appear completely nonsexual to other individuals.

CYBORGS, FREAKS, AND ONLINE EMBODIMENT

Acknowledging the body's simultaneous existence as both a physical presence and a discursive configuration provides an understanding of how it is that the somatic remains always already present in online social relations. It is through their performative engagement with this discursive apprehension of the physical that interactants on these channels effectively integrate the body into their online activities. Though it is always possible that the symbolic body presented online diverges radically from the corporeal form, for those interacting on these channels an intense eroticism is achieved precisely because online discourses are expected to reference some physical reality. This is especially the case for individuals seeking to engage offline in those erotic practices discussed online (such as gaining and muscle worship).

In light of these online erotic discourses, the "cyborg" proves a useful trope for conceptualizing a subjectivity predicated on the constructedness of the body, especially in regard to sexual identity. Introduced by Manfred Clynes and Nathan Kline in 1960, the term cyborg—short for cybernetic organism—refers to a creature that "deliberately incorporates exogenous components extending the self-regulatory control function" (Clynes and Kline, 1960, p. 31). The concept of the cyborg was originally developed for the National Aeronautic and Space Administration (NASA) as a possible way for adapting humans for travel and colonization in space, with the first creature actually designated a cyborg being a 220-gram laboratory rat at New York's Rockland State Hospital with a "tiny osmotic pump implanted in its body" (Haraway, 1995, p. 11). Since that time, the image of the cyborg has evolved considerably in both social science and science fiction.

The understanding of the cyborg I am most interested in here is that of the postgendered technological hybrid articulated in Donna Haraway's so-called "Cyborg Manifesto." Haraway contends that we become cyborg subjects when two fundamental boundaries are transgressed: first, the boundary between human and animal, which twentieth-century biological science increasingly deconstructed, and second, that boundary between the animal-human (organism) and the machine. As Haraway (1985) suggests, "Late twentieth-century machines have made thoroughly ambiguous the difference between natural and artificial, mind and body, self-developing and externally designed, and many other distinctions that used to apply to organisms and machines" (p. 152). This dissolving distinction between organic and technological not only concerns the human at the computer interface having sex with someone half a world away but also addresses all ways technology impacts the body: pacemakers and prosthetic limbs, pharmaceuticals and vaccinations, engineered nutrition and Nautilus machines, cosmetic manipulation and augmentation. All of these demonstrate the blurring of the distinction between the organic and the techno-social. Haraway's metaphorical cyborg has significantly influenced academics exploring the increasingly complex relationship of individual subjectivity to emerging technologies, including

Stone (1996) who uses physicist Stephen Hawking to exemplify this utterly transgressed border between organism and technology.[9]

This cyborg subjectivity, however, should not be viewed as inherently liberating. For, as Balsamo (1995) suggests, the American hyperawareness and monitoring of the body's organic functions through technological means—"electronic scales, home pregnancy kits, diabetes tests, blood pressure machines and fat calipers" (p. 216)—undermines notions that technological embodiment will result in bodily transcendence. Indeed, as this awareness of the biological body extends into society's surveillance of various populations—"random urine testing among high-school teenagers and adult workers, covert blood testing for HIV, and genetic finger-printing" (p. 216)—the body may be technologically transformed into a self-contained Foucauldian panopticon. Balsamo (1995) offers the phrase "technologies of the gendered body" to describe the means by which society utilizes new medical technologies to (re)inscribe cultural codes onto the very body it has fragmented—cultural codes reinforcing preexisting social schema, such as those surrounding gender or race.

Still, the image of the cyborg proves helpful in theoretically comprehending the subjectivity of those individuals utilizing pharmacological technologies to significantly alter their physical bodies. For the populations of #gaymuscle and #gaymusclebears, this may involve the administration of exogenous hormones into the body in an effort to achieve a self-identified "freakish" physical state. This is congruent with Lindsay's identification of the contemporary bodybuilder as a postmodern cyborg that delights in the transgression of the boundaries between organic and *man*ufactured. As Lindsay comments, "For Haraway, as for the sympathetic spectator of bodybuilding shows, this freaky subject is a wondrous being, a hybrid blurring the lines between true and produced freak" (1996, p. 366). Discourses emerging on #gaymuscle support Lindsay's contentions, for it is not uncommon to find self-identified bodybuilders and powerlifters referring to themselves as "cybernetic organisms" or exclaiming that "natural sucks!" I am not, however, contending that the cyborg represents some liberated subjectivity that can simply remake itself at will. Like Balsamo, I view the cyborg as a subject negotiating its existence in a society in which the very technologies that appear emancipatory can, in fact, be used to reinscribe restrictive social schema onto the body. Yet I would suggest that these interactants position themselves as cyborgs when they intervene upon their own bodies in an effort to reconstruct themselves as their erotic ideals, even when such refashioning produces a body that would be stigmatized within the context of mainstream society (such as the freak or the chub).

Here I identify cyborg subjects as those individuals who render the constructedness of their own bodies evident through the radical reshaping of their physical forms to conform to their particular understandings of the erotic. If, for instance, the sexual experience of being worshiped dictates that the body must possess extensive muscle mass, then those individuals desiring this experience may employ various practices and technologies to dramatically increase the muscularity of their bodies, thereby transforming themselves into an object of sexual attention both online *and* offline. In this sense, the body is made to correspond to the erotic practice and not the reverse— form, in essence, follows function. This is very much the case with **Msclfreak,** an individual who has admitted to transforming his body through technological means to become the "muscle man" in the worshiper-worshipee relation:

> **John:** how would you describe yourself?
> **Msclfreak:** 100% chemically assisted

"Steroids or not," Sam Fussell (1996) observes that "a natural bodybuilder is an oxymoron" (p. 44), likewise the gainer laboring to expand his girth. Both the gainer and the bodybuilder incorporate various technological formations into their intervention upon the body to make it more erotic and then utilize computer-mediated communication technologies as means of "displaying" their reconstructed bodies to potential sexual partners. It is through online communication that these individuals flaunt their social fabrication and, in turn, become cyborgs par excellence. Arguably, what makes the "freak" so desirable online and so unsettling offline is his rendering conspicuous the artificiality of not only his own body but also, in comparison, the "normal" body. "Freaks," such as **Msclfreak,** are dangerous precisely because they revel in their own constructedness as sexual entities. By incorporating technologies into their constitution of self, the cyborg and the freak become conterminous. The resistive power of both the cyborg and the freak rests not in their existence outside the relations of power but rather in their refusal to be rendered naturalized "others."

In discussing the resistive potential of the cyborg or the freak, it is critical to keep in mind the productive capacity of power. As Foucault and Butler have both argued, modern economies of power relations do more than repress or censor or conceal what already exists. Rather, these power formations have the capacity to produce—primarily through a proliferation of knowledges or "truths" about the world— that which they then appear only to subjugate or deny. Thus, a mere multiplicity of sexualities, sexual types, or sexual practices is not, in itself, liberating. To be clear, the fact that in these virtual spaces we witness the exploration and expression of alternative modes of sexual practice (muscle worship, gaining) or new configurations of the sexual body (bodybuilders, musclebears, chubs) does not suggest that these individuals are emancipated from dominant power relations or that these individuals are not equally capable of reproducing repressive hierarchies. However, there is cause to argue that these alternative sexual constellations surrounding the body do indicate the constructedness and artificiality of binary understandings of sex (male/ female) and sexuality (heterosexual/homosexual), and therefore hold the potential of unsettling those "truths" fundamental to dominant power structures.

Regarding the constructedness of gender, Butler (1990a) also argues there is the potential of undermining universalized images of this discursive regime: "If the regulatory fictions of sex and gender are themselves multiply contested sites of meaning, then the very multiplicity of their construction holds out the possibility of a disruption of their univocal posturing" (p. 32). Upsetting any "univocal" position on sex and sexuality represents the strongest subversive potential of discourses emerging from these online communities. When discourses on the three channels conflict as to what fundamentally constitutes a sexual act, what is erotic, and what is desirable, normative understandings of sex and sexuality are momentarily disrupted. Although these interactants may identify overwhelmingly as gay and exclusively as male, their antithetical understandings of the sexual throw into question received understandings of the erotic. It is in this unsettling of comfortable truisms in Western understandings of sex and sexuality that we find discourses potentially fuelling a progressive politics of pleasure and a pleasurable mode of resistance.

None of this is to deny the materiality of the body, for bodies do have a tangible existence outside of social relations. For my discussion to be read as a repudiation of the reality of physical bodies would be an instance of what Butler refers to as "unfortunate grammar." We are, without question, material beings, but we are material beings negotiating life through a reality utterly permeated by discourse. As Butler points out, "We may seek to return to matter as prior to discourse to ground our claims about sexual difference only to discover that matter is fully sedimented with discourses on sex and sexuality that prefigure and constrain the uses to which that term can be put" (1993, p. 29). Penises and vaginas as constitutive parts of the body are very real, but they acquire distinction and meaning only within a social universe.

Likewise, I should not be misunderstood as lauding the patrons of these channels as political subjects. This is by no means a triumphant discussion, for the ease with which these individuals naturalize their very particular understandings of the sexual is discouraging: for those into muscle worship, it is impossible not to see enormous muscles on a male body as beautiful; for those into gaining, it is inconceivable that a prodigious gut would not be a turn on. Even in this erotic playground, ideals of beauty arise and contend with one another. As troubling are some of the oppressive notions regarding gender and race that are readily reproduced in these virtual environments. However, from a theoretical vantage point, the discursive practices played out on these channels do usefully call into question the "naturalness" of sex and sexuality, even if their participants remain oblivious to such implications. Out of their own exploration of the erotic, these interactants are complicating normative understandings of the body and transfiguring themselves, even if only momentarily, into freaks and cyborg subjects.

Chapter 5

Guts and Muscles and Bears, Oh My!

The awful thing is that beauty is mysterious as well as terrible. God and devil are fighting there, and the battlefield is the heart of man.

Fyodor Mikhailovich Dostoevsky
The Brothers Karamazov, 1880

To Bear is human, to Chub divine!

A topic of the day on the channel #gaychub, 2001

The story of how I came to know **Younghung** is perhaps one unique to cyberspace. By the summer of 1997 I had established myself as a regular on the channel #gaymuscle. Having yet to return to school, I would generally log on to IRC in the evenings while eating dinner. Where once I would have my meal alone watching television, now I would dine with company in a virtual space. One particularly muggy evening in the heart of summer, I logged on to find a new face on the channel, so to speak. He wasn't participating in any of the conversations on the main window, just watching mutely from the sidelines. I joined in the discussion with those other regulars who, like myself, spent their evenings after work on #gaymuscle—**PECS, Umgawa, Britannic, WorkOut, BIGrGUY**—but I kept glancing in the direction of this reticent newcomer. During a quiet moment after an especially energetic exchange among several of us on the channel, the newcomer messaged me individually. Opening a separate window, we began our private chat:

Younghung: hi
John: Hey there.
Younghung: how are ya?

John: OK. Just eating dinner, hanging out, relaxing. Long day. you?

Younghung: good. just got back from the gym and stilled pumped. thought I'd check out this channel to see if any big guys hang out here.

From this our conversation continued well into the night. **Younghung** revealed himself to be a young bodybuilder of immense size and physical strength living in northern Florida, far from the glamour and excitement of Miami and South Beach. He described himself as six-foot-three-inches tall, weighing in excess of 300 pounds, with enormous shoulders and arms. As he was only twenty-one years old, he expected to be able to grow significantly larger. He characterized himself as one of those rare genetically gifted individuals who is able to acquire muscle mass with relative ease. He told me about the many years he spent working at his father's construction company and how such physical labor starting at a very early age had granted him remarkable muscular development. Now he was considering pursuing competitive bodybuilding because he had been told that he had the natural ability to become an elite contender. Though his personality initially read as charmingly cocky—stereotypically befitting someone with his build—by the end of the evening I detected a certain subtle vulnerability. Throughout our conversation, I had the distinct sense he was looking to me for some form of affirmation, and perhaps I even found such insecurity endearing.

After this first encounter, I would find **Younghung** waiting on the channel whenever I logged on. Though I never saw him chatting on the channel itself, he always messaged me as soon as I arrived and we would begin our friendly conversations. He would tell me about his daily experiences impressing all the other men at the construction site with his strength. He would also relate incidents at the gym where he awed much older weight lifters with his mass and muscular development. Even competitive bodybuilders with years of experience were encouraging him to enter contests, he would tell me. Our chats became composites of flirting and gossip, discussions of favorite movies and books, and news about other online personalities and our offline social lives. Sometimes our dialogues became intensely intimate, both of us discussing our sexual desires and lamenting the absence of a romantic partner in our lives.

In time, **Younghung** asked me to send him a picture of myself, explaining that he would not be able to return the gesture because he didn't have access to a scanner. Up to that point I had always followed a general rule that I only traded pictures, meaning that I send pictures only to those who can reciprocate. However, whereas I already considered **Younghung** a friend, I was content with sending him pictures in the understanding that when he did finally have digital images of himself he would send them to me.

Younghung also formed a strong friendship with another person I knew from the channel, **Britannic**. Despite chatting with several people on #gaymuscle and being messaged by a great many more due to his nickname, he repeatedly commented that he considered **Britannic** and me to be his closest friends online. I recall **Younghung** consoling me when a brief but passionate relationship of mine ended abruptly. Somehow it was especially comforting to think that this physically imposing individual—a person that certainly embodied those characteristics idealized on #gaymuscle—would think that I was an attractive man. As the summer months drew to a close and I prepared for the move to western Massachusetts to attend school, **Younghung** and I had established what I believed to be a sincere friendship based on mutual affirmation and respect.

Then, a few days before I was to move and during a particularly heartfelt conversation in which I confessed my self-doubts about returning to school after so many years, **Younghung** revealed that he needed to tell me something important that might impact our friendship. I reassured him that I doubted anything he could say would jeopardize our relationship. There was a long pause, and then:

> **Younghung:** I haven't really been honest with you. . . . I'm not what I've been telling you I am
> **John:** What do you mean?
> **Younghung:** I'm not a bodybuilder . . .

Younghung went on to explain that although he was in fact a twenty-one-year-old man living in Florida, he did not weight train, he was not muscular, nor did he work at his father's construction company. In fact, he had not even seen his father in years. He lived with his mother, who, as a single parent, raised both him and his sister. Though he was six-feet-three-inches tall, as he had said, he viewed himself as considerably obese and physically unattractive. The aggressive and convivial bodybuilder persona he had assumed online was only an elaborate performance intended to conceal the shy and insecure person actually sitting before the keyboard.

My initial response to this revelation was an odd mixture of disbelief coupled with bewilderment. Other people had pursued such charades on the channel, but generally they were quickly exposed. How was it that I had been so utterly convinced by **Younghung**'s performance? Did this mean that what I had come to view as a cherished online friendship was itself an illusion? Did his affirmations that I was an attractive man suddenly carry less weight? At least this explained why he never had any pictures of himself to send me. **Younghung** made the same revelation to **Britannic,** and we wondered how it was that both of us had been so taken in by this performance. Though both **Britannic** and I experienced an initial sense of betrayal, we also agreed that there was something understandable in **Younghung**'s enactment of virtual body bending. After all, would I have been so eager to become **Younghung**'s friend if I had known he was an out-of-shape security guard still living at his mother's house in the first place? How could I deny that believing **Younghung** represented some paradigm of muscular development made our evening conversations all the more delicious? Perhaps I so readily accepted his performance because I was so enamored with the notion that someone possessing such a physique should find me (a man in his late twenties with an average build and a gut) attractive.

During an interview a year later, **Younghung** discussed his construction of this fantasy-man role, a role he referred to as simply "the stud," a role **Younghung** described as "a man good, too good to be real, perfect in most everyway." During this same interview, **Younghung** provided some indication of why he assumed this "stud role":

> **John:** When Britannic first messaged you, he asked for stats?
> **Younghung:** yes, so he'd know what i looked like
> **John:** Where your "stats" how you saw yourself offline?
> **Younghung:** no, they weren't
> **John:** How did Britannic react when he received your "stats"?
> **Younghung:** he was very excited from what i could tell
> **John:** How did you feel when he responded that way?
> **Younghung:** it was fun, exciting . . .a sexual release
> **John:** Why was it a sexual release?
> **Younghung:** it was a sexual release . . . sexual role playing . . . living out a fantasy for each of us.
> **Younghung:** just britannic didn't know it was a fantasy.

In this same interview, **Younghung** also explained why he ultimately exposed his performance to **Britannic,** and I assume the same rationale applies to me as well:

> **John:** Did you ever tell Britannic that you were not in the real world as you described yourself on-line?
>
> **Younghung:** yes, I did, I started feeling bad about lying, I have a conscience and when I started seeing him as a true friend, not as some guy, I had to tell him. . . . I felt too guilty

Shortly after conducting this interview, I had a conversation with **Britannic** about his experiences with **Younghung**. I was particularly interested in how his relationship with **Younghung** had developed over the year since the revelation of the fantasy-man performance. I was also interested in **Britannic**'s thoughts on why **Younghung** had assumed this stud role online. Despite **Younghung**'s comments, I suspected that there was more than sexual role-play at hand.

> **John:** You use to chat with someone that went by the nick of Younghung?
>
> **Britannic:** Yes, Jim.
>
> **Britannic:** I still do.
>
> **Britannic:** Not as much as I used to, but we still chat.
>
> **John:** how do you feel about him?
>
> **Britannic:** I think he's a sweet kid. Nice. A good imagination and fun to talk to.
>
> **John:** Did you know he was not what he originally presented himself to be?
>
> **Britannic:** Eventually, yes.
>
> **Britannic:** He's not the first person who's done that.
>
> **John:** How did you feel when that happened?
>
> **Britannic:** Well, I was a little disappointed he lied, but it's easilly forgiven. I understand that need to be something that your not and how IRC can give you that since there is no way someone can verify that.
>
> **Britannic:** I easily forgave him for it and we're still friends.
>
> **John:** WHy do you think he did it?
>
> **Britannic:** Because he's unhappy with who he is in real life and what he looks like and how people treat him, so he created this alternate persona with what he thought other people wanted so that he could gain some acceptance on IRC that he can't seem to find in real life.

As **Britannic** noted, **Younghung**'s "stud role" performance is certainly not the first instance in which someone has utilized computer-mediated communication as a means of enacting a constructed online persona dramatically departing from the offline person. Perhaps the most infamous occurrence of this is the case of New York psychiatrist Sanford Lewin, who, in 1982, logged onto a CompuServe chat room and presented himself as Julie Graham, a woman who had been rendered paraplegic in an automobile accident (Stone, 1996). Lewin claimed the motivation behind his elaborate online performance was one of professional curiosity—he wanted to determine if women would be more open to him as a mental health authority if they thought *he* were a *she*. However, I suspect the motivations behind **Younghung**'s "stud" enactment are much more complicated than Lewin's expert curiosity, even more complicated than the sexual fantasy role-play **Younghung** himself professes.

Looking a bit closer at those physical particularities **Younghung** described in glorious detail during his performances offers some indication: in addition to being tall and immensely muscular, this constructed persona was young (like **Younghung** himself), blond-haired and blue-eyed (not so like **Younghung** himself), smooth, hard, and, of course, white (which **Younghung** is as well). On the channel #gaymuscle, where the competitive bodybuilder is the image put on high that all should desire and revere, these physical characteristics are valued above all others and come to constitute a form of social capital. **Younghung** did not assume just any male form—he did not enact an older body, a hairy body, or a soft body—he presented himself as what he believed was universally understood as desirable. As **Britannic** observed, **Younghung** presented himself as what he thought other gay men want—young, muscular, smooth, white—so he would feel accepted. The fact that **Younghung** assumed this very specific male form out of the belief that this was what gay men *should* desire suggests the existence of a social phenomenon I identify as the "gay male beauty myth."

In this chapter I build on the work of feminist Naomi Wolf in an effort to interrogate this gay male beauty myth. I examine how hierarchies of beauty are imposed on gay men in their understandings of their own bodies and the bodies they should desire, and how these oppressive notions are reinforced by narrow representations of the attractive male physique in the mainstream media. I also endeavor to demonstrate how this constricting constellation of mediated representations motivates some individuals to construct virtual spaces in which absent or derided male forms, such as the obese or hairy male body, can be affirmed and celebrated. In doing so, I contend that some individuals are unsettling those beauty archetypes surrounding the male form online. However, rather than witnessing the abandonment of beauty hierarchies in cyberspace, I hold that what is in fact taking place is a proliferation of competing beauty myths. I will begin this discussion by explaining what I have in mind when referring to the gay male beauty myth.

THE GAY MALE BEAUTY MYTH

Though a number of writings address the depiction of gays and lesbians in the mass media, few studies directly examine mediated representations of the gay male body. The majority of studies addressing the representation of gay males in the media focus on the general absence of meaningful queer representation and the confinement of homosexual men to the stereotypical images of the victim, the villain, or the AIDS-infected person (Gross, 1991, 1993; Reardon and Richardson, 1991; Watney, 1993). In contrast, those studies specifically addressing body images in the media and the social implications of those images have, to date, largely focused on the images of the heterosexual female body (Silverstein et al., 1986; Thomas, 1989). One of the most influential of these latter works is *The Beauty Myth: How Images of Beauty Are Used Against Women* by Wolf (1991). In her feminist discussion of the societal construction of the "attractive woman," Wolf notes that the "beauty myth is not about women at all. It is about men's institutions and institutional powers" (p. 13). For her, this "political weapon against women's advancement" (1991, p. 10) is a patriarchal index imposed upon and by which women must measure their self-worth, an index that naturalizes its own fabrication under the objective and universal. I contend that the beauty myth as articulated by Wolf can also be applied to how gay men conceptualize themselves, their bodies, and their own self-worth in a heterosexist society. I refer to this image imposed on gay men in their understanding of their own bodies as the gay male beauty myth. Although this dominant model of male beauty propagated in the mass media and fueled by the lucrative fitness and beauty industries also impacts how heterosexual men view their own bodies, my focus in this discussion remains on how it restricts the images gay men are presented with as desirable.

Les Wright, in a discussion of the gay male bear subculture, asserts that gay men "have fallen for mass media images of what we *should* consider the gay male ideal beauty" and "have acquiesced or collaborated in our own subjugation as quasi-women" (1997b, p. 8, emphasis original). Wright also contends that when a bear-identified gay man makes the statement "that he is not a 'woman,' not a 'twink,' not a 'heterosexual,' he is using his body to participate in changing social practice and challenging hegemonic power" (1997b, p. 9). Wright touches on how one's own body can be used to signal a defiance of societal norms. As discussed in Chapter 4, the chub and the freak both inscribe their sexual desires on their flesh, and in so doing, their bodies come to symbolically defy normative assumptions regarding the attractive male body; certainly both the chub and the freak constitute images of the male body that are often marginalized within the context of the mainstream media.

In his extensive examination of depictions of men in the mass media, Philip Locke (1997) finds very restrictive norms surrounding what constitutes the attractive male body. As Locke point outs, men's bodies are increasingly prevalent in the media, and, like "images of women, male forms in the media images fit within a narrowly defined spectrum of 'desirable' male beauty" (p. 104). Locke indicates how the lack of diverse bodily representation in the mainstream media is compounded for gay men:

> For gay men, the obvious solution to feelings of marginalization caused by lack of gay images in the mainstream "straight" media would be to turn to the gay mass media for support and validation. There is not a lot in the way of specifically gay-oriented television, but there is a variety of magazines, including both erotic and nonerotic publications, as well as videos and films. But an examination of male images presented in gay mass media reveals that they do not do better than their straight counterparts at presenting an accepting view of male body types that fall outside of a particular standard of beauty. (pp. 104-105)

In his study, Locke finds a predominant set of conventions surrounding those representations of the male body appearing in the mainstream media: body hair is generally depicted as a negative physical attribute (especially back hair); facial hair (i.e., beards), though less derided, remains equally rare among males depicted as desirable and males depicted as gay; and obese male bodies and the particular attribute of the male gut are uniformly depicted as undesirable and unhealthy. Locke's conclusions concur with Wright's discussion of "fat discrimination" and Kathleen LeBesco and Jana Evans Braziel's (2001) interrogation of societal "fat phobia," in which heavy bodies are generally viewed as unattractive in Western society. This is certainly reflected in those male images explicitly presented to the public as desirable or "sexy." For instance, in *People Magazine*'s "Sexiest Man Alive 2002" issue, thirty-year-old, six-foot-two-inch actor Ben Affleck is presented as a paradigm of male attractiveness by the editors. Of course, Affleck's body—tall, lean, smooth, and young—signals by negation those physical characteristics considered unappealing: short, fat, hirsute, and old.

Locke (1997) finds, however, there is no more significant diversity in mainstream publications targeted at gay men (such as *The Advocate*): "almost all of the men whose bodies show up in these magazines are on the slimmer side of average and would definitely be classified as 'trim' and/or 'toned' and/or 'muscular'" (p. 111). As Locke notes, "Heavier-than-average men almost never appear in photos," and when the "husky" male body does appear, it is generally the "before" self in an ad for cosmetic surgery (i.e., liposuction) representing the flawed body that can be "fixed" through medical technology (1997, pp. 111-113).

In his seminal work, *White*, Richard Dyer (1997) finds comparable attributes ascribed to the idealized white male body in Western media. In his examination of Tarzan films and American action films of the 1980s (e.g., *Conan the Barbarian* [1982], *First Blood* [1982], *Rambo: First Blood Part II* [1985], *The Barbarians* [1987]), Dyer notes that "the formal properties of the built body carry connotations of whiteness: it is ideal, hard, achieved, wealthy, hairless and tanned" (p. 150). These attributes, Dyer argues, are utilized by the media to depict the white male body as the heroic body, the body socially superior to the nonwhite body. Based on these narrow media representations, the implication is that not only is the "nonwhite" body inferior, so is the soft, "natural," hairy, and/or pale body.

These narrow depictions are not confined to television and film. Edisol Wayne Dotson (1999) demonstrates how fitness magazines targeted primarily at men, such as *Muscle & Fitness* with its 600,000 subscribers, not only provide narrow representations of the male body but also impose humiliation on those who do not possess these idealized muscular bodies. As Dotson indicates, in these publications, not "only are the lack of muscles and an overweight body dead giveaways of being unmasculine, they are also shameful" (p. 115). The bodies presented in these publications (including *Flex, Ironman Magazine, Muscular Development, MuscleMag International,* and even the more mainstream *Men's Health* with a paid circulation of over 1.5 million in 1997[1]) are not only muscular and hard but also smooth (hairless) and tanned, conforming to Dyer's discussion of the idealized white male body depicted in film.

A "special report" by Jack Del Rio in an issue of *MuscleMag International* (2000) exemplifies this narrow media representation of the male body discussed by both Dotson and Dyer. The report concerns "the extraordinary physique transformation made by 30-year-old Vern Runnalls," who shed some "80 pounds of fat while gaining over 20 pounds of lean, rock-hard muscle" (p. 77). What proves most striking about this "special report" are the "before" and "after" photos juxtaposed prominently on the first page (p. 76). In the before photo, Runnalls is grimacing (almost as if in pain), his face unshaven, his body, though smooth, very pale, and his considerable gut protruding strikingly over his tattered cutoff jean shorts. In the after photo, Runnalls is smiling, his face clean-shaven, his body deeply tanned, and his hard abdominal muscles apparent over his bright spandex gym shorts. The coding apparent in these photos is consistent with Dyer's discussion: Runnalls's earlier body (soft, "natural," facially hairy, pale) is inferior to his transformed body (hard, achieved, smooth, tanned). Even the shorts Runnalls wears—from cheap-looking tattered jean cutoffs to expensive designer spandex—signal an improvement of social status as a result of his bodily transformation. As Del Rio blatantly states, Runnalls's "perseverance, dedication, and goal-setting" transformed him from "flab to fab, chunk to hunk, paunch to prince, blubber to babe magnet, zero to hero, geek to sheik" (2000, p. 77). There is little subtlety to the imposition of shame the man with the fat (pale, hairy, poor) body should feel according to the publishers of *MuscleMag International.*

Dotson finds equally restrictive depictions of the male body in gay-produced and -consumed media, especially gay pornography. As

Dotson contends, the men represented sexually in gay male pornography "are the archetypes of gay male beauty. They are the gods, in all their physical and naked glory" (1999, p. 132). Of course, as Dotson (1999) notes, these archetypes are muscular, young, smooth, and generally white:

> Sometime in the course of evolution of gay male pornography, body hair became passé, and men with body hair all but disappeared from such videos. It is difficult to pinpoint the origins of gay male body shaving. Perhaps it was an idea lifted from the world of competitive bodybuilding, since contestants shave their body hair to better display their muscles. (p. 132)

Richard Mohr (1992) also notes the norm of the smooth body in gay male pornography, ascribing it to a focus on the desirability of youth: "Hairiness is dropped from gay male porn, for while it is naturally male, it socially connotes age, and the typical consumer of porn does not want age in his fantasies unless he is specifically looking for a daddy or bear type" (p. 148). The hairless body then becomes a norm of male attractiveness not only in straight mainstream media but also in gay mainstream media. This is reflected in the increasingly ubiquitous advertisements for laser (permanent) hair removal in mainstream gay publications.

This idealized image of the erotic male body is not entirely novel, as demonstrated in Waugh's (1996) historical survey of gay male erotic imagery up to Stonewall. As Waugh indicates, the so-called physique culture idealizing the muscular and athletic male body finds its roots in the muscular Christianity movement and strongmen of the late nineteenth century. It was first in the visual representations of carnival strongmen (such as the renowned Eugen Sandow) that a new ideal image of the male emerged: "The undraped, muscular, mature body of the proletarian hero encoded new ideals of social mobility, strength, popularity, leisure, consumption, and triumph" (1996, p. 178). This, in turn, transformed the male body (like the female body before it) into "an object of media consumption: it not only worked, presided, and earned but also played and competed, and was displayed, recorded, endlessly reproduced, sold, consumed, preserved, admired, emulated—and desired" (pp. 178-180). This mass mediation, consumption, and admiration of the muscular, athletic, youthful, strong (and principally white) male body was solidified in the post–World

War II physique culture of North America and western Europe
through a proliferation of physique magazines (notably *Physique
Pictorial, Trim, Tomorrow's Man,* and *Face and Physique*), the clear
and queer forerunners to the more mainstream bodybuilding magazines of today. Indeed, as Waugh (1996) indicates, this cultural image
of the muscular male body as an erotic ideal would come to dominate
the 1950s and 1960s—that "golden age of the male body beautiful,"
with its "eroticization of muscle, strength, and combat" (p. 176).
What does appear new, however, is the pervasiveness of this image of
the muscular male body and the increasingly impossible dimensions
of this idealized form. Harrison Pope, Katharine Phillips, and Roberto
Olivardia (2000) argue that widespread use of pharmacological drugs
(most notably anabolic steroids) since the 1980s has made it feasible
to widely portray a body image that is impossible for most men to actually achieve without the aid of such drugs.

These idealized images of the increasingly muscular male body
are certainly not confined to print or broadcast media. Such images
now appear in the toys young boys play with, most notably action figures. Feminists and social scientists such as Jacqueline Urla and Alan
Swedlund (1995) have interrogated the impossible image of a woman's
body that the contemporary Barbie doll presents to young girls.
Noting that if today's Barbie were the height of an average woman
(five feet, four inches) her waist measurement would be only seventeen inches, Urla and Swedlund contend that "Barbie truly is the un-
obtainable representation of an imaginary femaleness" (p. 298).
Equally impossible images of the body are now being presented to
boys through the action figures they play with. As Lynne Luciano
(2001) comments, just "as Barbie grew less like ordinary women,
G.I. Joe, with his enhanced muscularity and definition, has become
less like ordinary men" (p. 175). Not only have G.I. Joe and other
similar action figure toys come less to represent an "ordinary" male
body, but the body they do represent is one that is virtually impossible
for any man to achieve. In their examination of anxieties surrounding
male body image, Pope, Phillips, and Olivardia (2000) demonstrate
how these action toys present a male body that "has evolved in only
about thirty years from a normal and reasonably attainable figure,
such as that of the Vietnam-era G.I. Joes, to a hugely muscular figure
that we believe no man could attain without massive doses of steroids" (pp. 43-44).

What I am suggesting here is that American society has become permeated by an idealized image of the male body that is just as restrictive and just as impossible for most men to achieve as that idealized image of the female body imposed on women. Pope, Phillips, and Olivardia (2000) argue that as a result, men are experiencing a growing preoccupation and dissatisfaction with their bodies based on a distorted understanding of what the male body *should* look like. They refer to this condition as the Adonis complex which is, they contend, exacerbated by the commercial media:

> [R]esearch shows that sociocultural influences, such as the media, tend to make women feel worse about their bodies, and preliminary studies of these influences suggest the same is true for men. In addition, there seems little doubt that over the last generation our culture has placed a growing emphasis on the male body image—as exemplified in toys, comic books, magazines, newspapers, television, the movies, and advertisements of all types. (p. 60)

For those gay men possessing and/or desiring a body not conforming to these idealized criterians of attractiveness, mainstream media and even many forms of gay media prove inherently unsatisfying. This may well constitute another physical-world motivation for online interaction—to find or construct representations of the attractive and desirable male body that do not conform to (or reject outright) those images presented in the mainstream media. With this in mind, I now turn to an examination of how individuals on these channels perceive those images of the male body presented in the mainstream media and how they respond to this gay male beauty myth.

THEY NEVER SHOW: REACTIONS TO MEDIA REPRESENTATIONS OF THE MALE BODY

In Chapter 3, I examined some of the reasons cited for first venturing into these particular cyberspaces. Within that discussion, it became clear that some individuals turned to these channels to compensate for some absence in their offline lives, such as physical isolation resulting from either the loss of a loved one or illness. I further that discussion here by exploring another physical-world circumstance motivating individuals to seek out these particular channels—the narrow range of media representations of the desirable male body. Many of those I have interacted with on these channels, particularly individuals patronizing #gaychub and #gaymusclebears, expressed a general frustration at not being able to find images of the male body they either identified with or desired in mainstream straight or gay media. These same interactants, however, would frequently comment that virtual environments such as #gaymusclebears afforded them an opportunity to speak of bodies commonly marginalized or rendered completely invisible in the media—to speak of the obese body, to speak of the hairy body, to speak of the older body—in a context that affirmed their own desires and self-image. Thus, it is possible to view these particular channels as resistive efforts to broaden cultural understandings of what constitutes the attractive, the healthy, and the erotic male body.

In her discussion of the beauty myth imposed on women, Wolf (1991) comments on how the real problem is one of "lack of choice" (p. 272), the compulsion to make the body fit a singular idealized index of beauty. I would contend the same holds true in regard to the gay male beauty myth. The narrowness of the spectrum of what constitutes the desirable male body in the mainstream media became apparent in discussions with individuals on all three channels, including **Top_Bear,** a thirty-four-year-old computer professional from Washington, DC, who chats primarily on #gaymusclebears:

> **John:** When you look at the mainstream media do you find any men that look like you?
> **Top_Bear:** only in the pro football/wresting area not much else
> **John:** How does that feel?
> **Top_Bear:** disturbing only in the fact that the media and advertisers are trying to sell everyone the way they should look not be happy with the way they are

Similar sentiments were expressed by those who chat on the channel #gaychub, as reflected in this discussion with **Big_Wolf** about whether forms of mainstream media present images of men he finds attractive:

> **Big_Wolf:** No the media men are variations on the same basic theme . . . so its like General Motors products mainstream media men . . . a few bits of hair and, muscle in different places but in effect all the same package fitted out to look distinctive on the cheap.

Big_Wolf: Like the chrome bits and, bobs that add to similair cars to make them unique.

Big_Wolf's comments clearly relate his discontentment with the lack of diversity in those male body images presented as desirable in mainstream media fare. **Big_Wolf**'s observations support Jerry Mosher's (2001) conclusions regarding the representation of heavy or fat male bodies in American prime-time television. In his examination, Mosher notes how the fat man is customarily absent from leading roles and, if present at all, is a marginal presence confined to narrow range of stereotypes: the bumbling oaf, the effete servant, and the discriminating gourmet (p. 171). In all such representations, the fat male body is never positioned as sexual or desirable but rather is restricted to an object of amusement, spectacle, and even pity. As he notes, televised representations "of fat men thus are broadly drawn from contradictory impulses: they are rendered ordinary but deviant, average but grotesque, male but not masculine" (p. 187). Looking at such media representations, it seems inconceivable that the fat body could be understood as an attractive body and fat itself could be viewed as erotic: "on television fat desire, like homosexuality, is still marginalized as deviant behavior, even when the fat desire involves straight heterosexual sex" (Mosher, 2001, p. 185).

However, those turning to forms of mainstream gay media, such as *The Advocate,* may find themselves as frustrated by the similar absence of body images they seek. Remarks from patrons on all three channels indicated that those images of the male body appearing in most gay publications are as restrictive and unsatisfying as those images appearing in the mainstream straight media, especially in regard to fat desirability. This became apparent in conversations with **BIGrGUY, SFBigCub,** and **Big_Wolf:**

> **John:** In general do you find images of men in mainstream gay publications such as THE ADVOCATE attractive? What about images of men in the mainstream straight media?
>
> **BIGrGUY:** I find muscle mass sexually attractive in a man . . . I also find a large belly to be erotic on that frame
>
> **BIGrGUY:** I'm sure the muscle could be found in the media, but the belly would not
>
> **BIGrGUY:** I prefer a belly, not perfect abs you see everywhere in the media

John: In general do you find the images of men in mainstream gay publications such as THE ADVOCATE attractive?

SFBigCub: well, they have classically attractive faces usually . . . and that's nice. but their bodies, are not really anything special to me.

SFBigCub: I like men who are bigger than I am—either chubbier or muscular; and generally bearish sorts of men.

John: What do you mean by "bearish"?

SFBigCub: facial hair, body hair, rugged-looking.

John: do you find that image in the mainstream media?

SFBigCub: not really, no

John: do you find the men you see in mainstream gay publications (like THE ADVOCATE) attractive?

Big_Wolf: Well I have nothing against them mind you . . . but NO I would leap across all of the ADVOCATE and, other mainstream men to let a BIG man walk on my feet as he leaves the building.

Certainly this treatment of the male body in both mainstream straight and gay media supports Brown's (2001) contention that the dominant "culture continues to see fat men as funny, happy souls to be laughed at, or at best *with*—but never desired" (p. 43, emphasis original). While this certainly reflects society's general fear of fat desire and the sexuality of the corpulent body, it also reflects the immense influence of the multi-billion-dollar diet and fitness industry. Those "perfect abs you see everywhere in the media" that **BIGrGUY** refers to are the keystones of an industry that depends on less-than-perfect bodies wanting those idealized abdominal muscles.

For some on these channels, the frustration surrounding this restrictive spectrum of male body images available within the mainstream media included an antipathy toward those mediated representations of the gay male body. Comments frequently indicated that individuals on these channels believe they neither look like nor can identify with those images of gay men appearing in such mainstream fare as NBC's successful sitcom *Will & Grace,* in which one of the central characters, Will Truman (played by Eric McCormack), is presented to the viewer as a model of the attractive gay urban professional. Mosher (2001) notes how mainstream media representations of the gay male body can be even more restrictive than those surrounding the straight male body, commenting that the "identification of a singular gay male body type, thin and effeminate, proves to be just as reductive as are hard-bodied notions of heterosexual masculinity" (p. 186). In addition to not resembling or desiring the image of the gay man represented by the character of Will Truman, participants often did not want to be associated with such a body image by virtue of a shared (homo)sexual identity. On all three channels, patrons exhibited a resentment toward the notion that they should have to conform to a particular model of the male body (that epitomized in the character of Will) by virtue of identifying as gay men.

This distress with the constricted constellation of mediated representations of the gay male body was apparent in a conversation with **Younghung:**

> **John:** In general, do you find images of gay men in the mainstream media (TV or Film) attractive?
>
> **Younghung:** not really
>
> **Younghung:** they tend to be the very flamboyant, very fem, very skinny guys, i don't find that attractive
>
> **John:** Do you find images of gay men in the mainstream media that you can identify with?
>
> **Younghung:** no, they don't portray the kind of man i want to be or i like as gay, ever
>
> **John:** what do you mean?
>
> **Younghung:** they never show the football linebacker, or the pro wrestler or the powerlifters as gay, they are always the totally str8 ones that bash gay men
>
> **John:** How does that make you feel?
>
> **Younghung:** it feels like they are telling you that if you are gay, you should be skinny, vulnerable, and fem

Younghung's dissatisfaction with mainstream media representations of gay men originates from what "they never show"—the large, muscular, brawny male body as a gay body, a body that is not only an object of same-sex sexual attraction but is itself a body deriving pleasure from same-sex sexual activities. Conventionally, these larger male bodies are coded as both sexually undesirable (that is, they are generally positioned as the functional athletic body that should be appreciated *only* for what they can accomplish on the playing field or in the ring and not for their aesthetic qualities) *and* fiercely heterosexual. **Younghung** also views the gay male body as portrayed in the mainstream media as a vulnerable body, arguably a body rendered safe and nonthreatening for straight audiences. For gay men looking to the media, they may find a void of images resembling their own bodies or the bodies they desire, and those images that are presented as idealized gay male bodies may well be physical forms they perceive as degrading.

Even those idealized "types" emerging from these channels may be understood as reactions to a mainstream media that fails to provide images that speak to the erotic desires or identifications of these particular gay men. Arguably, these channels represent efforts to speak differently about the male body, to speak of the fat body or the hairy body or even the extremely muscular body as attractive, desirable, and queer. The centrality of such rearticulation in fashioning a positive understanding of their own sexual identities for these individuals should not be underestimated. Butler (1990b), for instance, discusses both the importance of alternative discourses for comprehending embodiment for those occupying a marginal status within society and the damage caused when those of marginalized status understand their own identities only through a discourse of denigration: "Discourse becomes oppressive when it requires that the speaking subject, in order to speak, participate in the very terms of that oppression—that is, take for granted the speaking subject's own impossibility or unintelligibility" (p. 116). This perhaps represents the greatest importance of these online communities to those interacting there—the ability to construct alternative discursive realities based on acceptance and affirmation not only of their sexuality but also of the bodies they both possess and desire. Certainly channels such as #gaychub can prove invaluable resources for their patrons both in offering alternative representations of the attractive male body and in providing spaces in which fat desirability is affirmed and even celebrated. Essentially, such channels function as havens against the demeaning repercussions of societal fat phobia.

SUBVERTING/RECONSTRUCTING BEAUTY HIERARCHIES IN CYBERSPACE

Not all oppressive indices of male beauty are imposed solely from outside these communities. Though many of those interacting on these channels arguably come to such cyberspaces to find representations of the male body unavailable in the mainstream media, these same individuals can themselves establish new and equally restrictive standards of beauty online. Even in Locke's largely celebrational discussion of alterative male images appearing in publications oriented toward the bear community, he fears that a new idealized model of the gay male body—such as the so-called glamour bear—will simply be substituted for that model found in more mainstream media. In particular respects, Locke's concerns have come to pass on channels such as #gaymuscle, where idealized images of the male form (in this instance, the bodybuilder) have come to dominate discussions surrounding the desirable body. As a result, some of those initially entering these channels to explore their erotic interests come to feel painfully inadequate about their own bodies.

Here I examine the experiences of two individuals, **WorkOut** and **Younghung,** who both chatted on #gaymuscle until they came to feel uncomfortable not only with the physical paradigm glorified on that channel but also with the expectations of other patrons that they should conform to this exacting model. The primary reason for focus-- ing on #gaymuscle is because the male form adulated there aligns with what Pope, Phillips, and Olivardia (2000) identify as the "supermale image" increasingly prevalent in the commercial media: "smiling bodybuilders with massive shoulders, rock-hard pectorals, and impossibly sculptured and chiseled abdominal muscles" (p. 2).

WorkOut's frustration with this supermale image and the expectations of others on the channel was apparent in his discussion of why he no longer chats on #gaymuscle:

> **John:** Do you ever chat on #gaymuscle or #gaychub?
>
> **WorkOut:** I started out on #gaymuscle, but when I found out about #gaymusclebears, I started hanging out there as well and eventually dropped #gaymuscle from the list of places I usually hang out.
>
> **John:** Why don't you go to #gaymuscle anymore?
>
> **WorkOut:** I started at #gaymuscle because I enjoy working out and I'm very attracted to men who work out and build muscle too. I dropped it, though, because of the people on the channel. They were very full of themselves, too often just looking for some net.sex or just someone to fluff their ego. Not that it's bad in itself but it just wasn't what I was looking for; what I wanted to hang around with. I also didn't like the attitude of the bodybuilders on there.
>
> **John:** What about the attitude of the bodybuilders on the channel did you not like?
>
> **WorkOut:** Just their general attitude. If you're bis or pecs aren't big enough, or if you bodyfat is too high they thought you weren't good enough to talk to them. One even told me I wasn't a real bodybuilder. They only want to be around other guys that look like pro bodybuilders.

Additional discussions with **WorkOut,** a novice bodybuilder from
Minnesota, revealed that part of his discomfort with #gaymuscle origi-
nated from the fact that the more advanced bodybuilders on the channel often refused to acknowledge his commitment to the bodybuilding lifestyle. As **WorkOut** commented one evening, "they don't take
me seriously," lamenting the fact that his body had yet to exhibit the
dedication he invests in weight training and diet. As discussed in
Chapter 4, the body of the bodybuilder is expected to identify itself
through its conspicuous muscle mass and extraordinarily low body
fat. In social spaces such as #gaymuscle, a man's bodybuilding identity is affirmed by his musculature, and should he lack sufficient
muscle mass, his claim to that lifestyle may be disputed by others.
WorkOut's decision to remain "natural"—that is, not to take anabolic steroids or other drugs designed to increase muscle mass—impedes
his ability to achieve that body image extolled on #gaymuscle and to
be recognized as a peer of those bodybuilders and weight lifters on
the channel who do employ such pharmacological aids.

    Younghung expressed similar sentiments when discussing why he
stopped frequenting #gaymuscle less than two years after he had first
ventured onto the channel. For **Younghung,** the expectations of other
patrons on the channel only exasperated those feelings of physical inadequacy he often experienced in his offline social relations:

> **John:** When I first met you, you were chatting on #gaymuscle. Do you
> chat on #gaymuscle anymore?
> **Younghung:** no, i don't
> **John:** why not?
> **Younghung:** i found that most guys on that channel are typically more
> . . . stuckup, less talkative outside their own clicke of friends, they
> tend to make outsiders feel VERY out of place unless they are mod-
> els of physical perfection, the other channels are more open, less
> intimidating
> **John:** What are those "models" of physical perfection?
> **Younghung:** perfectly lean, perfectly ripped bodybuilders are what the
> guys in there are typically after
> **Younghung:** when you tell them your stats and yer not a bb or
> powerlifter they tend to shun you, some can be very rude about it
> **John:** How did you feel about yourself when you were chatting on
> #gaymuscle?
> **Younghung:** they tend to make one feel less confident about them-
> selves . . .
> **Younghung:** making you feel like you are not as good as they are be-
> cause you are not built like them

Although **Younghung** initially ventured into the virtual space of #gaymuscle because he is attracted to the image of the male bodybuilder, the expectations of others on the channel often caused him to feel deficient about his own body. **Younghung**'s experience is by no means unique, nor is such antagonism toward particular body types confined to online communities. For instance, Patrick Giles (1998) discusses the pain experienced as an overweight gay man living in New York City and not conforming to those body images idealized in urban gay male culture: "In seventeen years of being out of the closet, none of the shit I've dodged from the straight world has matched the hostility, ostracism, and enforced anonymity flung in my face by my own queer kind" (p. 355). Mosher (2001) clearly notes that fat gay men are often "disappointed to find that fat-phobia is even more evident in gay culture than in heterosexual culture" (p. 186). It is not only the fat body that can be derided in gay culture but also fat desire. Despite being thin himself, Brown (2001) discusses how his identification as a "chubby chaser"—that is, a gay man attracted to fat or chubby male bodies—resulted in himself being positioned as deviant even within the gay community: "Here I am among my own kind, having only struggled out two or three years before—and they are ridiculing me in their ignorance, unable to accept the object of my desire" (p. 41). Like Brown, I found it difficult to locate those receptive to my desires prior to my experiences in cyberspace. Among my gay friends (thin and overweight alike), my attraction to exceptionally large men with broad shoulders, round faces, and nicely proportioned guts was characterized as incomprehensible. In contrast, I understood the objects of their attraction—young, smooth, "buff" men with perfect abdominal muscles—as what I was supposed to desire but did not. Speaking from my own experience, even today I find my models of the desirable male body not in gay male pornography but in those televised world's strongest men competitions. Thus like so many on these channels, I found affirmation of my desires not in physical-world gay bars but in cyberspace.

Indeed, the multiplicity of social scenes in cyberspace offers an important contrast to offline gay urban culture, especially in the ability to formulate communities around diverse understandings of the desirable body. Although **Younghung** experiences marginalization in virtual environments such as #gaymuscle, the vast assortment of channels on IRC presents the opportunity to find alternative online spaces where his body and his desires are accepted and celebrated:

> **John:** How do you feel about yourself when you chat on #gaymuscle-bears or #gaychub?
> **Younghung:** accepted, better, they appreciate me for me, some even like the way i look, since i've chatted there i realize there are guys who like how i look, or would like to help me get more muscular

My experiences on #gaymuscle suggest that **Younghung** and **Work-Out** are far from the only individuals on the channel experiencing feelings of inadequacy surrounding their own bodies. Indeed, the supermale image idealized on #gaymuscle proves daunting to most individuals I spoke with. However, not all feel so overwhelmed by this idealized male form that they leave the channel altogether. Rather, some find a camaraderie with others struggling to achieve this body image, using the channel as a space to express their frustration at not being bigger or harder or more ripped to a sympathetic community.

Though one might expect those bodybuilders patronizing #gaymuscle to be confident in their own bodies, I often found that beyond the facade of security, they too harbored misgivings about their physiques, worrying that their bodies are not sufficiently muscular or symmetrical. For instance, **Msclfreak** has added a tremendous amount of muscle mass to his body during years that I have known him. Online acquaintances that once characterized him as "big" now categorize him as "huge," making frequent comments about the remarkable development of his body. Despite this, **Msclfreak** continues to express doubts about the adequacy of his physique, as demonstrated in this recent conversation:

> **John:** You look incredible Magnus. It's amazing what you've done to your body!
> **Msclfreak:** thanks john, but I see guys my height 10 years younger that is already bigger though, wonder what the hell they are taking! I need to get bigger!

In light of the fact that he is already much larger than the majority of men, **Msclfreak**'s dissatisfaction with his size and muscularity may be incomprehensible for most people. Individuals such as Pope, Phillips, and Olivardia may even hold that **Msclfreak** suffers from a psychological condition they term *muscle dysmorphia,* in which the individual has a consuming preoccupation with his or her own muscularity. They describe this condition in relation to anorexia nervosa:

> The body image distortions of men with "muscle dysmorphia" are strikingly analogous to those of women (and some men) with anorexia nervosa. In fact, some people have colloquially referred to muscle dysmorphia as "bigorexia nervosa" or "reverse anorexia." People with anorexia nervosa see themselves as fat when they're actually too thin; people with muscle dysmorphia feel ashamed of looking too small when they're actually big. (p. 11)

I am not convinced, however, that muscle dysmorphia adequately describes the social dynamics underlying **Msclfreak**'s endless quest for more mass. In my conversations with **Msclfreak** over the years as we have interacted online suggest that he is quite aware of the impressive muscularity of his own body. This is especially evident in his eagerness to exhibit his body online and to be worshiped by gay men offline. What I see at hand is a twofold social phenomenon: First, there is a certain eroticism at play in **Msclfreak**'s desire to grow larger. As discussed in Chapter 4, the sexual practice of worship shifts the erotic focus to the musculature of the male body, and thus the greater the amount of muscle mass, the greater the erotic intensity. For bodybuilders such as **Msclfreak,** there is an autoeroticism driving the years of weight training, diet, and steroid use—an autoeroticism encapsulated in the comments of Arnold Schwarzenegger: "Seeing new changes in my body, feeling them, turned me on."[2] As Fussell (1996) notes, it should be of little surprise that the correlate of pumping iron is "vacuum pumping," an erotic practice in which men "shave their scrotum and the base of the penis to highlight the organ and extend its length through daily stretching through a custom-ordered modified vacuum tube" (p. 47). The erotic fantasy essential to both practices is that of growth without boundaries, of infinitely enlarging biceps and balls, pecs and penises.

The second side of this phenomenon is an erotic model of the body that is so extreme no human can actually achieve it. This idealized image—especially prevalent on #gaymuscle—is that of the "freak" as personified in those morphed pictures of already exceptionally massive bodybuilders traded online. As the state of true freakiness is, by definition, humanly impossible to obtain, individuals such as **Msclfreak** continue to feel inadequate in the face of this sexual ideal. At least on the surface, it appears that these individuals can fall prey to the very idealized images of the erotic body they participated in formulating, thereby contributing to the dissatisfaction they experience toward their own bodies. However, I should qualify this discussion by noting that merely desiring to possess unusually larges amounts of muscle mass should not be viewed in and of itself as psychologically unhealthy. Bracketing those health issues related to taking substantial amounts of anabolic steroids (which may indeed be serious cause for concern), the desire to construct an unusually large body should not be immediately positioned as negative and perhaps can be seen through a more celebratory lens if one views **Msclfreak** and those other bodybuilders on #gaymuscle as inscribing their erotic desires directly onto their bodies for all to read. To stigmatize a body simply because it possesses an exceptional amount of muscle mass (mass phobia) is not in form much different than disparaging a body because it possesses an unusually great amount of fat mass (fat phobia). My point here is that how a body is read in regard to its desirability or attractiveness is dependent on the specific cultural context. In cyberspace where there is a multifaceted assemblage of beauty myths reflecting diverse erotic desires, bodies looked upon as unattractive or unhealthy within the larger social milieu may be rearticulated as desirable or admirable.

Though an examination of any one particular channel would reveal the existence of a potentially repressive beauty myth, a broader view of the constellation of channels indicates a subversion of any universalized notions of beauty and the erotic. Although idealized images of the body are not abandoned in cyberspace, they must contend with conflicting understandings of the desirable and the attractive in the virtual, effectively undermining the supremacy of any one hierarchy of beauty. As interactants move from channel to channel, they in effect unsettle any naturalized standards of beauty, and even the notion of the *natural* body itself becomes a relative reference. Indices of beauty remain, but none can be positioned as objective or universal. This certainly meets Grosz's (1994) articulation of a feminist retheorization of the body that abandons singular models "based on one type of body as the norm by which all others are judged" (p. 22). While some individuals promote constricting images of male attractiveness on one channel, others construct alternative spaces where the disdained male body is embraced. Thus any desire to celebrate or condemn these channels as political arenas is again complicated, for within cyberspace there "is no one mode that is capable of representing the 'human' in all its richness and variability" (Grosz, 1994, p. 22).

DON'T HATE ME BECAUSE I'M BEAUTIFUL...

Those queer scholars studying mainstream forms of American media have noted the furthermost marginal position and, until recently, often complete absence of gay and lesbian representation (Gross, 1991, 1993; Russo, 1981). Though the last decade has witnessed a quantitative increase in queer representation in the media, critical issues remain regarding the diversity of such depictions (Gross, 2001). Consistently, during online interviews and casual conversations, interactants expressed a particular displeasure with how the gay male body is depicted in American television and film. Participants frequently commented that images of the male body they either identify with or desire—the obese body, the hairy body, the extremely muscular body—are marginalized, stigmatized, portrayed as abnormal or unattractive, or simply absent. This deep dissatisfaction with mediated images of the desirable body was apparent in the comments of **Top_Bear:**

> **Top_Bear:** they need more images of stocky well built men similiar to what they have done with the heavier women in the advertising industry recently . . . it is a shame that most mainstream media only focuses on thin men with no body hair . . . it is as if being big is ugly, it is not

For individuals on these channels, the marginal representation of gay men in the mainstream media is compounded by the paucity of images of the male body they can identify with. These same interactants, however, indicated that IRC channels such as #gaymusclebears and #gaychub open spaces where they can speak affirmably of bodies generally marginalized or completely invisible in film and television. This, in turn, appears to have helped some interactants to conceptualize their sexual identities and their own bodies in more positive terms. In this respect, the comments of **Younghung** warrant repeating:

John: How do you feel about yourself when you chat on #gay-musclebears or #gaychub?

Younghung: accepted, better, they appreciate me for me, some even like the way i look, since i've chatted there i realize there are guys who like how i look, or would like to help me get more muscular

Seeking out virtual spaces where their own bodies or the bodies they desire are affirmed and even celebrated represents yet another way in which these individuals incorporate computer-mediated communication technologies into their negotiation of daily life. By entering these virtual spaces, patrons are clearly not endeavoring to escape the body but rather are looking to reconcile social understandings of the desirable body with those bodies that are part of their immediate experience. In essence, some are using these channels as social arenas in which to come to terms with the gay male beauty myth.

Still, some may mistake the story of virtual body bending opening this chapter as evidence of the transcendent nature of online interaction. However, when one looks a bit closer, it is clear that **Younghung** constructed and performed a particular image of the body he believed would be desirable based on his physical-world experiences. He was not transcending his corporeal state as much as he was disguising a body he had been taught was unattractive and undesirable by a society and a commercial media that stigmatize obesity. Perhaps stories of virtual body bending should lead us to question a bit more critically why some individuals feel compelled to present themselves so differently online. Are these individuals displeased with their own appearance because they see themselves as failing to achieve an image of male beauty few men can actually fulfill? Are incidents of virtual body bending symptomatic of some pervasive dissatisfaction men experience toward their own bodies when bombarded by supermale images in the mainstream media? Although comprehensive answers are beyond the scope of this modest study, such questions do usefully remind us of the need to contextualize online interaction within a larger social universe permeated by mass media images.

Chapter 6

Getting Off Online

You can never plan the future by the past.

Edmund Burke
Letter to a member of the National Assembly, 1791

During the summer evenings of 2002, I frequently found myself chatting about the development of this book on #gaymusclebears. Several of the regulars on that channel had participated in the original study, and they often expressed a keen interest in how my work was progressing, what conclusions I was reaching, and what my opinions were on various topics related to online interaction. I certainly welcomed these open discussions on the main window of the channel, as they periodically produced useful analytical fruit. During one such occasion late into the summer months, a regular who had not participated in the actual study and who generally only logged on to the channel quite late—usually long after I had logged off for the night—inquired about the specific focus of the book. **BigJoe** had heard that someone on the channel was writing a book about chat rooms, but those details he garnered secondhand were too vague to provide any real appreciation for the project. When I informed him that the book was looking at the uses gay men make of particular IRC channels, the following conversation ensued on the main window:

```
<BigJoe> irc is dead anyway[1]
<John> why is irc dead?
<BigJoe> dunno
<BigJoe> not really any new users
<BigJoe> outside the realms of warez channels
<BigJoe> ie, its been replaced by other more successful chat mediums
<John> what do you see as superceding IRC?
<BigJoe> gay.com and stuff
<BigJoe> the success of aol
```

<BigJoe> in general, the people here are mostly bitter anti-aol
<BigJoe> more computer savvy in general
<John> except for me :)
<John> computer savvy that is
<BigJoe> im an exception as well
<BigJoe> i just stumbled upon this years ago
<BigJoe> and made some friends along the way
<John> same here
<BigJoe> and i cant afford aol
<John> is that why you keep chatting on IRC—to maintain friend-ships?
<BigJoe> and dont really need the chat room stuff anymore since i settled down with someone
<BigJoe> yeah
<BigJoe> and i make new ones along the way
<BigJoe> but take Hairybeef for example
<BigJoe> ive known him for about 6 years now
<John> wow
<BigJoe> since i was 18
<BigJoe> basically i talk to him, jim, kim, and couple other people
<John> is that how long you've been chatting on irc—6 years?
<BigJoe> yeah
<BigJoe> something like
<BigJoe> maybe a little more
<BigJoe> was the first chat medium i found
<BigJoe> so ive really watched it decline
<John> decline? how so?
<BigJoe> harder to get on servers, less servers
<BigJoe> less people
<BigJoe> less conversation
<John> I have noticed that it is harder to find a server to get on these days
<BigJoe> yeah
<RedBear> have you updated MIRC?
<BigJoe> yup
<RedBear> seems to be more that work now
<BigJoe> a little
<John> yeah, I have the latest version—still can't DCC on this new version
<BigJoe> i think it used to have issues with more firewall software
<BigJoe> yeah haha, i cant dcc either
<John> how are we suppose to share porno if we can't DCC?! After all, isn't that what the internet was created for!
<BigJoe> haha
<BigJoe> porno, viagra, and debt consolidation
<John> *grin*
<BigJoe> but i meet new people along the way
<BigJoe> like jim i met only maybe 3 years back

<BigJoe> maybe 4 now
<BigJoe> i think anyway the whole sex aspect behind some of the gay channels has dissolved
<BigJoe> in favor of other means
<John> what other means? are you thinking of video chat services like ICUii?
<BigJoe> remember when you used to get stat-line after stat-line
<RedBear> I've met a lot of guys from IRC
<BigJoe> yeah, i think thats big
<BigJoe> icu2
<BigJoe> i never got a cam so i dont really know about all those things
<RedBear> I don't like ICU . . . really unfriendly people
<BigJoe> but they seem to be popular
*** TechnoBear has joined #gaymusclebears
<TechnoBear> Grrrrrrrrrr
<John> Hey Jim-we're having a great conversation about the rise and fall of IRC
<BigJoe> its alive!
<TechnoBear> Oh really?
<BigJoe> lol
<TechnoBear> IRC is still the largest facility of its kind.

BigJoe's comments about the demise of IRC haunted me like a childhood melody playing incessantly in the back of one's brain. I often found myself pondering the future of IRC during the writing of this book. Indeed, much has changed in the realm of computer-mediated communication since the advent of online chat. When IRC came on the scene, so to speak, the World Wide Web had yet to exist, let alone Java-based chat rooms on commercial Web sites, online video chat services, and streaming audio and video over the Internet. The late 1990s witnessed a fundamental shift in the character of online chatting with the introduction of a more private mode of one-on-one online synchronous communication, instant messaging (IM). Although instant messenger applications such as ICQ (intended to be read as "I seek you") function well for maintaining existing social networks—particularly for keeping in touch with distant friends—they do not offer the same opportunities to explore diverse social scenes as online chat rooms. Still, I wonder what role IRC will play in this ever expanding computer-mediated universe?

Certainly IRC is now far from the only venue in cyberspace in which individuals discuss their erotic desires and practices. From online newsgroups such as Yahoo! Groups to AOL chat rooms, gay men are constructing spaces to explore such sexual activities as bondage, gaining, muscle worship, and vacuum pumping (sometimes all on the same site). What this proliferation of cyberspaces dedicated to the sexual suggests is that many individuals are less committed to any specific online medium than they are focused on exploiting the range of virtual locations where they can share their interests with like-minded others. Thus, those interested in gaining may continue to chat on #gaychub while also frequenting particular chat rooms on AOL as well as posting messages on newsgroups dedicated to the practice. What then are the implications for IRC as an online medium?

BigJoe sees a clear decline in the state of IRC, believing that newer modes of computer-mediated communication are superceding this older model of online chat. Certainly in terms of numbers, America Online is the predominant method of online chatting for those residing in the United States. **TechnoBear,** however, disputes **BigJoe**'s assessment. For him, those interacting in cyberspace are now moving fluidly between different means of synchronistic online communication, not so much abandoning IRC as expanding their repertoire of online venues. As he commented to me during a private conversation, "nothing is actually replacing irc . . . people are just exploring all the different ways of communicating over the internet . . . each has its pros and cons, but irc will always be here." **TechnoBear** himself epitomizes this new Internet user, employing multiple modes of online communication concurrently, such as chatting on IRC while simultaneously logging on to a video chat network. Many of the participants in this study have, over the past few years, begun experimenting with other modes of online communication, making their presence on IRC increasingly sporadic.

Though I still encounter individuals such as **TechnoBear, Umgawa, Bennoe, Big_Wolf, Mage78,** and **Mad_Hatter** fairly regularly on IRC, others such as **Britannic** and **PHLguy** appear only infrequently on these channels, often logging on solely to get in touch with old online acquaintances. For some, such as **SFBigCub,** online chatting has lost its novelty in their lives and faded into the background as simply another communication technology, much like the telephone. **SF BigCub** now uses e-mail as his primary means of staying in touch with those he has met online. The presence of **PECS** on these channels began to diminish after he moved from the relative isolation of rural New Hampshire to the cosmopolitan bustle of Montreal in the spring of 2000 (yet another example of how offline circumstances inform online behavior). At some point in 2001, I lost contact with **Younghung** and have not spoken to him since. When last we did speak, he had become involved with a man he met on #gaychub and was moving to central Florida to live with him. I hope **Younghung**'s absence from these channels is a testament to the happiness and fulfillment he has found in that relationship. **GremlinBear** also left IRC in 2001, preferring to chat primarily on Internet video chat services such as ICUII and iSpQ VideoChat. Through these services interactants are able to combine textual chat with real-time visual images of themselves (providing they have access to a webcam). Despite the poor quality of the images and the slower pace of communication, these services seem to be increasingly prevalent. Like **GremlinBear, Msclfreak** now chats solely on Internet video chat services. The particular appeal of such a mode of online communication for individuals such as **Msclfreak** is that they can now visually display the body once performed only through textual description, heightening the sense of immediacy and erotic intensity (see Figure 6.1).

The growing popularity of these video chat services suggests that we remain intensely visual creatures, supporting Ken Hillis's (1996) identification of vision as "the most noble organ" in Western belief (p. 71). If not the most noble, then for individuals such as **Msclfreak,** vision is unquestionably the most erotically charged mode of perception. The societal importance ascribed to actually seeing the body conflicts with those grand aspirations of corporeal transcendence. Far from becoming abstract creatures of pure thought in cyberspace, such practices as showing off one's muscular development through Internet video chat services demonstrates how invested we remain in the titillation of the flesh.

The majority of participants in this study, such as **IrishCrop, BIGrGUY,** and **WorkOut,** now employ a broad spectrum of online communication mediums, moving between video chat services and more traditional chat rooms on IRC and AOL as well as instant messaging. I am certainly one of these individuals, spending less and less time on IRC as I expand the terrain of cyberspaces I visit. In addition to IRC, I now chat on AOL, use various instant messenger applications, and on occasion venture onto Internet video chat services (fully clothed, of course). As a result, I question whether I can still be characterized as a regular on these channels. Am I still a native in these virtual spaces? Was I ever actually a native?

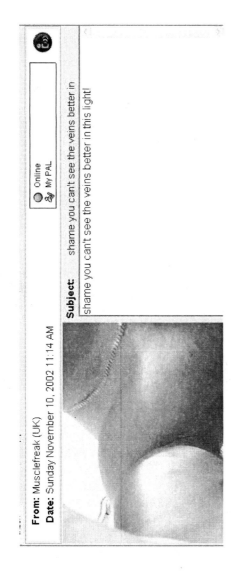

From: Musclefreak (UK)
Date: Sunday November 10, 2002 11:14 AM

Online
My PAL

Subject: shame you can't see the veins better in

shame you can't see the veins better in this light!

FIGURE 6.1. **Msclfreak** attempting to display the veins on his biceps through an Internet video chat service

In this concluding chapter, I offer some reflections on what these virtual playgrounds of the erotic reveal about the physical world we inhabit. Returning to the thought of Foucault, I examine the implications of embodied identity online, noting how some of the discourses emerging on these channels unsettled naturalized understandings of the body. Of particular interest is Foucault's understanding of the generative quality of power and how that is manifest in these cyberspaces. I also touch on the debate surrounding the use of ethnography in cyberspace, confronting the question of whether a meaningful ethnographic account can be constructed solely through online inquiry. First, however, I want to examine some of the sociological implications surrounding claims to nativeness in this narrative.

WHO'S NATIVE TO CYBERSPACE ANYWAY?

In tracing the development of gay and lesbian studies within anthropology, Kath Weston (1998) holds that "the best work in this field uses ethnographic material in classic relativist fashion to denaturalize Anglo-European conceptions of gender and sexuality" (p. 175). While this book is positioned at the anthropological junction of gay and lesbian studies and the study of social formations in cyberspace (sometimes referred to as cyberculture studies), I do hope it meets Weston's call in bringing into question some of the cultural assumptions underlying sex, sexuality, and the sexed body. I equally hope that my unique position relative to the communities I study provides novel insights into the online experiences of sexual minorities.

However, there is a risk involved in proclaiming my membership in these communities. This particular risk lurks not in the ethnographic account I actually produce but in how this account will be received by academic audiences. As Weston (1998) poignantly points out, queers who study queers are not generally afforded the same academic legitimacy as ostensibly heterosexual researchers who study ostensibly heterosexual populations. Too frequently gay and lesbian researchers writing about the lived experiences of sexual minorities are read by academic critics as simply writing about themselves, reiterating that pejorative stereotype conflating same-sex sexual attraction with obsessive narcissism. These researchers are often relegated to the position of "insider" by those critics failing to acknowledge either the rigor of their work or the complexity of the communities they study. Of course, such positioning begs the question: "Inside what? An unbounded, heterogeneous population that can be neither counted nor defined?" (Weston, 1998, p. 203).

I anticipate that some will read me as if speaking from the position of "insider" or "native," as opposed to ethnographic researcher. As a result, my work may be interpreted as a form of advocacy rather than an instance of critical analysis. ("Isn't he just championing the cause of his people?") To view myself and populations I study so uni-dimensionally is to ignore the complex ways sexuality intersects with other axes of identity, including gender, race, ethnicity, class, religion, and age. It is to reduce gays and lesbians to their sexual identity alone, as if their sole constituting components are their sexual acts. It is my hope that this book helps to reveal the immense heterogeneity within a population so often seen as homogeneous. In fact, this is a population seen as unified only from without. From "within," gay men and lesbians are often united only by their shared experience of marginalization within a heterosexist society. "Sexual minorities," Larry Gross (2001) notes, "differ in important ways from the 'traditional' racial and ethnic minorities," as with "other social groups defined by forbidden thoughts or deeds, we are rarely born into minority communities in which parents or siblings share our minority status" (p. 13). To speak of *the* gay community is at best to speak of some more abstract "imagined community"—in Benedict Anderson's (1983) sense of the term—in which all queers supposedly share membership by virtue of their sexual identity. Despite the alarmist rhetoric of the religious right, "*the* gay community" is little more than a fiction around which diverse groups muster for a common set of purposes.

Despite the more conventional style in which I have authored this text,[2] I hope the self-reflexive incorporation of my own experiences online have shattered any pretenses to objective "truth." This is not to diminish the methodological or analytical rigor of my research. Rather, this is to remind the reader that I, like all researchers, remain a positioned subject. Although I believe such introspective interrogation of my own social position produces a more critical account, I am aware that reflexivity alone is no guarantee of one's work being received as legitimate scholarship. Incorporating the self into one's work as a means of examining the researcher as positioned subject can be misconstrued as egotistical indulgence. While reflexivity, as Weston (1998) notes, "has the advantage of calling attention to differences that make a difference," it does not "automatically confer credibility" (p. 200).

However, the reflexive moments in this text should call the reader's attention to the tentativeness of my membership in these communities. I came to participate on these particular channels not out of some essential element of my character but out of my exploration of my own erotic desires and interests. Building upon the closing discussion of Chapter 3, I, like so many others on these channels, "drifted" into the social scenes I would later study. There was nothing inevitable about my becoming part of, if only momentarily, these online communities. Though I would identify myself as a "regular" on or "patron" of these channels, I would avoid the use of the term "native" with its essentializing connotations. Native is so often a designation assigned from without that denies the agency of subjects in laying claim to their own identification. The very term "native" smacks of the European colonialist project from which anthropology first emerged, an identification connoting social hierarchies predicated on the construction of an essentialized "Other." As Weston (1998) notes, whether someone "becomes nativized—much less primitivized—depends upon matters of history and power that extend well beyond the academy" (p. 197). As no one actually lives in cyberspace, claims to nativeness online remain at best problematic. We are all colonists in this foreign virtual landscape where understandings of self/other and us/them may need to be discarded in favor of more fluid ontologies of identity.

EMANCIPATION FROM THE BODY?

Another challenge to academic credibility arises from the decision to study online communities, a social phenomenon still being established as worthy of investigation in the more conventional fields of anthropology, sociology, psychology, and that disciplinary newcomer, communication. When conducting the original study upon which this book is based, I recall colleagues confronting me with such trivializing comments as "Isn't that cyberspace stuff all hype?" or "How meaningful can relations over the Internet truly be?" Although questions of validity haunt any new terrain of social science inquiry, the ephemeral quality of social interaction in cyberspace seems to render this field of research particularly susceptible to scholarly dismissal by its critics. Fieldwork in cyberspace yields no physical artifacts that can later be displayed in a museum or kept as trophies on one's desk, little proof of actually having "been there" as Clifford Geertz (1988) would say. For the researcher of online social relations, there are generally only transcripts of conversations and interviews conducted through the Internet—a vast collection of print—from which an entire social world must be reconstructed. As a result, an unresolved methodological controversy continues to enshroud online inquiry.

Much of this controversy centers on whether meaningful ethnographic accounts can be constructed solely from observations made and interviews conducted in cyberspace. On the self-acknowledged conservative side of this debate are individuals such as Sherry Turkle (1995), Daniel Miller and Don Slater (2000), and David Hakken (1999), who contends that the "misappropriation of ethnography is one reason why intellectuals find it hard to construct a convincing account of culture in cyberspace" (p. 45). These scholars generally hold that valid and verifiable accounts of online interaction can be constructed *only* by examining firsthand the offline experiences of such populations, suggesting that research is only "real" if it is conducted face to face or at least confirmed through some form of physical-world contact. I am not convinced of this prerequisite of physical-world contact for meaningful scholarship. Returning to the question of whether ethnographies can be conducted solely in cyberspace, the answer is simple: of course they can; this book is a testament to that fact. Ethnographies can be conducted online just as they have been conducted in workplaces, schools, hospitals, nightclubs, science-fiction conventions, and a vast array of other social scenes. The object of this debate, however, is fundamentally misdirected. The question that merits consideration is not whether ethnographies can be conducted online but rather what *claims* can be meaningfully made from such research. My online ethnographic mode of inquiry is ideally suited to my primary interests in those discourses surrounding sexuality and embodied identity appearing on these channels.

Although some may characterize this study conducted online as a "virtual ethnography," I am reluctant to employ such a designation myself. For me, the "realness" of an ethnography is not determined by the site of investigation but by the commitment the researcher has made to the community or social formation under study. As Hammersley and Atkinson (1995) point out, despite the observational skills of the researcher, ethnographers remain largely dependent on what accounts subjects elect to share, and I would hold that these accounts remain valid cultural artifacts whether they are gathered in physical copresence or in cyberspace. I fail to grasp how the stories informants provide us with are rendered any less meaningful simply because they are mediated through computer technology.

Of course, this suspicion surrounding online inquiry has been exasperated by the overly romantic rhetoric that initially greeted cyberspace. I am inclined to agree with Annette Markham's (1998) concluding thoughts that "we academics who write about the transcendence of the body, the fragmentation of identity in cyberspace, the hyperreal, etc., may be making too much of the entire phenomenon" (p. 222). In this remark I do not read Markham as suggesting that cyberspace does not constitute a social phenomenon worthy of interest but instead that the romantic images of an idealized public sphere and bodily transcendence endemic to so much of the early literature on cyberspace buries in hype the more ordinary ways individuals incorporate Internet technologies into their lived experience. Without doubt, many of those early utopian declarations heralding the arrival of cyberspace were poorly thought out. For instance, to claim that individuals overcome racism, sexism, and other discriminatory ways of perceiving people by transcending their bodies online is to suggest that such social problems are intrinsic components of embodied experience, which, in turn, effectively denies the mechanisms by which such oppressive formations are culturally constructed and socially instituted. Could any notion be more pessimistic than the belief that the only way to truly realize an equitable society free of hierarchy is to abandon our bodies?

As is evident in the discourses emerging from the channels examined in this study, oppressive notions surrounding race and gender remain entrenched in online social dynamics. Although individuals may be turning to these virtual environments to escape the marginalization of their sexual identities within a heterosexist society, they are unfortunately quite capable of bringing with them their preconceptions surrounding race, gender, body type, and even sexuality. In the opening of this book I questioned whether those discourses emerging online reinforce the oppressive deployment of sexuality in

Western societies or undermine such naturalized understandings. The answer to this question it seems is both: although the erotic practices of gaining and muscle worship unsettle dominant notions of the healthy and the erotic, the ease with which these individuals naturalize their own erotic interests while marginalizing the desires of others suggests that many individuals maintain their existing physical-world mind-set online, a mind-set encompassing racist and sexist views.

One of the key points of this study, which may be clear only in retrospect, is that those practices with which one identifies are far too easily rendered "natural," while those practices or identities one does not share are often viewed as unhealthy and alien. It is disturbing how easily we justify as "normal" those things that bring us pleasure while stigmatizing the pleasures of others. What should be apparent to any member of a sexual minority or other nondominant group is the oppressive character of those discourses that invoke the "natural." Worthy of interrogation is the very impetus to be viewed as "normal." Why is there such moral authority invested in these notions of naturalness and normalcy? Individuals interacting on these IRC channels should be in the position to readily view identities as socially constructed and therefore alterable. Yet some of them perpetuate the very discourses by which they are subjugated, effectively reinscribing themselves within hierarchies of power. In contrast to much of the celebratory rhetoric surrounding computer-mediated communication, my observations suggest that online interaction in itself does *not* radically alter the worldviews of those venturing into cyberspace.

Of interest is how this reproduction of oppressive social formations in cyberspace supports Foucault's "theory of power." In delineating his conceptualization of power, Foucault warns of viewing power as simply "a group of institutions and mechanisms that ensure the subservience of the citizens to a given state" (1978, p. 92). Though this understanding of power may prove convenient for political organizing, it fails to address ways in which power dynamics produce and permeate social relations. It is worth noting that Foucault has been criticized for his abstract articulations of power. If power is everywhere, then how can it be resisted, critics ask. However, Foucault's refusal to essentialize power—in other words, his refusal to station power in a single location—allows for the interrogation of power dynamics within any social relationship. It allows us to conceptualize power as both a repressive and productive force, constituting those very societal formations it then appears only to suppress. Foucault vehemently rejects simplistic views of power as exclusively negative and external:

> We must cease once and for all to describe the effects of power in negative terms: it "excludes," it "represses," it "censors," it "abstracts," it "masks," it "conceals." In fact, power produces; it produces reality; it produces domains of objects and rituals of truth. The individual and the knowledge that may be gained of him belong to this production. (1977, p. 194)

Foucault's primary objective in his reconceptualization of power is interrogating those "truths" fundamental to our understanding of the world and ourselves, even those truths that are positioned as the objective products of science. For Foucault (1977), "power and knowledge directly imply one another" (p. 27), and to adequately understand how it is we came to see the world the way that we do, we must first understand how knowledge is produced within historically specific economies of power relations.

Through this production of knowledge, power is able to ever more effectively permeate all life processes, administering birth as well as death, sexual relations as well as physical hygiene, mental dispositions as well as physical illnesses. This, Foucault argues, is a historically and culturally specific development, and this new mode of power that came to supercede that of sovereignty "is more dependent upon bodies and what they do than upon the Earth and its products" (1980, p. 104). As Foucault (1978) holds,

> Power would no longer be dealing simply with legal subjects over whom the ultimate dominion was death [as it had under sovereignty], but with living beings, and the mastery it would be able to exercise over them would have to be applied at the level of life itself; it was the taking charge of life, more than the threat of death, that gave power its access even to the body. (pp. 142-143)

These modern matrices of power have utterly permeated the human body, whether through the medical gaze in the clinic or the panoptic gaze in the prison, and it is this body entrenched in power relations that is reproduced in cyberspace.

Such an understanding of power helps to explain how it is that the very individuals turning to cyberspace to escape restrictive social models surrounding sex and sexuality themselves reproduce problematic conceptions of gender and race. Even in their efforts to escape those narrow representations of the body in the mass media, these individuals construct new models of the desirable body that are often just as constraining. Despite the rhetoric of bodily transcendence, many of the social practices that render individuals docile bodies in the Foucauldian sense (such as beauty hierarchies) are replicated online.[3] The body and all the sociocultural ways the body is apprehended—the gendered body, the raced body, the classed body, the sexualized body, the ethnic body, the aged body—do not simply cease to hold valence when one enters cyberspace. When we look more critically at what people actually do in cyberspace, we see that race, gender, sexuality, class, age, ethnicity, religion, and looks continue to be differences that make a difference in online social relations. This is not to deny that online textual interaction can indeed expose the artificiality of how the body is socially apprehended. Rather, this is to point out the hold these historical-cultural constructs have on how we understand ourselves and those we interact with.

In contrast to those fantastical images of the protean self in cyberspace, I have found that the identities individuals construct online generally reflect those offline characteristics foremost in their understandings of themselves. This should not be surprising, for if individuals venture into cyberspace to meet existing physical-world needs or desires—as we have seen on these channels—then these offline drives are likely to shape and contain the identities people will forge online.

SANCTUM SANCTORUM IN CYBERSPACE

In relating the story central to this book, I should not be read as heralding the Internet as some liberating technological force, nor should I be seen as celebrating the individuals patronizing these channels as political subjects. Rather, I recount this narrative to illustrate how one particular group of individuals incorporates emerging communication technologies into their day-to-day lives to meet their existing needs and desires. Based on the experiences of these individuals, I would argue the emancipatory potential of cyberspace lies not in some disembodied subjectivity but in the opportunity to bring to the fore those aspects of embodied existence concealed within the dominant society and absent within the mainstream media.

This tale of bodybuilders and musclebears and chubby chasers suggests that far from being a means of escaping the body, online interaction constitutes a mode of rearticulating our relationship to the physical body and, at least for these interactants, resisting dominant models of beauty and the erotic. No bodily transcendence is found in going online, though the dream of such speaks volumes about Western society's ontological division between mind and body. As the story told here demonstrates, online and offline experiences bleed into each other, and therefore it is doubtful that encounters in cyberspace will radically reformulate how people understand the physical world they inhabit. Even those who come to redefine their sexual identity as a result of their online experiences are not necessarily likely to view sexuality itself as socially constructed and artificially imposed.

However, these channels do offer important discursive resources to their members. For some, these are spaces of companionship and consolation during times of isolation and loss. For others, these are spaces of erotic exploration and self-discovery where sexual desires are affirmed and new understandings of the self are forged. And for many, these are spaces of fraternity where old friendships are maintained and new ones are established. Indeed, the importance of these virtual spaces was suggested in **Britannic**'s response to the question of how he believes patrons such as himself view these channels:

> **Britannic:** As their sanctum sanctorum, I guess.
> **John:** Sanctum Sanctorum?
> **Britannic:** It's latin . . . it means a place of safety.
> **Britannic:** Their personal sacred space.

There is, of course, also a certain pleasurable politics at work on these channels. When one's pleasures are coded (or stigmatized) by society as nonnormative, then engaging in those pleasures becomes, in itself, a political act. Furthermore, the very construction of these online environments can be read as a form of political resistance. As Nina Wakeford notes (2000), queer online spaces, or "cyberqueer spaces" as she refers to them, "are necessarily embedded within both institutional and cultural practices, and are a means by which the lesbian/gay/transgendered/queer self can be read into the politics of representation and activism confronting homophobia" (p. 408). By using computer technology to construct communities celebrating forms of erotic desire stigmatized within the dominant society, these individuals can be seen as engaging in a politically subversive act. However, the vital question that refuses a definitive answer is to what degree, if at all, will these seditious online experiences inform offline political practices? I would like to think that on some level these individuals will view with suspicion those cultural constructions positioned as "natural" and "normal," though I have no evidence to support this wishful thought.

The objective of this study has not been to provide definitive answers regarding the role Internet technologies play in contemporary Western society. Rather, it has been to provide a more particular understanding of how the positionalities of individuals within the physical universe inform their use of computer-mediated communication technologies and, consequently, signal the need for more grounded investigation into online practices. Though multiple and complex, it should now be clear that the offline daily experiences of individuals shape their online activities. This seemingly self-evident assertion has too often been disregarded in favor of sweeping generalizations touting the social and technological wonders of cyberspace.

Ideally, those individuals patronizing these virtual spaces would be able to safely explore their sexual desires offline. Ideally, those desires would be accepted within the larger cultural milieu as healthy and not branded as deviant. Ideally, such sexual expression and exploration would not be accompanied by very real risks to employment, familial relations, and even life. However, in a society that is far from ideal for many, certainly for members of sexual minorities, it is vital we understand those physical-world needs fueling online social relations.

Appendix

IRC Interviewee Profile

Nick	Sexuality	Race/ Ethnicity	Profession	Chat from Work?	Age	Education	Region
Bennoe	Gay	White	Police officer	No	36	HS	Australia
Big_Wolf*	Gay	Black	Disabled/ unemployed	N/A	40	BA in progress	Maryland
BIGrGUY	"I don't identify it"	White	Industrial relations	No	30	BA	Canada
BluCollar*	Gay	White	Machinist	No	47	HS	Michigan
Britannic	Gay	White	Computer programmer	Yes	31	BS	New Jersey/Boston
GremlinBear*	"Openly gay"	White	Sales	No	36	BS	West Coast, United States
IrishCrop	Gay	White	University administrator	Yes	26	BA	Minnesota
Mad_Hatter	GWM [gay white male]	White	Data entry clerk	Yes	29	BA	Florida
Mage78	Bisexual	White	Student (un-dergraduate)	School primarily	21	BA in progress	Kentucky
Masculin	"Homo-sexual not gay"	White	Computer professional	No	35	BS	Canada
Msclfreak	Gay	White	Publisher	Yes	30	BA	Manchester, United Kingdom
PECS	Gay	White	Exotic birds breeder	N/A	40	GED	New Hampshire/Montreal

Nick	Sexuality	Race/ Ethnicity	Profession	Chat from Work?	Age	Education	Region
PHLguy (PHLguy28)	"Not straight, bisexual"	Latino	Secretary/ temp	No	28	BS	Philadelphia
Quixote	Gay	White	Web designer	No	40	BA	New York City
SFBigCub	Gay	White	Public policy consultant	Yes	32	MA	California
TechnoBear*	"Varies"	White	Network engineer	No	37	BS	New York City
TexMuscle*	Gay	White	Insurance	Yes	43	BS	Texas
Top_Bear*	Gay	White	Computer professional	No	34	BS	Washington, DC
Umgawa	Gay	White	Computer security	Yes	33	BS	Massachusetts
WorkOut	Gay	White	Legal secretary	Yes	28	BA	Minnesota
Younghung	Gay	White	Night security guard	Yes	23	HS	Florida

*Indicates interviewee requested nickname be changed

Note: Education refers to the highest level of formal education completed. HS indicates high school, or secondary school graduate, or the equivalent of such abroad. GED indicates a general equivalency degree for those not completing secondary school. BA or BS indicates a four-year college bachelor's degree, or the equivalent if abroad. MA indicates master's degree.

Notes

Chapter 1

1. It is worth noting, however, that many of those media scholars drawing on the work of de Certeau came under criticism for bestowing upon the consumers of mass media too much agency. Although it is important to understand how individuals incorporate communication technologies into their particular experiences of everyday life, this should not be done at the expense of examining the larger political and economic forces shaping society. By focusing on how a particular group of people employ Internet technologies to meet their specific needs, I am not ignoring the existence of powerful corporate entities that seek to transform the Internet into a target-market media outlet with shop-at-home capabilities. However, unlike traditional mass media— television, film, and radio—the technological structure of the Internet currently allows for significant and varied individual expression. This is precisely why I avoid a simplistic technological determinist position in favor of a more complex understanding of cyberspace as a culturally contested technological *and* social phenomenon.

2. I have elected not to disclose which IRC network the channels examined in this study exist on. Although I use the actual channel names for obvious reasons, I hope that by concealing the network identity I can offer some privacy to those interacting on these channels.

3. These estimates were devised by checking the reported numbers of people online according to my IRC interface (mIRC) every weeknight for twelve consecutive weeks, starting June 21, 1999, and ending September 17, 1999. All figures were gathered between 7 p.m. and 10 p.m. EST. The number of channels devoted to some form of nonnormative sexuality was devised by running a "list" function on my IRC interface for channels with the words "gay," "queer," "lesbian," "man for man," "woman for woman," or "bisexual" in their designation. I then examined the resulting list to determine the topic of discussion for each channel.

Chapter 2

1. I have changed both the online handle and offline name of my friend.

2. To preserve the complexity and uniqueness of online interaction, the portions of interviews presented remain fundamentally unchanged from the way they appeared on the computer screen at the time.

3. This "posting" was accomplished by using a feature on my IRC interface that allows me to compose a long standardized message (posting) and then display that message at any time using a preset command. Each time I entered a channel for

research purposes, I would use this preset command function to bring up my standardized message, indicating to all those on the channel that I was interested in interviewing individuals about their online experiences. The following is the actual text of my posting: "Hello everyone. Many of you already know me. My name is John and I'm a graduate student at the University of Massachusetts–Amherst. I'm currently conducting research on the online experience of gay men on this IRC channel. I am looking for people willing to be interviewed for this project. You will remain completely anonymous, and the interview will only take as long as you want it to. If you're interested in being interviewed, or would like to learn more about my project, please message me. Thanks."

4. An additional advantage of online interviewing is provided by my IRC interface which can be set to automatically transcribe my online conversations. Concerning the transcription of oral narratives, Catherine Kohler Riessman (1993) indicates that transforming "spoken language into a written text" is a serious endeavor, involving theoretical and interpretive decisions "because thoughtful investigators no longer assume the transparency of language" (p. 12). Riessman continues: "Different transcription conventions lead to and support different interpretations and ideological positions, and they ultimately create different worlds" (p. 13). However, research in cyberspace presents different considerations because the very technologies underlying computer-mediated communication can also provide the researcher with analyzable data from online interactions. The fundamental difference, however, is that this transcribed text is static, whereas at the time of the interaction it appeared fleeting. Here the text can be read slowly, with sufficient time to reread any unclear passages. Then, however, to keep up the appearance of real-time conversation, the text would have scrolled swiftly by on the screen.

Chapter 3

1. By referring to these channels as "stable" spaces, I am noting the fact that the channel remains consistently open and running even if all interactants leave the channel. This is not the case with most IRC channels, which simply cease to exist when the last interactant has departed. However, with these particular channels, "bots"—special programs designed to maintain a channel or space on IRC—have been developed by the interactants to keep the channel running even if no one is present.

2. By "open," I refer to the fact that any individual logged on to the channel can participate in these conversations at any time. This is different from those private spaces patrons create with other members of a channel to engage in more intimate discussions.

3. As indicated in the more technical literature on IRC, any individual on a channel can be given operator privileges (thereby becoming a channel moderator) by anyone already possessing such privileges. When an interactant first creates his or her own channel, he or she is automatically granted by the system software all of the operator privileges governing that particular virtual space. As a channel grows, it is common for the founder to delegate these operator privileges to other individuals, thereby involving them in the maintenance of a particular channel. When channels become very well established, a group of individuals with the technical skills will

generally compose a modest system program (often referred to as a channel "bot") with two functions: first, keep the channel running continuously, even in the event of all interactants logging off that chat room; second, automatically bestow operator privileges to any individual on a list of designated moderators. In the case of **#gaymuscle,** many of those interacting consistently on the channel for several years and who are well known to (and at least to some extent well respected by) other members of the community are generally added to the automatic list of channel moderators in the "bot" program.

4. Though Danet, Ruedenberg-Wright, and Rosenbaum-Tamari (1997) have argued that discussions appearing in the main window of a channel represent "public" discourses and are therefore open to social science examination, I believe there are always additional considerations. In this instance, there are complicating circumstances in that the discussions appearing on these channels identify interactants as members of a sexual minority. Thus, in this example, I have elected to alter all of the nicknames to conceal each individual's online identity while maintaining the exact form and content of the discussion.

5. In case the reader is wondering, yes, **Umgawa** is actually seven feet tall. Having met him several times in person, I can attest to this fact, which, as the reader might suspect, makes him a conspicuous individual in any offline setting and also quite popular online.

6. Information regarding state and federal antidiscrimination legislation as well as the actual statistics reported by the FBI on hate crimes is available on the Human Rights Campaign Web site (http://www.hrc.org/index.asp).

7. Obviously, offline privacy is not always assured. This was poignantly demonstrated in the 1998 case of U.S. Navy Master Chief Petty Officer Timothy R. McVeigh (not to be confused with Oklahoma City bomber Timothy James McVeigh), who was dishonorably discharged by the military after seventeen years of honorable service because he identified himself as a "gay" on his America Online profile (Napoli, 1998). Though McVeigh's discharge was later overturned in federal court as violating the military's "Don't ask, don't tell" policy and America Online issued a formal apology, the incident exemplifies the delicate nature of online privacy for members of sexual minorities.

8. I have substituted pseudonyms for the actual offline given names listed by **Umgawa.**

9. Reviewing the interview transcripts, I later debated the appropriateness of this question. Whether it was my place to inquire about such a clearly personal matter as a researcher is a complex ethical question. What if my questioning had caused this interactant to reexperience painful emotions he perceived as resolved? However, I have decided to present this conversation to show how questions often arise spontaneously in online interviewing.

10. This was, according to **WorkOut,** in 1990.

Chapter 4

1. By "here," **Big_Wolf** refers to the channel **#gaychub,** which represents the site he usually frequents. The use of spatial terms in cyberspace is indicative of the sense of "presence" interactants experience.

2. This is not the interactant's actual online nickname. Given that this comment was made outside the context of a formal interview, I have elected to conceal his online identity.

3. Tom Prince is a professional bodybuilder well known within the elite competitive bodybuilding world for his remarkable muscular development and immense mass.

4. The assumption is always that a less muscularly developed individual will present himself as a bodybuilder and not that a bodybuilder will present himself as someone with less muscular development. This bespeaks what images of the male body are idealized in these virtual spaces.

5. For an analysis of one instance of online erotic fantasy play, see John Edward Campbell's (2003) article "Always Use A Modem: Frames of Erotic Play and Performance in Cyberspace" in the *Electronic Journal of Communication.*

6. Purely for accurately representing what would be generally acknowledged as constituting "big" or "huge" stats on the channel **#gaymuscle,** those stats used here are the actual stats of **Msclfreak.**

7. Wright (2003) defines "erotic folk art" as an "Aesthetic category of art objects, which are produced using means readily available (such as pencil, pen-and-ink, photography, digital imagery), manifesting a technical skill level (whether it is the artist's apparent skill level or a deliberate artistic effect) consistent with untrained, self-taught, or 'naïve' folk art styles, typically drawing upon the visual language of commercial pornography ("soft-core" or "hard-core"), erotic art traditions, and the artist's personal vision, with the intent of expressing the artist's vision (dream, fantasy, desire), typically a sexual utopian vision." Wright's discussion of erotic folk art originating from within gay male bear subculture can be found on the Nashoba Institute Web site (http://bearhistory.com).

8. During my years of interacting on these channels, I have repeatedly encountered individuals who have turned to IRC out of frustration at not being able to locate others who shared or appreciated their erotic desires or interests in conventional offline venues, such as gay bars or clubs.

9. Stone (1996) discusses how Hawking, an individual afflicted with amyotrophic lateral sclerosis, is able to lecture to auditoriums filled with people through a computer, a specialized interface, and a speech synthesizer. For Stone, Hawking's utilization of computer technologies to communicate with those around him raises critical "boundary debates, borderland/*frontera* questions" (p. 5), where the cybernetic organism emerges.

Chapter 5

1. This figure was reported by Pope, Phillips, and Olivardia (2000).

2. As quoted in Fussell (1996, p. 47) from Arnold Schwarzenegger and Douglas Kent Hall's *Arnold: The Education of a Bodybuilder* (1977).

Chapter 6

1. I have substituted pseudonyms for all of the nicknames and offline given names appearing in this transcript. In all other respects, the transcript remains unaltered.

2. For a more experimental approach to the authoring of an online ethnography, see Frank Schaap's work, *The Words That Took Us There: Ethnography in a Virtual Reality* (2002).

3. Could anything better exemplify Foucault's notion of "disciplining power" enacted on bodies than such sites as <www.RateMyBody.com> where individuals (gay and straight) post pictures of themselves so other online users can assign standardized numerical values reflecting the sexual attractiveness of their bodies? The subtext of this site is far from subtle: make your body conform to these dominant standards of beauty or be publicly marked as unattractive and flawed.

Bibliography

Alter, J. (1999). Bridging the digital divide. *Newsweek,* September 29, 1999, p. 55.

Althusser, L. (1971). Ideology and ideological state apparatuses. In *Lenin and philosophy and other essays* (pp. 123-173). London: New Left Books.

Anderson, B. (1983). *Imagined communities: Reflections on the origin and spread of nationalism.* London: New Left Books.

Argyle, K. and Shields, R. (1996). Is there a body in the net? In R. Shields (Ed.), *Cultures of Internet: Virtual spaces, real histories, living bodies* (pp. 58-69). London: Sage Publications.

Atkins, D. (1998). Introduction: Looking queer. In D. Atkins (Ed.), *Looking queer: Body image and identity in lesbian, bisexual, gay, and transgender communities* (pp. xxix-li). Binghamton, NY: Harrington Park Press.

Balsamo, A. (1995). Forms of technological embodiment: Reading the body in contemporary culture. In M. Featherstone and R. Burrows (Eds.), *Cyberspace/cyberbodies/cyberpunk: Cultures of technological embodiment* (pp. 215-237). London: Sage Publications.

Baym, N. (1995). The emergence of community in computer-mediated communication. In S. Jones (Ed.), *Cybersociety: Computer-mediated communication and community* (pp. 138-163). Thousand Oaks, CA: Sage Publications.

Beemyn, B. (1997). Introduction. In B. Beemyn (Ed.), *Creating a place for ourselves: Lesbian, gay, and bisexual community histories* (pp. 1-7). New York: Routledge.

Bell, D. and Valentine, G. (1995). Introduction: Orientations. In D. Bell and G. Valentine (Eds.), *Mapping desire: Geographies of sexualities* (pp. 1-27). London: Routledge.

Blotcher, J. (1998). Justify my love handles: How the queer community trims the fat. In D. Atkins (Ed.), *Looking queer: Body image and identity in lesbian, bisexual, gay, and transgender communities* (pp. 359-366). Binghamton, NY: Harrington Park Press.

Boswell, J. (1989). Revolutions, universals, and sexual categories. In M. Duberman, M. Vicinus, and G. Chauncey Jr. (Eds.), *Hidden from history: Reclaiming the gay and lesbian past* (pp. 17-36). New York: Meridian Books.

Breslow, H. (1997). Civil society, political economy, and the Internet. In S. Jones (Ed.), *Virtual culture: Identity and communication in cybersociety* (pp. 236-257). London: Sage Publications.

Bromberg, H. (1996). Are MUDs communities? Identity, belonging and consciousness in virtual worlds. In R. Shields (Ed.), *Cultures of Internet: Virtual spaces, real histories, living bodies* (pp. 143-152). London: Sage Publications.

Brown, L. (2001). Fat is a bearish issue. In L. Wright (Ed.), *The bear book II: Further readings in the history and evolution of a gay male subculture* (pp. 39-54). Binghamton, NY: Harrington Park Press.

Browning, F. (1993). *The culture of desire: Paradox and perversity in gay lives today.* New York: Vintage Books.

Bruckman, A. (1996). Gender swapping on the Internet. In P. Ludlow (Ed.), *High noon on the electronic frontier: Conceptual issues in cyberspace* (pp. 317-326). Cambridge, MA: MIT Press.

Budd, M., Entman, R., and Steinman, C. (1990). The affirmative character of U.S. cultural studies. *Critical Studies in Mass Communication* 7, 169-184.

Butler, J. (1990a). *Gender trouble: Feminism and the subversion of identity.* New York: Routledge.

Butler, J. (1990b). Performative acts and gender constitution: An essay in phenomenology and feminist theory. In S. Case (Ed.), *Performing feminisms: Feminist critical theory and theatre* (pp. 270-282). Baltimore, MD: The Johns Hopkins University Press.

Butler, J. (1993). *Bodies that matter: On the discursive limits of "sex."* New York: Routledge.

Califia, P. (1994). *Public sex: The culture of radical sex.* Pittsburgh, PA: Cleir Press.

Campbell, J.E. (2003). Always use a modem: Frames of erotic play and performance. In N. Baym (Ed.), *Electronic Journal of Communication/La revue electronique de communication* 13(1). Available online at <http://www.cios.org/www/ejcmain.htm>.

Chauncey, G. (1994). *Gay New York: Gender, urban culture, and the making of the gay male world, 1890-1940.* New York: HarperCollins Publishers.

Clynes, M. and Kline, N. (1960). Cyborgs and space. In C. Gray (Ed.), *The cyborg handbook* (pp. 29-34). New York: Routledge.

Connell, R. W. (1995). *Masculinities.* Berkeley: University of California Press.

Correll, S. (1995). The ethnography of an electronic bar: The lesbian café. *Journal of Contemporary Ethnography* 24(3), 270-298.

Curtis, P. (1996). MUDding: Social phenomena in text-based virtual realities. In P. Ludlow (Ed.), *High noon on the electronic frontier: Conceptual issues in cyberspace* (pp. 347-374). Cambridge, MA: The MIT Press.

Danet, B. (1998). Text as mask: Gender, play, and performance on the Internet. In S. Jones (Ed.), *Cybersociety 2.0: Revisiting computer-mediated communication and community* (pp. 129-158). Thousand Oaks, CA: Sage Publications.

Danet, B., Ruedenberg-Wright, L., and Rosenbaum-Tamari, Y. (1997) "Hmmm . . . Where's that smoke coming from?" Writing, play and performance on Internet Relay Chat. In B. Danet (Ed.), *Journal of Computer-Mediated Communication*

(JCMC) 2(4), Hypertext publication available online at <http://cwis.usc.edu/dept/annenberg/vol2/issue4/danet.html>.

de Certeau, M. (1984). *The practice of everyday life* (S. Rendall, Translator). Berkeley: University of California Press.

Del Rio, J. (2000). Vern Runnall's success story. *MuscleMag International* 216 (June), 76-84.

Dery, M. (1994). Flame wars. In M. Dery (Ed.), *Flame wars: The discourse of cyberculture* (pp. 1-10). Durham, NC: Duke University Press.

Désert, J. (1997). Queer space. In G. Brent Ingram, A. Bouthillette, and Y. Retter (Eds.), *Queers in space: Communities, public places, sites of residence* (pp. 17-26). Seattle, WA: Bay Press.

Dotson, E. (1999). *Behold the man: The hype and selling of male beauty in media and culture.* Binghamton, NY: The Haworth Press.

Dyer, R. (1997). *White.* London: Routledge.

Featherstone, M. and Burrows, R. (1995). Cultures of technological embodiment: An introduction. In M. Featherstone and R. Burrows (Eds.), *Cyberspace/cyberbodies/cyberpunk: Cultures of technological embodiment* (pp. 1-20). London: Sage Publications.

Fernback, J. (1997). The individual within the collective: Virtual ideology and the realization of collective principles. In S. Jones (Ed.), *Virtual culture: Identity and communication in cybersociety* (pp. 36-54). London: Sage Publications.

Fiske, J. (1987). *Television culture.* London: Routledge.

Foucault, M. (1977). *Discipline and punish: The birth of the prison* (A. Sheridan, Translator). New York: Vintage Books.

Foucault, M. (1978). *The history of sexuality: An introduction,* Volume I (R. Hurley, Translator). New York: Random House.

Foucault, M. (1980). *Power/knowledge: Selected interviews and other writings 1972-1977* (C. Gordon, L. Marshall, J. Mepham, and K. Soper, Translators and C. Gordon, Ed.). New York: Pantheon Books.

Fussell, S. (1996). Bodybuilder americanus. In L. Goldstein (Ed.), *The male body: Features, destinies, exposures* (pp. 43-60). Ann Arbor: University of Michigan Press.

Geertz, C. (1988). *Works and lives: The anthropologist as author.* Stanford, CA: Stanford University Press.

Giles, P. (1998). A matter of size. In D. Atkins (Ed.), *Looking queer: Body image and identity in lesbian, bisexual, gay, and transgender communities* (pp. 355-357). Binghamton, NY: Harrington Park Press.

Goffman, E. (1959). *The presentation of self in everyday life.* New York: Anchor Books.

Gross, L. (1991). Out of the mainstream: Sexual minorities and the mass media. In M. Wolf and A. Kielwasser (Eds.), *Gay people, sex, and the media* (pp. 19-46). Binghamton, NY: Harrington Park Press.

Gross, L. (1993). *Contested closets: The politics and ethics of outing.* Minneapolis: University of Minnesota Press.

Gross, L. (2001). *Up from invisibility: Lesbians, gay men, and the media in America.* New York: Columbia University Press.

Grosz, E. (1994). *Volatile bodies: Toward a corporeal feminism.* Bloomington: Indiana University Press.

Hakken, D. (1999). *Cyborgs@cyberspace? An ethnographer looks to the future.* New York: Routledge.

Halperin, D. (1995). *Saint Foucault: Toward a gay hagiography.* New York: Oxford University Press.

Hamman, R. (1996). *Cyborgasms: Cybersex amongst multiple-selves and cyborgs in the narrow-bandwidth space of America Online chat rooms* [Online]. Available at <http://www.socio.demon.co.uk/>. Accessed June 1, 2000.

Hammersley, M. and Atkinson, P. (1995). *Ethnography: Principles in practice,* Second edition. London: Routledge.

Haraway, D. (1985). Manifesto for cyborgs: Science, technology, and socialist feminism in the 1980s. *Socialist Review* 80, 65-108.

Haraway, D. (1991). A cyborg manifesto: Science, technology, and socialist-feminism in the late twentieth century. In D. Haraway (Ed.), *Simians, cyborgs and women: The reinvention of nature* (pp. 149-181). New York: Routledge.

Haraway, D. (1995). Cyborgs and symbionts: Living together in the new world order. In C. Gray (Ed.), *The cyborg handbook* (pp. xi-xx). New York: Routledge.

Hebdige, D. (1979). *Subculture: The meaning of style.* London: Routledge.

Hillis, K. (1996). A geography of the eye: The technologies of virtual reality. In R. Shields (Ed.), *Cultures of Internet: Virtual spaces, real histories, living bodies* (pp. 70-98). London: Sage Publications.

Hillis, K. (1999). *Digital sensations: Space, identity, and embodiment in virtual reality.* Minneapolis: University of Minnesota Press.

Hine, C. (2000). *Virtual ethnography.* London: Sage Publications.

Hoggart, R. (1957). *Uses of literacy.* London: Chatto and Windus.

Ihde, D. (2002). *Bodies in technology.* Minneapolis: University of Minnesota Press.

Ingram, G., Bouthillette, A., and Retter, Y. (1997). Lost in space: Queer theory and community activism at the fin-de-millénaire. In G. Ingram, A. Bouthillette, and Y. Retter (Eds.), *Queers in space: Communities, public places, sites of resistance* (pp. 3-16). Seattle, WA: Bay Press.

Ito, M. (1997). Virtually embodied: The reality of fantasy in a multi-user dungeon. In D. Potter (Ed.), *Internet culture* (pp. 87-110). New York: Routledge.

Jacobson, D. (1996). Contexts and cues in cyberspace: The pragmatics of naming in text-based virtual realities. *Journal of Anthropological Research* 52, 461-479.

Jenkins, H. (1992). *Textual poachers: Television fans and participatory culture.* New York: Routledge.

Johnson, D. (1997). The kids of fairytown: Gay male culture on Chicago's near north side in the 1930s. In B. Beemyn (Ed.), *Creating a place for ourselves: Lesbian, gay, and bisexual community histories* (pp. 97-118). New York: Routledge.

Jones, S. (1995). Understanding community in the information age. In S. Jones (Ed.), *Cybersociety: Computer-mediated communication and community* (pp. 10-35). London: Sage Publications.

Jones, S. (1997). The Internet and its social landscape. In S. Jones (Ed.), *Virtual culture: Identity and communication in cybersociety* (pp. 7-35). London: Sage Publications.

Kauffman, B. (1992). Feminist facts: Interview strategies and political subjects in ethnography. *Communication Theory* 2(3), 187-206.

Kendall, L. (2002). *Hanging out in the virtual pub: Masculinities and relationships online.* Berkeley: University of California Press.

Kennedy, E. and Davis, M. (1997). I could hardly wait to get back to that bar: Lesbian bar culture in Buffalo in the 1930s and 1940s. In B. Beemyn (Ed.), *Creating a place for ourselves: Lesbian, gay, and bisexual community histories* (pp. 27-72). New York: Routledge.

Klein, A. (1993). *Little big men: Bodybuilding subculture and gender construction.* Albany: State University of New York Press.

Kohler Riessman, C. (1993). *Narrative analysis: Qualitative research methods series 30.* London: Sage Publications.

Kollock, P. and Smith, M. (1999). Communities in cyberspace. In M. Smith and P. Kollock (Eds.), *Communities in cyberspace* (pp. 3-25). New York: Routledge.

Leap, W. (1996). *Word's out: Gay men's English.* Minneapolis: University of Minnesota Press.

LeBesco, K. (2001). Queering fat bodies/politics. In K. LeBesco and J. E. Braziel (Eds.), *Bodies out of bounds: Fatness and transgression* (pp. 74-87). Berkeley: University of California Press.

LeBesco, K. and Braziel, J. E. (2001). Editor's introduction. In K. LeBesco and J. E. Braziel (Eds.), *Bodies out of bounds: Fatness and transgression* (pp. 1-15). Berkeley: University of California Press.

Lindsay, C. (1996). Bodybuilding: A postmodern freak show. In R. Thomson (Ed.), *Freakery: Cultural spectacles of the extraordinary body* (pp. 356-367). New York: New York University Press.

Locke, P. (1997). Male images in the gay mass media and bear-oriented magazines: Analysis and contrast. In L. Wright (Ed.), *The bear book: Readings in the history and evolution of a gay male subculture* (pp. 103-140). Binghamton, NY: Harrington Park Press.

Luciano, L. (2001). *Looking good: Male body image in modern America.* New York: Hill and Wang.

Lupton, D. (1995). The embodied computer/user. In M. Featherstone and R. Burrows (Eds.), *Cyberspace/cyberbodies/cyberpunk: Cultures of technological embodiment* (pp. 97-112). London: Sage Publications.

Malinowski, B. (1922). *Argonauts of the Western Pacific: An account of native enterprise and adventure in the archipelagoes of Melanesian New Guinea.* London: Routledge.

Markham, A. (1998). *Life online: Researching real experience in virtual space.* Walnut Creek, CA: AltaMira Press.

Marvin, C. (1988). *When old technologies were new: Thinking about electric communication in the late nineteenth century.* New York: Oxford University Press.

Matza, D. (1990). *Delinquency and drift.* New York: Transaction Publications.

McLaughlin, M., Osborne, K., and Smith, C. (1995). Standards of conduct on Usenet. In S. Jones (Ed.), *Cybersociety: Computer-mediated communication and community* (pp. 90-111). Thousand Oaks, CA: Sage Publications.

McRae, S. (1997). Flesh made word: Sex, text and the virtual body. In D. Potter (Ed.), *Internet culture* (pp. 73-86). New York: Routledge.

McRobbie, A. (1991). *Feminism and youth culture: From Jackie to Just Seventeen.* London: Routledge.

Miller, D. and Slater, D. (2000). *The Internet: An ethnographic approach.* New York: Berg Press.

Mills, R. (1998). Cyber: Sexual chat on the Internet. *Journal of Popular Culture* 32(3), 31-46.

Mohr, R. (1992). *Gay ideas: Outing and other controversies.* Boston: Beacon Press.

Mosher, J. (2001). Setting free the bears: Refiguring fat men on television. In K. LeBesco and J. E. Braziel (Eds.), *Bodies out of bounds: Fatness and transgression* (pp. 166-193). Berkeley: University of California Press.

Napoli, L. (1998). Sailor says Navy is using AOL profile to oust him. *The New York Times,* January 9, 1998, p. A11.

Nguyen, D. T. and Alexander, J. (1996). The coming of cyberspacetime and the end of the polity. In R. Shields (Ed.), *Cultures of Internet: Virtual spaces, real histories, living bodies* (pp. 99-124). London: Sage Publications.

O'Brien, J. (1999). Writing in the body: Gender (re)production in online interaction. In M. Smith and P. Kollock (Eds.), *Communities in cyberspace* (pp. 76-104). New York: Routledge.

Oikarinen, J. (2000). IRC history. IRC.org [Online]. Available at <http:// www.irc. org/history_docs/jarkko.html>. Accessed June 15, 2002.

Oldenburg, R. (1991). *The great good place: Cafés, coffee shops, community centers, beauty parlors, general stores, bars, hangouts and how they get you through the day.* New York: Paragon House.

Plant, S. (1996). On the matrix: Cyberfeminist simulations. In R. Shields (Ed.), *Cultures of Internet: Virtual spaces, real histories, living bodies* (pp. 170-183). London: Sage Publications.

Pope, H., Phillips, K., and Olivardia, R. (2000). *The Adonis complex: The secret crisis of male body obsession.* New York: The Free Press.

Radway, J. (1984). *Reading the romance: Women, patriarchy, and popular literature.* Chapel Hill: University of North Carolina Press.

Radway, J. (1988). Reception study: Ethnography and the problems of dispersed audiences and nomadic subjects. *Cultural Studies* 2(3), 359-376.

Reardon, K. and Richardson, J. (1991). The important role of mass media in the diffusion of accurate information about AIDS. In M. Wolf and A. Kielwasser (Eds.), *Gay people, sex, and the media* (pp. 63-75). Binghamton, NY: Harrington Park Press.

Reid, E. (1991). *Electropolis: Communication and community on Internet relay chat.* [Online]. Available at <http://www.aluluei.com/work.htm>. Accessed September 1, 1998.

Reid, E. (1995). Virtual worlds: Culture and imagination. In S. Jones (Ed.), *Cybersociety: Computer-mediated communication and community* (pp. 164-183). London: Sage Publications.

Reid, E. (1996a). Communication and community on Internet relay chat: Constructing communities. In P. Ludlow (Ed.), *High noon on the electronic frontier: Conceptual issues in cyberspace* (pp. 397-412). Cambridge, MA: MIT Press.

Reid, E. (1996b). Text-based virtual realities: Identity and the cyborg body. In P. Ludlow (Ed.), *High noon on the electronic frontier: Conceptual issues in cyberspace* (pp. 327-346). Cambridge, MA: MIT Press.

Reid, E. (1999). Hierarchy and power: Social control in cyberspace. In M. Smith and P. Kollock (Eds.), *Communities in cyberspace* (pp. 107-133). New York: Routledge.

Retzloff, T. (1997). Cars and bars: Assembling gay men in postwar Flint, Michigan. In B. Beemyn (Ed.), *Creating a place for ourselves: Lesbian, gay, and bisexual community histories* (pp. 227-252). New York: Routledge.

Rheingold, H. (1991). *Virtual reality.* New York: Simon and Schuster.

Rheingold, H. (1993). *The virtual community: Homesteading on the electronic frontier.* Reading, PA: Addison-Wesley.

Robins, K. (1995). Cyberspace and the world we live in. In M. Featherstone and R. Burrows (Eds.), *Cyberspace/cyberbodies/cyberpunk: Cultures of technological embodiment* (pp. 135-156). London: Sage Publications.

Russo, V. (1981). *The celluloid closet: Homosexuality in the movies.* New York: Harper and Row.

Schaap, F. (2002). *The words that took us there: Ethnography in a virtual reality.* Amsterdam, Netherlands: Aksant Academic Publishers.

Schwarzenegger, A. and Hall, D. K. (1977). *Arnold: The education of a bodybuilder.* New York: Simon and Schuster.

Shaw, D. (1997). Gay men and computer communication: A discourse of sex and identity in cyberspace. In S. Jones (Ed.), *Virtual culture: Identity and communication in cybersociety* (pp. 133-145). London: Sage Publications.

Silverstein, B., Perdue, L., Peterson, B., and Kelly, E. (1986). The role of the mass media in promoting a thin standard of bodily attractiveness for women. *Sex Roles* 14(9/10), 519-532.

Silverstone, R. (1989). Let us return to the murmuring of everyday practices: A note on Michel de Certeau, television and everyday life. *Theory, Culture and Society* 6, 77-94.

Stenberg, D. (2002). History of IRC (Internet relay chat) [Online]. Available at <http://daniel.haxx.se/irchistory.html>. Accessed June 15, 2002.

Sterne, J. (1999). Thinking the Internet: Cultural studies versus the millennium. In S. Jones (Ed.), *Doing Internet research: Critical issues and methods for examining the net* (pp. 257-288). London: Sage Publications.

Stone, A. R. (1992). Will the real body please stand up?: Boundary stories about virtual cultures. In M. Benedikt (Ed.), *Cyberspace, first steps* (pp. 81-118). Cambridge, MA: MIT Press.

Stone, A. R. (1996). *The war of desire and technology at the close of the mechanical age.* Cambridge, MA: MIT Press.

Stratton, J. (1997). Cyberspace and the globalization of culture. In D. Potter (Ed.), *Internet culture* (pp. 253-276). New York: Routledge.

Terranova, T. (2000). Post-human unbounded: Artificial evolution and high-tech subcultures. In D. Bell and B. Kennedy (Eds.), *The cybercultures reader* (pp. 268-279). New York: Routledge.

Thomas, V. (1989). Body-image satisfaction among black women. *The Journal of Social Psychology* 129(1), 107-112.

Thorpe, R. (1997). The changing face of lesbian bars in Detroit, 1938-1965. In B. Beemyn (Ed.), *Creating a place for ourselves: Lesbian, gay, and bisexual community histories* (pp. 165-182). New York: Routledge.

Turkle, S. (1995). *Life on the screen: Identity in the age of the Internet.* New York: Touchstone.

Urla, J. and Swedlund, A. (1995). The anthropometry of Barbie. In J. Terry and J. Urla (Eds.), *Deviant bodies* (pp. 277-313). Bloomington: Indiana University Press.

Wakeford, N. (1996). Sexualized bodies in cyberspace. In W. Chernaik, M. Deegan, and A. Gibson (Eds.), *Beyond the book: Theory, culture, and the politics of cyberspace* (pp. 93-104). London: University of London.

Wakeford, N. (2000). Cyberqueer. In D. Bell and B. Kennedy (Eds.), *The cybercultures reader* (pp. 403-415). New York: Routledge.

Watney, S. (1993). The spectacle of AIDS. In H. Abelove, M. Barale, and D. Halperin (Eds.), *The lesbian and gay studies reader* (pp. 202-211). New York: Routledge.

Watson, N. (1997). Why we argue about virtual community: A case study of the Phish.Net fan community. In S. Jones (Ed.), *Virtual culture: Identity and communication in cybersociety* (pp. 102-132). London: Sage Publications.

Waugh, T. (1996). *Hard to image: Gay male eroticism in photography and film from their beginnings to Stonewall.* New York: Columbia University Press.

Wellman, B. and Gulia, M. (1999). Virtual communities as communities: Bet surfers don't ride alone. In M. Smith and P. Kollock (Eds.), *Communities in cyberspace* (pp. 167-194). New York: Routledge.

Weston, K. (1991). *Families we choose: Lesbians, gays, kinship.* New York: Columbia University Press.

Weston, K. (1998). *Long slow burn: Sexuality and social science.* New York: Routledge.

Wiegers, Y. (1998). Male bodybuilding: The social construction of a masculine identity. *Journal of Popular Culture* 32(2), 147-161.

Willis, P. (1977). *Learning to labor: How working class kids get working class jobs.* London: Saxon House.

Willis, P. (1978). *Profane culture.* London: Routledge.

Winner, L. (1986). *The whale and the reactor: A search for limits in an age of high technology.* Chicago: University of Chicago Press.

Wolf, N. (1991). *The beauty myth: How images of beauty are used against women.* New York: Anchor Press.

Wolfe, M. (1997). Invisible women in invisible places: The production of social space in lesbian bars. In G. Brent Ingram, A. Bouthillette, and Y. Retter (Eds.), *Queers in space: Communities, public places, sites of resistance* (pp. 301-324). Seattle, WA: Bay Press.

Woodland, R. (2000). Queer spaces, modem boys and pagan statues: Gay/lesbian identity and the construction of cyberspace. In D. Bell and B. Kennedy (Eds.), *The cybercultures reader* (pp. 416-431). New York: Routledge.

Wright, L. (1997a). A concise history of self-identifying bears. In L. Wright (Ed.), *The bear book: Readings in the history and evolution of a gay male subculture* (pp. 21-40). Binghamton, NY: Harrington Park Press.

Wright, L. (1997b). Theoretical bears. In L. Wright (Ed.), *The bear book: Readings in the history and evolution of a gay male subculture* (pp. 1-17). Binghamton, NY: Harrington Park Press.

Wright, L. (2003). The Nashoba Lexicon. Available at <http://bearhistory.com/lexicon.htm>. Accessed September 1, 2003.

Index

GETTING IT ON ONLINE

Cyberspace, Gay Male Sexuality, and Embodied Identity

_____in hardbound at $37.46 (regularly $49.95) (ISBN: 1-56023-431-8)

_____in softbound at $14.96 (regularly $19.95) (ISBN: 1-56023-432-6)

Or order online and use special offer code HEC25 in the shopping cart.